Riko

Seductions of an Artist

DENISE B. DAILEY

Throughout this book you will find a sampling of Riko's work. For an online look at more or to add to the collection of photographs of Riko's paintings, please visit Flickr.com:
https://flic.kr/s/aHsm7mkkSL

Riko: Seductions of an Artist Copyright © 2017 by Denise B. Dailey

Published in the United States by Denise B. Dailey.

PUBLISHER'S CATALOGING IN PUBLICATION DATA
Names: Dailey, Denise B.
Title: Riko : seductions of an artist / Denise B. Dailey.
Description: New York : Denise B. Dailey, 2017.
Identifiers: ISBN 978-0-9994069-0-8 (hardcover) | ISBN 978-0-9994069-1-5 (pbk.)
Subjects: LCSH: Artists--Czech Republic--Biography. | Prague (Czech Republic)--
    Biography. | World War, 1939-1945--Czech Republic--Biography. | Jews--Czech
    Republic--Prague. | Immigrants--United States--Biography. | BISAC:
    BIOGRAPHY & AUTOBIOGRAPHY / Artists, Architects, Photographers.
    | HISTORY / Europe / Eastern. | HISTORY / Modern / 20th Century.
Classification: LCC N44.M55 D35 2017 (print) | LCC N44.M55 (ebook)
| DDC 700.92--dc23.

Printed in the United States of America

Photographs within this book are shared with permission from Denise B. Dailey, Jacques Schmied, and Chaim Tabak. Please contact Denise B. Dailey with questions or permission-related queries.

For information about special discounts available for bulk purchases, sales promotions, fund-raising and educational needs, contact the author at daileytd@aol.com

Also by Denise B. Dailey, available on Amazon in paperback and e-book:
Listening to Pakistan: A Woman's Voice in a Veiled Land

Book design by Katie Holeman

To my family

He was absolutely a siren as far as women were concerned. He was really incredible and he knew it, of course. He knew his charm. He knew he could seduce just about anybody, male or female. The women would fall in love with him; the men would become his fast friends. He had a great gift of relating to people within a very short time, and doing so on a very intimate basis. He elicited that from people. I don't know what that quality was, but it was a kind of special gift he had. Besides his art, it may have been his greatest talent.

—ED SCHECKMAN, photographer, psychiatrist,
Riko's NYC student and friend

Austro-Hungarian Empire before 1918.

Jan Emmerich (Riko) Mikeska

In his mid-forties, around the time of his
arrival in the United States in 1948

Historical Timeline of Vitkovice, Czechoslovakia

First noted in mid-1300s, a Hussite community from 1400s.

1828   Changes from agricultural to heavy industrial center

Rise of iron and steel works originally owned by Roman Catholic archbishops of Olomouc.

1843   Iron and steel works purchased by the Viennese banker, Salomon Mayer von Rothschild, who finances the extension of Emperor Ferdinand's Northern Railway from Vienna to Ostrava (Vitkovice).

1873   Rothschild heirs found Witkowitzer Bergbau-und-Hüttengewerkschaft, largest iron and steel works in the Austro-Hungarian Empire, with Rothschild owning 51% of the shares, Viennese Wilhelm Ritter von Guttman 49%.

1908   Emperor Franz Joseph I declares Vitkovice an Independent Municipality.

1924   Vitkovice becomes a part of Greater Ostrava.

1939   Germans "aryanize" iron and steel works, which becomes Reichswerke Hermann Göring Conglomerate.

1945   Czech state socializes the industry, names it Klement Gottwald after Chairman of the Communist Party and fifth President of the Republic of Czechoslovakia, who succeeded Edvard Beneš.

1998   Coal extraction stopped.

2002   Closed industry declared a National Cultural Monument of the Czech Republic.

Riko's and Greta's Timelines

1900   Greta Schmied born in Prague April 1, 1900.

1903   Jan Emmerich ("Riko") Mikeska born in Vitkovice, Moravia on August 1, 1903.

1919–1926   Riko travels to Vienna, Berlin, Amsterdam, Paris and Brittany to paint and study.

1920   Greta Schmied marries Rolf Passer in her parent's home in Prague.

1921–1923   Greta studies art in Berlin and Paris.

1927   Rolf Passer recalls her to Prague to meet Riko, "an exceptional new artist who has joined the Prague Secession."

1929   Greta divorces Rolf Passer to marry Riko.

1938   Greta escapes Nazi threat in Prague to go to Great Britain. Riko follows suit in March of 1939, days before Nazis invade.

1939–1949   Greta in London, moves to Warwickshire to teach art in a girls' school; moves on to become a secretary to Professor Korner in Scotland.

Riko in London and Warwickshire, where he takes over Greta's teaching job at girls' school.

1949   Greta and Riko move to New York City.
Summers in Ischia, Croatia and Martha's Vineyard, Massachusetts
Gallery Shows, painting and teaching in New York City through 1980.

1983   Riko dies at Beth Israel Hospital in New York City at age 79 of bowel cancer.

1998   Greta dies at 98 of old age at Riverdale Home, New York City.

Riko's Academic Training, Exhibits and Collections

TRAINING:

- Vienna University
- Academy of Berlin
- Ecole des Beaux-Arts, Paris
- Sorbonne, Paris
- Académie Moderne, pupil of André Lhote and Jean Metzinger
- A founder with Maxim Kopf and Oskar Kokoschka of The Prague Secession

EXHIBITIONS:

- Academy of Berlin, 1925
- Salon d'Automne, Prague, year unkown
- Salon des Indépendents, Prague, 1929-'37
- Galérie André, Prague, 1930
- Czech State Exhibition, year unkown
- Arts Council of Great Britain, 1945-'49
- Winter Art Festival, New York City, 1958
- Argus Gallery, New Jersey, 1962
- Burgos Gallery, New York City, 1964
- Hirschl and Adler Gallery, New York City, 1965
- Bernard Dannenberg Gallery, New York City, 1970
- Dorsky Gallery, New York City, 1982

PAINTINGS IN:

- National Gallery of Prague*
- Ministry of Education, Prague*
- Modern Gallery, Prague*
- German Museum, Neurenberg*
- Galerie de l'Art Moderne, Luxembourg*
- Art Institute of Cincinnati
- Syracuse Gallery of Art
- Wichita Art Museum
- Private collections in North America and Europe

*hidden, moved and/or destroyed during the Second World War.

Greta and Riko,
Probably in late 1920s, southern France

Table of Contents

Introduction

As EARLY AS 70,000 YEARS BCE, a red ochre stone with cross hatchings informed hunter-gatherers that beings of specific craft and sensibilities existed amongst them. *We live. We are here*, they said on this stone from the Western Cape of South Africa. They said other things: *I have changed this stone to attract you. See you've stopped. You've picked me up. You feel my shape and temperature. You note my color. Your finger tips trace the lines I've exed. I go over it too, because my touch reassures me that my marks remain. My stone will be here when I, or anyone else, return to it. Do you believe I have left it as a gift for someone in need, or for someone who has died? Or will you take it as a decoration for a burial mound you made for one of your own? I won't mind. We all unite in death. And birth. Perhaps you will take it to the woman who has given birth to your child. Or perhaps you will keep it simply because you like it because, for what-ever reason, it has meaning for you. Perhaps you will copy what I have done. It is all good. I attracted you and made you pay attention, and you are as pleased as I am that we now feel things in another way. I pass on my life and my art.*

For millenia, farmers, builders, and archeologists have dug up different stories in the form of artifacts: a limestone statue of a Rubenesque woman in what is now Willendorf, Austria, the Franco-Cantabrian lions in silhouette sniffing out prey, the human and animal prints in caves in Brazil, in Indonesia, in Russia. These artists crafted materials to confer identity, reassurance, embellishment and posthumous existence. They knew how to seduce us and we, the discoverers, craved to succumb to the seduction of these universal mysteries and desires. This was a reciprocal art.

This story began about Riko alone, but it soon became apparent that there were at least two protagonists: the artist and his wife. Then more people appeared, each with a testimonial that added a complex of color, texture, depth and narrative to the canvas of the Mikeskas' lives.

These students, teachers, family members, friends, art critics, colleagues and historians did so in person, by phone calls, via lengthy hand-written letters in Italian, German, Czech, French and English. All correspondences, which I left unedited in the original and in translation, showed that if Riko was the skilled seducer, we were the giddily seduced, attracted as much by the aesthetics of his intellect as of his art.

In peeling the different layers of Riko's creative life, I found myself questioning how societies evaluate an artist. How and when do they promote him, and what are their expectations in return? What are those of the artist? To what extent is the artist able to act from unbridled passion and ambition, mindless of popular and academic recognition? How is it possible to express artistic freedom without satisfying the basic necessities of life? Where do the favors of chance play a part? And what is it about the public that is willing—nay, hungry—to be convinced by the sheer artistry of the effort?

Whether speaking with Riko in his studio in New York City, or being held captive behind coils of razor wire in his hometown in Czechoslovakia (and wondering if researching his life was worth my inquiry), my experiences shed light on those questions. Nothing was orderly, direct or easy, but it all was illuminating, and it all mattered in my pledge to record his life.

I invite the readers to tumble into the Mikeskas' worlds, as I did.

1

A Proposal

There's a painter I want you to meet. His name is Jan Emmerich Mikeska, Riko, for short. If you'd like, I can set up a meeting with him.

And then Lars added the real reason he was bringing up this topic:

He's fallen on hard times.

Lars Björling was a frequent guest at our house in New York City, to which he came from Stockholm for coaching in voice. We had met him and his wife, Veronica, on a visit to Sweden in 1980. All of us were avid followers of the arts, so it was not a surprise when he mentioned the painter the next time we saw him in New York, the fall of that same year.

We met the Mikeskas in the late '60s when Veronica and I summered in Ischia at the Casa Antica, Lars told us. *They used to rent a villa on the hillside and Riko liked to vary painting landscapes with painting portraits. He spotted us in a market one day when a vegetable vendor started hectoring Veronica to buy a fennel: "With this you make babies!" Riko was so insulted on behalf of my young wife, that he intervened, apologized for the crude behavior of the vendor, and asked us to join him and Greta for an apéritif.*

Riko charmed the Björlings with his old-fashioned manners, good looks and courtesy. He was quick to make the connection to Lars's world renown father, the tenor Jussi Björling, and he stunned Veronica by his deep knowledge of Chinese porcelains and ink pots, items Veronica's family collected in their manor home in Ekolsund.

Yes, you see, Riko said, *I have a friend, Fritz LowBeer, whose family also collected East Asian Art. I was lucky enough to see the glazed wonders in their home before they gave them to the Linden Museum in Stuttgart. Undoubtedly, your family knows their collection intimately.*

The pedigrees each side claimed might have seemed like a display of one-upsmanship, but I was to learn both Riko and Greta had an astounding knowledge of artistic artifacts, and attracted a surprising list of *dramatis personae.*

In Ischia, Lars and Veronica joined Riko and Greta on the balcony overlooking the Adriatic for the first of many evening drinks and conversations, but it was Veronica's blue eyes, fair skin, and fly-away blond curls that entranced Riko. He asked if he might make a few sketches.

When the Björlings left the island that summer, Riko gave them two oil portraits of Veronica to take home with them. *We have bought other paintings since, including a fine one of Marcel Marceau with whose speechless persona Riko came to identify,* Lars remarked with no further clues.

When Lars told us Riko had fallen on hard times, we guessed Lars expected us to help Riko out of those, but what we did not know is that Lars had previewed this hope to Riko himself, thus setting up the first of many conflicts of expectations.

Within the week, Lars arranged for my husband, Tom, and me to visit first Riko at his studio, then Greta at their home in Chelsea. Shortly thereafter, Lars left for Sweden, Tom concentrated on his surgical practice, and while our three children, aged eighteen, sixteen and eleven, were in school, I adopted much older and needier children: the Mikeskas.

2.

Meeting Riko

THE RARE STAND-ALONE white filigreed building on the south-west corner of 17th Street and Union Square looks like an Italian palazzo from the outside. Inside, it has high ceilings and huge windows, an optimal habitat for all the artists that claim space within it. Turpentine, paint and linseed oil perfumed our ascent in a caged elevator to Riko's studio on the eighth floor.

When I called to arrange an appointment, I heard his soft European-accented voice answer: *This is Riko the painter*, a saluta-tion I came to learn as his verbal signature. And so we met.

Madame, were his first words to me as he raised my hand to his lips, looked over my shoulder, and took a professional gander at Tom's 6'6" height and sculpted face. I felt he was evaluating Tom as a subject just as he had Veronica in Ischia and, indeed, Riko ended up making several sketches of Tom's head, but those came later.

Riko was neatly dressed in grey slacks and an Indian-collared white cotton shirt. He fixed us with his blue eyes and a melodic, quiet voice whose accent was clearly European, though not readily identifiable. Having celebrated his 80th birthday two months before, he still moved gracefully, like an athlete, and waved us to a couch he must have used as a day bed. A painting lay covered on the easel, and his black beret hung from a clothes stand next to the door. Cubbies of different sizes holding his watercolors, sketches and oils lined up on the wall by the couch and along the wall that made a right angle to it. His paints and palettes, brushes, charcoals and sketch pads were neatly arranged on a counter running the length of the wide windows which faced north towards the Empire State Building.

Perhaps it was our reaction to the uncommon October light slanting in the big windows that started him speaking.

Yes, I like it. My studio in Prague, nothing more than a garret, overlooked the Moldau and had the most wonderful light imaginable, but of course I had to abandon it when the Germans invaded. They destroyed my work and my studio. Stupid people. Ignorant. No knowledge of anything except how high up they could raise their arms in a salute to Hitler.

May I offer you some tea? I haven't much food here, but I can boil up some water.

He seemed to want to interrupt his tirade, but when we signaled we wanted nothing to eat or drink, he continued to fan the live embers of his anger.

I heard the stomping of booted feet coming up the stairs. The space was full of canvasses in sketched, half and wholey-painted states, and the scents of our oils, glues, linseed oil and turpentine permeated every surface. It was near my favorite café, the Edison, where all of us— painters, musicians, and therapist friends—gathered for long coffees and longer talks. This is where I intended to stay for the rest of my life, but on that day, I opened the door to the German soldiers.

"Open up or we'll bash down the door."

'No need for that,' I replied in German, a distinct advantage over the Czech I might have used. I allowed them entry, then asked: 'What do you want from me? I am a painter.' I hoped the soldiers would not take the obvious clarity of that statement for sarcasm, but they had no nuance to worry about.

"Are you Jan Emmerich Mikeska?" *they asked.*

'Friends call me Riko but, yes, my name is Jan Mikeska.'

"That is not the name on the lease."

'My wife's name is on the lease.'

"Well then, where's your wife?"

'Not here,' I said, wondering how on earth I would avoid answering the questions sure to follow.

"It is important you tell us where she is."

'And why would that be?'

"We are looking for Jews," *the older of the two soldiers said.* "She is Jewish."

'Yes, indeed, she is Jewish, but she is no longer in country.'

"Where is she?"

'For that, you will have to ask the authorities.'

"We *are* the authorities."

'Well, then, you must know where you took her. I know you are very efficient. She was taken away in May, four months ago,' I lied.

"We have no record of that, and we keep very careful records. Be careful, Herr Mikeska, we count on your cooperation or you, too, will find yourself going away."

'I am not Jewish,' I said, feeling both relief and shame.

"It doesn't matter. This studio is in her name and no Jews are allowed to own property in Prague. As long as it is in her name, you will not be able to work here."

Instead of confiscating my paintings then, or shackling me to take me to a police station, or putting a new lock on the door, the soldiers left inexplicably. I knew they would be back. Idiots, *Riko muttered in shaking rage and fear, reliving what had passed nearly thirty years before. The authorities I alluded to taking Greta away were friends, not the Nazi party, but the word 'authority' alone veered the Germans off course. They were careless listeners when following a single-minded pursuit.*

Initially, we did not speak specifically of art, not his, nor of art in general. He monopolized the conversation as older people do when they have not had much company. He had a lot to say. He kidnapped Tom and me with his knowledge of history—the dissolution of the Austro-Hungarian Empire *(I felt so happy, fool that I was!),* of geography's role in shaping history (the detours in Alexander's advances towards Persia); of poetry (all German—Schiller, Heine, Goethe) and, ultimately, of art (the disarticulation of narrative in minimalism). His restless hands toyed with a small clay figure of a horse a young pupil had given him, but he was reluctant to slide out any of his works from the series of open cubbies that lined his studio.

Some two hours later, Riko revealed some of his pieces, and after he felt we had established our true interest in his paintings, in the sunny palette he favored for watercolors, in the abstract tumult of a circus series for which he revealed a notebook full of realistically rendered pencil sketches, Tom and I left his studio cradling a canvas we had bought, thus accomplishing the true purpose of Lars's introduction.

The oil was of a cityscape looking north from his studio, a bright splash of orange reflecting the sun bouncing back from one of the windows of a brick building opposite him. In reality, other buildings near-by showed off classical faces, gargoyles, stuccoed arabesques that might have reminded him of the European architecture he had left. In the painting, Riko left them out. Its size was roughly 36 x 48 inches and labeled *At Night*.

As we left him that afternoon, Riko's parting comment as we left was, *Dorothy Dehner paints down the hall.*

Riko dropped this seeming non-sequitur with a slight upturn of his mouth, the guarded smile I was to recognize that had both casualness and purpose: to invite admiration, verification and questions.

At Night

3

Meeting Greta

What did you bring me? were the first words out of Greta's mouth when I called at their home, a ritual by now of two year's standing. The brownstone in which they lived at 414 West 20th Street was on the south side of a leafy street of four-storied houses all the same height, and across from the beautifully-bricked Episcopalian Theological Seminary. But for the fact the Mikeskas lived on the third floor, it was an ideal spot for two aesthetically susceptible artists. In the early 1950s, when they had moved in, the available next-to-last floor had attracted Riko for its light, but now, nearly thirty years later, with both of them arthritic and advancing into their 80s, climbing the staircases that listed disconcertingly to one side grew burdensome.

Greta never answered the bell to any unseen person, so the only way she had of verifying who was pushing the outside buzzer was to open the window and look out. Her hair stood like a white corolla round her head, and her raspy voice had a whine to it.

I would park my bike, which I rode from the upper East 80s, and lift from its back-wheel baskets the items Greta asked me to bring. Routinely I called to ask her if I might come by and, if so, was there anything she wanted or needed? No matter that I went down the checklist Greta had dictated, it was as if she would not grant me entry unless I had every item, and then some. Riko and Greta were pretty much destitute by this time, so the purchases were always an understood gift.

When she verified I had what she wanted, she would withdraw her head sideways, like a crab, and leave me waiting on the sidewalk until she festinated her way to the inner buzzer. *Bring up the mail, will you?* was another constant.

The mail for all the apartments was thrown into disorganized piles onto a dark refectory table in the hall where a lamp of meager lumens made me decipher with difficulty what mail was directed to Mikeska. I leaned against the wall to keep my balance on the warped stairs, and when I reached the third landing, Greta would be standing at the open door, backlit by the windows facing the street. The Parkinson's disease she suffered, as a result of having the Spanish flu in 1918, made one hand shake and slowed her progress. She preceded me with her tentative flat-footed shuffle along the hallway past many of Riko's canvasses braced between the floor and the dirtied chipped walls. We passed a small bedroom converted to a storage space for Riko's larger canvases, none easily accessible—in fact, hardly displayed. As we entered the kitchen-living room, only one wall was free of windows, kitchen cabinets, sink and entrance door and, on that wall, there were no discernible Mikeskas, as if at home his art was excessive.

She patted the enamel-topped table for me to set down the

mail and food parcels, then unpacked the things with grunts of approval or comments such as *I didn't ask for that.* She accepted the Sacher tortes or éclairs that were the treats I could find, but not until after she had questioned me where I had bought them.

Pain Chocolat? But they are not so good there. You should try at La Maison Française, or, better yet, at Café Wien.

"I tried them there last time, but you said you found them inferior. There's a new Hungarian bakery opening near us. I'll try there the next time," I would promise, knowing full well that the strudels, rugelach, truffles would be found wanting by the grande dame she still wished herself to be. Greta had been brave in her losses, and I knew full well she would have been disappointed if one day I did not bring her a taste from long ago. She and Riko spoke with longing of the pastries they ate in Vienna, Paris or Berlin, and their exiles had not been easy.

I watched her scuffle from table to pantry closets to sort out the Brillo pads or laundry soaps or Knorr soups she had ordered, then watched her set out plates, knives, forks, spoons and chipped tea cups for our lunch together, as often as not, some sardines and dark bread we both liked, or a soup I had made. The important thing was to share a meal and to talk. Over the course of months, Greta parceled out her own and Riko's history in the even rhythms and low tones of her German-sounding English. She spun stories slowly and well, a time of full control for her, a rarity in her life. That her recollections skipped around seemed fair enough, titillated me with what details the interstices might have provided and nudged me into questions I might ask on another day. I took to bringing my recording machine on my weekly visits thinking the tapes would be a welcomed set of memories to share with their friends.

Do I really sound like that? she would laugh when she asked me to play back a passage. *Wait. Let me sing you some 'Carmen' in German. You know, the girls at the sewing shop where I had my first work in this city used to make me sing it to them.* But she would not sing. *Where were we?* she said, looking up as if I had derailed her. What threw her off the track, however, was Riko's homecoming.

In the late afternoons, tired after his walk of eight blocks, five of them long crosstown ones, Riko entered their apartment. In cold weather, he would shed his black beret onto a desk top in his home study and shrug out of a long dark overcoat, left arm first, right one next to favor his painter's arm; in summer, he'd hang his wide-brimmed straw hat on a wall hook. He would pause briefly at the door into their kitchen-living room for two reasons: to be noticed (he never lost his physical beauty and needed the assurance that all eyes were on him), and to assess the light, its degree of slant from the sliver of southwestern view they had out their back windows. He would sniff at and comment on his supper on the hob, though he was seldom hungry.

His greetings to Greta were courteous, almost gallant, as they were to me. He would remain standing, a silhouette against the back-lit sky until the sun sank past the Hudson River and the Jersey Palisades. Only then would he sit, separate from us, in a chair by the window and wait for Greta to serve him his hot tea in a glass that she fitted into a silver holder and placed on a flimsy side table by his chair. She set a pot of opened cherry jam with a long spoon in it, so that he might stir the sweet fruit into his tea.

Even if he caught the tail end of Greta's and my conversation, he would ask me to update him on the subject of our discussions. Too often, he would scold Greta at a recollection he felt was unrepresentative: *You know nothing!* he would say with an exasperated exhalation, a dismissive turn of his Augustan head. But through the years of our talks, I never caught Greta in the wrong and, whenever we had our solitude, I let her talk on.

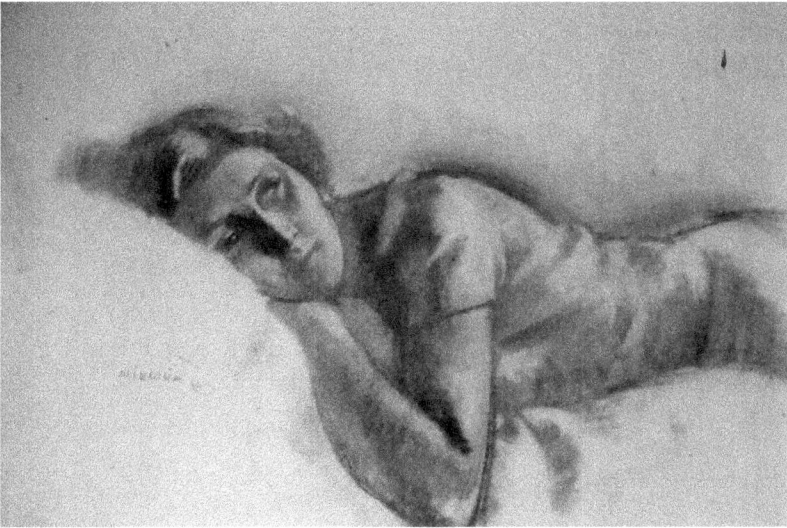

Study of Greta

4

Putting Pieces Together

OVER THE COURSE OF MONTHS, and once our shopping results, mail-sorting, tea-making rituals were set, Greta shared Riko's history. Her recollections were cogent and fluid, her narratives chronologic and compelling, but always interspersed with current affairs and gossip she followed avidly in the newspapers.

What do you think of the Reagan–Gorbachev meeting in Iceland? I think Gorbachev is handsome with that birthmark on his forehead. Looks like the map of the world. Appropriate for a leader, wouldn't you say? Or, *Do you believe in the détente between the US and Russia?* Or, *Princess Diana has improved the looks and wardrobe of the Royal family. I love it when they show lots of pictures of her. She's really pretty, don't you think so?*

I came to learn what topics she truly wanted comments on, but avoided offering opinions that might set her sharpening verbal knives. Greta spoiled for a fight, but I lacked the time and disposition to engage her challenges.

What ultimately refocused her historian's task was that Riko's strength was waning, his story-telling truncated, his hours away from home diminishing. For these reasons, Greta felt a new urgency to set straight everything she could think of about Riko's life starting from the beginning.

Riko's cultural origins were complex. His father, Kazimir, was born in Dobroslavice, a village that was sometimes part of Moravia, sometimes part of Silesia, but certainly of Slavic origin and Austrian domination.

Greta looked up to see if there might be confusion in my face about the geography that tripped off her tongue. *Bring me the Atlas! Americans know nothing*, she would say, sounding like Riko. She was partially right, of course, but the purpose of stating her doubt was a reminder that made clear she felt anyone on this side of the Atlantic was ignorant—ignorant of geography, and absolutely uninformed of European history in general, the Austro-Hungarian Empire in particular. She and Riko held in contempt the spoiled Americans who hadn't had soldiers destroy their property, demand and take everything that was most precious in their victims' lives, move people around as if they were cattle. Americans hadn't even been bombed on their home soil, for heaven's sake. What did any of us living on the American continent know about anything?

Her shaky right index finger first found Berlin for me; then, once on the page, moved surely in a southeastern direction across Prague and further south to Vienna.

Prague was at the center of the most traveled corridor between the two most important centers of European civilization for centuries. Everything came to Prague—all the Jewish culture that had accumulated in Vienna and all the German culture that crowded Berlin.

Now, from Prague, travel straight east almost two hundred miles, and there you find Ostrava. Vitkovice, where Riko was born, doesn't even show up; it was simply considered an appendage on the other side of the river Ostravice. Her finger circled the areas of Bohemia, Moravia, Silesia that sat in a northwest to northeast cap on her pre-World War One map of Czechoslovakia.

And then look, she said, now completely involved with the map in front of her. *Take a northeasterly direction into Poland to reach Krakow, not more than 75 miles away, and half-way there, you hit Auschwitz.* Here her eyes turned steely, her breath shortened for reasons I would find out presently. *Now, put away this atlas. I am getting ahead of Riko's father's time.* Finger to her lips to ensure I would not interrupt, she forged on.

In Dobroslavice, the Mikeskas were a well-to-do, long-established family of farmers. I met him after Riko proposed to me, when I was in my twenties. But you'll have to wait for that story, she said in a coy manner that did not suit her better matter-of-fact self.

Kazimir used to love to tell me stories, how he attended a one-room school house which was divided in two. Beginning students sat on one side of the room for three years, and then on the other—if the teacher advanced them—for another three years. The elderly school master taught both sides of the classroom more or less at the same time in the Czech language and smoked a pipe that Kazimir said looked two yards long. With this he would point to his pupils. When it was harvest time, he understood that the boys would work in the fields and not be in school, but he didn't have to worry about the girls who were educated at home.

Kazimir recalled winters were severe, there were few proper roads, and the march to school through the snow was long and uncomfortable.

Horses and sledges were reserved for those who couldn't walk. Many a child arrived in an agony of chilblains and frost bite.

At home, Kazimir's parents spoke Czech and Polish. They were Hussites in an area that was predominantly Roman Catholic.

You know what a Hussite is, don't you?

I was becoming used to her dares, understood this was a game of wits she liked to play, and listened to her explain—something she was set to do in any case—the life of Jan Hus and the Hussites.

She and Riko interested me as much for their intimate knowledge of wide-ranging subjects as for the factual bases. The Mikeskas had prodigious memories. Over the years, one of their friends took to checking what they reported, even to quotations. They were always exact.

And so Greta and I exclaimed over the improbability of Jan Hus's legacy, how long ago he had lived (1369-1415), how his simple adherence to the beliefs of the English preacher, John Wycliffe, landed Hus at the stake.

Both Wycliffe and Hus said people should be able to read the Bible in their own language, not just in Latin. In Bohemia, Hus complained loudly against the tyranny of the Roman Catholic Church, so of course they didn't like him very much.

Greta paused, gave me another professorial session and took me on a related tangent. *You understand the printing press had not been invented yet, and how burdensome it was to produce books, don't you? The monks went blind doing their copying by candlelight,* she said insinuating it was my fault. Then a weighty pause. *You <u>do</u> know when the printing press came into being, don't you?*

I disappointed her greatly by suggesting around 1440, one of those dates I learned in school like the dates of the Battle of Hastings or of the Magna Carta, though as a grown-up, I wondered if I remembered any facts correctly, or believed them if I did.

She sniffed and went on. *Anyone found with a vulgate edition* (painfully and lengthily hand-wrought, she reminded me) *would be executed. When Hus was tried as a heretic, he was tied and chained to a stake piled high with straw, the Wycliffe Bibles used as kindling.*

Greta looked up to see if the horror of this story had affected me appropriately (it had), then ended the account with one of her throw-away lines: *Hus sang for a living in churches.*

Pour me some tea, would you? I am talking too much, and it makes my mouth dry.

Any suggestion that we break off, Greta waved away. She took up her account of Riko's father as if she had merely stopped to pick up a stitch in knitting. She was happy in her reminiscences of her father-in-law, a man she found *handsome and easy to talk to.*

Kazimir was ambitious. His talents and enthusiasm for farming and bee-keeping—one of the more valuable skills he learned from his schoolmaster—were not enough for him. He was perhaps the first to leave his farming community to seek a living in the city, but first he had to serve in the military. He was lucky; he entered during a non-combative time and used the disciplines the army taught to his advantage: he learned to read, write and speak German fluently.

He found work in Vitkovice, which, like the schoolhouse he attended, was split in two. The river Ostravice cut the town into a

Polish half and a Moravian half, where Kazimir rented the same small house in which I met him and Mother years later.

The job he secured was in the foundry of the Vitkovice Bergbau-und-Geweldschaft, a commercial-industrial partnership whose steel works were owned originally by the Roman Catholic archbishops of Olmutz (Olomouc). When the archbishop died, the Church's funds were insufficient to expand the company in the way of the future so, by the time Riko was born in 1903, the steel works had passed into the Jewish hands of the Austrian Rothschilds and the Baron von Gutman. These were notable changes considering the political and re-ligious climate even then—even then. Ach! Jah![1] Religions!

Like Picasso's *Absinthe Drinker*, Greta came to lean her elbows on the table, twine her arms around one another, hold her graceful long-fingered hands in one another, and secure the palsied one that held her cigarette. Her palsy was one of the many compromising conditions she had and would encounter in her life, but she made no allusion to it then; instead, her still gaze and thoughts focused on the past. She might have been sitting for a portrait.

Kazimir told me he was not strong enough to work in the foundry, but along with his fine German, he had good clear penmanship. You have to remember the post office of this large international company still operated in pre-modern technological times, she said with another of her didactic reminders. *Even typewriters were rare, so it mattered that Kazimir had clear and beautiful penmanship. Ah, yes*, she said sarcastically, *for the Germans the beauty of his writing counted too. And, of course, those who worked in the post office*

---

[1] See Edward Crankshaw in Notes on page 256

had to read and write different languages, but especially German, the language of culture, business and politics of the Austro-Hungarian Empire. Moravia and Silesia were an integral part, you know.

She threw me one of her stares as if alerting me to an exam she would give after class. I learned to relax under her scrutiny by understanding her need to have the superior edge on facts, and the moral one on opinions. No question I was learning a lot.

Kazimir knew his geography, and he was quick at remembering how much postage went on what weight of letters and packages to which different countries. He could sort mail in various languages, and he could address envelopes legibly; in short, he was a prize and he rose to become head of the post office of this large concern.

Ha! she laughed. *Show me your handwriting. I want to see if you'd pass!*

Ha! she laughed again, indicating my failure by dismissively turning back to me the paper on which I had written *Czechoslovakia* in a script that did not even achieve the standard American Palmer requirements. Why I did not rise to her nettling was no mystery; I found her character fascinating and—alas—felt sorry for her. She was needier than I was. I thought I could walk away any time I wanted to. For now, she had my ear.

Kazimir met and married a beautiful young girl, Anna Brudy, also from Silesia. She came from a bourgeois family of German and Polish extraction where they spoke both languages at home, but almost no Czech. The Brudys were practicing Roman Catholics and considered themselves part of the established order, superior to the family of farmers their daughter was marrying into. Kazimir converted when his becoming a Roman Catholic became a pre-requisite to marrying Riko's mother.

After Anna married Kazimir, she was always referred to as Mrs. Mikeska, or Mother. She wore a black velvet ribbon round her elegant neck and seemed always to be bound by a corset. Her carriage was straight and proud. She wore her hair up in a chignon and kept an immaculate house. Kazimir and Riko both tyrannized and venerated Mother. She was terribly bossed on one level, yet set apart as the inviolable moral paragon on another. Riko grew up with a strong sense of two highly romanticized kinds of love for women. One was heavenly and pure, the other earthly and wanton. Mother was the epitome of the first.

And then, as if to shake any smidge of sentimentality in her account, she shifted her position in the chair and went back to the map. In aggressive strokes, as if she were gouging a new route across three longitudinal meridians, she again pointed out Berlin, Prague, Vienna and emphasized: *This was the most important corridor of culture throughout the Austro-Hungarian Empire. Even before! The Holy Roman one, too, she said, and even now. But what do you know? You have never even had a war on your continent!*

I was hesitant to mention the Revolutionary War or the Civil War that had occurred on American soil and left scars from which there seemed to be no healing. Greta's wounds were more recent, however, and the mutilations global. A competition did not seem to be in order.

Now, I am tired. Tell me what you are doing with the children. Are you making the Hungarian Easter eggs I told you how to make? Did you get the bees wax and the dyes on 6th Street near the Ukrainian church?

I did not have the heart, patience or energy to correct her, tell her it was a friend of mine who had introduced both my daughters and myself to the painstaking process of a kind of tie-dyeing of the egg shells, but Greta's studies had been in the visual arts. There was no doubt that she might have painted Ukrainian eggs. What would she have been like as a teacher, I wondered. Perhaps in her youth she had patience, but I now felt it was in short supply. What she needed and wanted was credit for all things, a credit she knew would evanesce as soon as she heard Riko's keys fit the lock.

Riko's mother, Anna Brudy Mikeska. Unsigned and undated.

5.

Entrapment or Negotiation?

I want you to write a biography of Riko.

Greta's greeting floored me. We had met sporadically since the previous fall; now, the leaves on the mountain ashes and sycamores lining 20th street shimmied yellow, and the ginkos gave off their signature stench. The weather was turning cold. In fair weather, and when my children were in school, my meetings with Greta were fairly regular, but there would be periods when three weeks would go by without a face-to-face. During those times, Greta would call with guilt-inducing tones in her voice.

Riko and I are old. How can you leave us alone? Have you forgotten about us so quickly?

I hated her wheedling. The first sentence was incontrovertible; the second made me want to remind her there were others she spoke of to whom she might apply for attention; the third was impossible. I felt caught in a web sagging with evidence of past prey, and it seemed the spider woman was before me ready to chew off heads as needed. Would that include her husband's? Not possible. Wasn't this about promoting him and his work? This last thought was as evasive as quick silver, but it niggled.

So why did I go back? Guilt? Yes. Respect for their age? Yes. Fascination? Certainly. They were living libraries who sustained themselves with something organic, like phagocytes swallowing nutrition where and when found. But that definition didn't satisfy, because they didn't entirely devour. They were better saprophytes, exotic orchids with tenacious roots that knew their lives depended on keeping their hosts compromised but alive and attracted.

I questioned if I returned because of loyalty. To whom? Would it be to Lars Björling, who had introduced us originally with a plea to help them? Although he returned to New York from time to time, I noticed he did not visit the Mikeskas. Were they now my sole responsibility? Surely not! Beyond my appeasing agreement that someone ought to write about Riko (no one had so far), Greta's proposition was a project I had not considered, and I told her so. I had no credentials to offer and my writing life was fully booked with short stories, travel articles, and writing proposals for courses in which I conflated different subjects for middle school classes, such as Teaching English through Science, and Teaching Science through Music. Why would I even contemplate one more enormous project?

Why else are you doing this? she shot back. *Look what I have for you!*

With a growing sense of restlessness, if not panic, she started bringing out artifacts from their past. She placed on the kitchen table between us papers and letters from Czechoslovakia, Italy and England that were kept in disorganized fashion in large manila envelopes, none identified by subject on the outside.

Here! A review by Johannes Urzidil, a leading art critic in Germany, who wrote a long article called 'Landscape.' 1936 he wrote it! Riko already had a name. It was published in 'Zeichnung,' a well-regarded magazine of the time. He focused the article entirely on Riko's work, how he evolved from basic drawing into painting, how he used the plasticity of colors, light and shade to achieve three dimentional representations. Greta interrupted her rush of enthusiastic reading to remind me of my shortcomings: *Of course you can't read it, because it's in German.*

She translated as she read, skipping here and there over short passages she thought were superfluous. In fact, the article was highly complimentary of Riko who had conquered two distinct talents—graphics and painting—according to Mr. Urzidil. *Whether in aquarelles, gouaches or oils, his landscapes and still lifes had become independent of the long experience of drawing which is used expediently. The works of Mikeska give you joy.*

Greta paused to search for another memento.

And here, a list of galleries that showed Riko's work in the United States. Read this aloud! she commanded. *It's in English.*

She handed me art historian, Doris Ast's, highly laudatory and philosophic review of Riko's retrospective work from his arrival in the United States in 1948 to November, 1962, exhibited at the Argus Gallery in Madison, New Jersey. In it, Ms. Ast highlighted Riko as a model among the European émigrés, whose shared plight was in adjusting socially, culturally and financially to the contemporary American scene.

*In Europe, artists were lionized, supported. Here he has to pro-
mote himself. He doesn't know how to do this. It is not his talent.
People must help him!*

By 'people,' and by Greta's intense look, she meant me at
that moment. She turned to two large pamphlets showing off
commercial projects she and Riko had done together for com-
panies in New Jersey. The first was an ad for *The Solution to
Your Drainage Problems*, in which Riko had sketched humorous
single-line cartoons of someone admiring drainage units that
looked like enormous bird condominia, or silos full of small
open rectangular windows.

The second was a brochure from *Your Textile Neighbor*, promoting what Hathaway Manufacturing Company was doing to
make things easier for their employees. Here, Greta had drawn
the graphics. They ranged from broken reels of cotton strips
entitled *The Old Way* to tidy taut reels delivering ribbons of material under the rubric of *The New Way*. There were companion
graphics of an old woman weaving at an ancient loom, and of
a Pilgrim-hatted clean-up man sweeping away shreds of cut
threads from beneath the loom. This depiction sat opposite to
that of a young man standing by a large sleek assembly with roll-
ers over which clean sheets of cotton wound round an immense
receiving roller—no floor clean-up here, it implied.

She gave me no sense that these works of illustration were
beneath the Mikeskas' ambitions as fine artists; on the contrary,
she looked at them proudly as creative money-makers, and was
pleased the Hathaway issue came to be known as 'the Mikeska'

issue. Despite Riko's prohibiting her from using their married surname in her art works—*There will be only one Mikeska, and that is me,* he had said early into their marriage—she had insisted that Hathaway use 'Greta Mikeska' as illustrator in their ad. She was good at it, and this assignment was a mere extension of her training at the Reimann School of Art and Design in Berlin.

Further, Greta's pleasure derived from her practical adaptabililty to a welcomed Americanization that freed her from the constraints of 'high art'. Riko's depictions in the first pamphlet were light-hearted. He would have seen the fun in making humorous cartoons, but I wondered if he did not feel some embarrassment or even debasement in contributing to such frank commercial art. I never risked asking him.

These were my scudding thoughts as Greta continued to shuffle papers under my gaze, and started to shove some back in the Manila envelopes. I became aware that Greta's thoughts were becoming more disjointed, her affect more manipulative.

You must speak with Doman and Halina Rogoisky, friends from Riko's school days in Vitkovice, Greta hectored. *Halina lives in Queens, I think; I know you can find her. And of course there are Eve Korner and Erika Kalmer—very important those two. Riko knew them from school and Prague, but it was their presence in England that made a difference in our lives. They stayed in London after the War. You'll have to find them there,* she said, offering no addresses.

I pictured myself in Hyde Park on a soap box bull-horning, "Does anyone know Erika Kalmer or Eve Korner? They might have different married names . . ."

The Bozzis, friends we spent our holidays in Ischia are in Italy—Bari, I think—and the Björlings are in Stockholm. Greta went on, adding contacts shamelessly but astutely, as if traipsing around eastern and central Europe would be the most natural steps for me to take in piecing together the history of Riko Mikeska. As to who would finance this venture, or how my family might react to such a plan, those would be my problems, clearly insoluble for the moment.

Three dusty African masks looked back at me inscrutably from one wall, and a two small Native American katchina dolls standing on a shadowed sill seemed to say 'don't look to us for answers.' In the nano seconds of stress-filled concentration, my eyes roamed the room for a pleasant distraction, but what I took in were faded magazine pages torn from catalogues of paintings by a medley of Medieval artists. They were taped ad hoc to the crackled yellowing walls of a room unpainted for years. But for a tiny framed Rembrandt sketch of a head, the absence of real art bespoke poverty, not lack of interest. A Janus-faced flower pot Greta had shaped in an art class at a near-bye Y tripled her presence in the room: one clay face was black, the other facing in the opposite direction was white, and then there was Greta's real face. I found no comfort.

We'll keep on with the interviews, is all I trusted my voice to offer her.

I left angry, conflicted and entrapped. Clearly, I was interested in her life and Riko's, and she knew it. Why else had I devoted so much time to them, made them part of my family by bringing them to dinner at our house, ensured that our puzzled children and Tom were kept abreast of this fixation of mine, gone to hear Greta vent week after week? I wanted to convince her I understood their lives mattered, that they would not be forgotten, but I was not ready to commit to a project I had not initiated. I, too, had lost worlds and family of my own, I wanted to tell her, but what remained of the Mikeskas' lives consumed them completely. I accepted that their grief, courage, talents and resilience deserved a pay-off, a validation wrought in words, if not art, to ink their histories, but…oh, so many buts!

I stomped down their dangerously uneven stairs continuing my vomitus of silent rebuttals to her. 'I esteem your disparate backgrounds, your complex and fascinating cultural histories, your multiple languages, your being born into an Empire whittled away by crumbling economics, religious persecutions, wars, insane rulers, lemming-like followers. Your double exiles aren't difficult to fathom!' I wanted to shout to the wind as I pedaled back home in a fury that did not cool even in the nearing-zero weather.

It was finally tempered before my next meeting with Greta when, unusually, Riko asked me to meet him at his studio, a place he held as a private sanctuary for his few students and fewer colleagues. Greta told me he did not allow her to come. *I make him nervous; he's afraid I will pass judgment, yet if he's painting a restless child, he wants me there to keep the child in order.*

Riko looked tired. I could see his day bed was mussed, the wide-striped wool cover drawn carelessly in place. I suspected he came to the studio to sleep as much as anything, although a book by his favorite mystery story writer, Dorothy Sayers, lay open to a page he was reading. There were food stains on his smock, and the smell of a Knorr's potato and leek soup lingered in a pan on his single spent burner. I exclaimed over a couple of notebooks open to his singularly beautiful charcoal and sepia portraits, but ignored the small still life studies smudged in browns and blacks. I did not want to be drawn into questions about them. I longed for the splashes of blues, whites, blacks and reds I found in his Marcel Marceau series, or in his energetic blasting abstracts of the circus, a life he found metaphoric of our larger one, but braver.

After my inquiries about his health (*Ach! Age!*), he asked, *How are you getting along?*

'You mean generally or with Greta?'

You are young and healthy and have a nice family, so I assume you are getting along generally fine, he said dismissively. *I mean with Greta. Is she giving you sufficient biographical material?*

So they were in cahoots. I almost laughed out loud at my naiveté. Despite my protestations that I knew nothing about writing a proper biography, the idea of my writing his had become their mutual goal. 'She's been telling me about your parents, about Vitkovice,' I said.

Riko came alive. *Well, then, I tell you my version!*

We lived in tidy but cramped two-storied houses that sat cheek by jowl to one another. My friends and I watched our mothers' daily struggle to keep lace curtains white, shut windows when bursts of coal burning turned the air especially rancid and sharp, but these were inconveniences compared to the suffering of the miners.

In winter, the coal miners were down in the shafts well before sunrise and came up again only after the sun had set, as if they were some counter weights on a pulley system that denied them light and warmth. If it didn't snow or rain on Sunday, their only day of rest, they might see and feel the sun veiled through coal dust.

It was barbaric. I cried the first time I saw a daisy push its way out of some filthied concrete. There it was showing us a miracle of beauty and vitality, yet no miner saw her.

Did she tell you that? he asked. His defensiveness took me aback as his description had seemed more like a private confession. He didn't care for an answer and went on.

The divisions did not start and stop at the entrance to the mines; there were no Czechs in high positions either. The German sense of national and cultural superiority overwhelmed the Slavonic, Polish, Bohemian, Moravian, Ruthenian and Jewish people that made up the diverse populations and languages of the workers.

Riko paced as he reminisced, his sense of anger and injustice apparently as emergent as the days in which he and his family were experiencing it. Riko worked his graceful hands as if he were wringing out the disgusts of his life. His long, thin fingers fisted in anger, then released, but he could not physically exorcise his fears, shame and sadness in the same way.

There we were, captives to an obsequious life, accepting visits from officers in the Austrian Army, people who wandered in and out of the prefectures under the Emperor, and who came regularly to visit the steel works and even our homes. It was one of them who started my interest in art. I must have been six.

The story was funny and harrowing at the same time. One of the visiting officers gave Riko a children's Bible that had simple depictions in black and white. In Riko's eyes, the great bundles of grapes and the fabrics on the men who returned with Joshua from the land of Caanan cried for color. He mentioned this to the officer who came up with colored pencils the next time he passed by Riko's father's office at the steel company.

For your son, he said. *After all, I am a painter myself,* the officer added.

As Riko eked purple and greens and crimson with his *not-so-good* colored pencils, he relived the stories of Moses pointing out the Promised Land—a land he was not allowed to enter himself—or of Jesus before Pilate and his tribunal, or of other heroes unconscionably wronged. Riko felt a special closeness to them and spoke to his father about the peoples' grievances.

Kazimir appreciated both the artistic and human engagement the Bible and pencils provided, so the day the officer asked if he might paint a portrait of Mrs. Mikeska, Kazimir's wife (*She is a handsome woman*), Kazimir felt both flattered and obligated to return some kind of favor.

The officer arrived with his dragoman, who carried the easel, the canvas and the paints into the Mikeska household. They set up a mini studio within the modest household, and the officer began his numerous calls to work on the portrait. It pleased Riko's parents to extend hospitality to them, and Riko took it all in with curious eyes.

Entrapment or Negotiation?

He noted how the officers arrived in smart braided uniforms, the painter with a bronze medal around his neck commemorating some battle in the occupation of Bosnia and Herzegovina.[2] The dragoman arrived with his own sketchbook in which he had drawn scenes from that same campaign. He showed Riko pantalooned Turkish Muslims against backgrounds of battle he had brought to life in watercolors. Riko admitted to me he found these depictions skillfully done, much better than the portrait the artist-officer produced, despite his mother's putting on her finest.

The officer began to appear for the painting sessions when Riko's father was absent, but when his father appeared unannounced one day and caught the painter manually repositioning Mrs. Mikeska for a better view, the painting sessions ended. Riko came to understand his father's careful possession and protection of his mother who became the *ne plus ultra* of the sainted woman, and diametric opposite to looser women Riko would encounter and cherish on a different level.

The rupture also made him fear the officer might exact some retribution from his father. The young boy was nothing if not sensible to the undercurrents of power in his father's world.

I was aware that despite my father's ability to speak, read and write in German, keep accounts and addresses legibly inscribed in beautiful penmanship, keep in memory what postage went on which letters and packages to different countries—in short, own all the talents that made him invaluable as head of the company's post office—he never spoke his native Czech or spoke of his farming roots as he feared those revelations might cost him his job.

[2] See Rebecca West in Notes on page 258

Riko feared what truly might have ruptured Kazimir's services to the company was his faithful attendance at the Czech underground meetings during the last three years of the War. A mustachioed, multi-ribboned officer of the Imperial army showed up at the Mikeska's house randomly and unexpectedly at night to check that his father was there. Kazimir never was caught, but Riko's anxieties over his father's safety grew.

There was a long silence in the room like a break in a film stopping just as a catastrophic wave is about to crash. When Riko resumed speaking, so did the propulsive wave, and I felt the stinging salt hit me.

I have told Bernie these stories. He has recorded them all.

I was back to 'Why?' What need for repeated history, then? I had other things to do.

Bernie Gurevitz, a student, friend and framer of Riko's art, had known how far to go: eight two-sided tapes of Riko's voice. Beyond that, he resisted the Mikeskas' double Siren song, but unlike Odysseus and his sailors, I neither had myself lashed to a mast nor plugged my ears. I swam to their voices and approached the shattering rocks. My pieces scattered but found moorings in Czechoslovakia and England, Italy and the United States, where friends would present and corroborate the extensive accounts I compiled over the next twenty years. These stories would be repeated and filtered through all of us who pledged to serve first Riko, then both Riko and Greta.

Did we flatter ourselves about our own specialness in being the Mikeska's chosen ones? Did the intimacy they invited—their con game, really—play into our deepest desires to believe in them as artists and victims of the times, or did it fool us into believing we really might succeed as enablers towards their road to success? It took two sides to play this game, and I felt I kept flipping a coin with increasingly indistinguishable faces on either side. If the Mikeskas were victims to their own narcissism and dependence, were not the rest of us—I, primarily—victims of naïveté, emotional vulnerability, and artistic appreciation? Almost to a person, we friends of the Mikeskas were exiles. Digging through the emotional layers of that condition became my compulsion. The intrigue was irresistible.

Whether told first-hand or through others, their stories unfolded, and our journeys came together in time and telling.

6

Compilations

My proximal journey into Riko's past began with my fingers rambling through a cache of letters written from Riko's parents to Riko and Greta after 1938. They were stuffed helter-skelter in one of the faded manila envelopes Greta pushed across the kitchen table at me.

My eyes can't focus on this difficult writing anymore. Maybe Halina can translate them for you, Greta said, recalling one of Riko's friends from Vitkovice who, herself, had escaped to New York.

I found Halina Rogoisky's name, address and telephone in the white pages of the phone book.

Yes, of course, I know Riko! We were such friends. And now you are. Isn't that wonderful!

Well, yes. Could be. Too early to tell, ran through my mind. I spoke with her about the possibility of translating the letters and, with her generous acquiescence, mailed them for her to review; in time, she invited me to come speak of them.

I met Halina at her apartment in Forest Hills, Queens. The windows were open to the warm breezes, an invitation for casual wear. Halina, however, was dressed elegantly in an emerald green suit. She sat me down to a beautifully laid table with a lace-edged table cloth, dainty matching napkins and silver service to offer me a tea with pastries and cookies that might have fed an orphanage. Over this generous repast, she first admitted she had not been able to decode more than a few letters.

As you see, Anna and Kazimir, she said, referring to Riko's parents by their first names, and waving some tissue-crackling pages in front of me, *they often wrote these in pencil and used both sides of the onion skin. The letters are almost indecipherable. Some letters are in German, most in Czech.*

I felt embarrassed to have burdened her with such obscure writing, but the contents she had been able to glean were eye-openers to the fears and love Riko's parents felt for the young couple as the Nazi advances in 1938 forced Riko's and Greta's ultimate departure from Prague.

My older brother, Doman, and I were friends from Riko's school days in Vitkovice. Our father worked as a physician in the same iron and steel works as the one in which Riko's father ran the post office. In German it was called the Witkowitzer Bergbau-und Hüttengewerkschaft, and it formed the basis of our communal lives, offering a gymnasium, a pool, excellent health services, and an extensively stocked library, which our fathers took advantage of to add to our education. The company guaranteed trams to transport the employees and their children, and in the second car reserved for students, Doman and Riko could discuss anything out of earshot of parents and teachers. They became inseparable friends, and our families were close.

My father was a physician of a higher rank in that enormous hospital of the Vitkovice Iron Works. The Austrians loved titles and used them always. My father's title beside the M.D. was in German 'Primararzt', which simply put him in the category of very respected members of the hospital community. When Riko's father got into some difficulties at his post, my father simply stated that he knows him very well and considers him an honest and hard-working person. These remarks coming from a 'Primararzt' were honored, and the matter closed.

Halina's smile and far-away look invited me back to scenes she held dear. She said she and her twin sister, Janina, used to hide behind the curtained windows of their home waiting for the boys to alight from the tram. *We never let Riko and Doman out of sight,* she said, and I wondered if Riko might have been their first crush.

Our family loved Riko for his courtly manners—even as a young boy—, his interest in so much history, his artistic talent, of course, but perhaps most especially, his sense of justice. It was born in the geography and history of Vitkovice that changed from an agricultural town to become, by the time of Riko's birth, the industrial giant.

Indeed, the coal deposits were there for those clear-eyed enough to carve deeper into the agricultural land and develop it with the help of the flanking river Ostravice, meaning sharp, as sharp in its course as in its social divisions, with the workers in Vitkovice on one side, the power rulers on the other. Halina paraphrased Greta's synopsis of the rise of the Vitkovice Iron Works.

In 1828, the Roman Catholic Bishops of Olomouc took over the land and founded the company. An ecclesiastical ancestor in Riko's mother's family was among them; mention of his name alone would come to Riko's aid when he served in the Army in the Second World War. Halina breathed this as an aside.

Three years later, when the ruling Bishop died, Salomon Rothschild expressed a desire to own the company. By 1873, it was in his hands with him owning 51% of the shares, and the Viennese Wilhelm Ritter von Guttman owning 49%. I can still see the plaque on the entrance wall to the foundry spelling out these facts. As a child, you remember.

Halina laughed at this. *Imagine! All these owners with different religions being in charge, but business was their single common focus. By extending the railway that connected Vienna to Vitkovice, the Rothschilds made the foundry into the preeminent manufacturer and deliverer of iron and steel for the entire Austro-Hungarian Empire through the end of the First World War.*

It was in this hay-day of the early 1900s that the Rogoisky and Mikeska parents raised their children. By 1939, German domination expropriated the highly successful company from its Jewish owners to 'Aryanize' it, but those changes lay in the un-imagined future.

When we still were young, Riko and his younger sister, Julci, found refuge on their grandfather's farm on the outskirts of town. Here in summer, they exchanged the town's coal-peppered atmosphere for fresh air and for the much needed milk their bones craved. They also gorged on honey from the bees their grandfather kept.

Riko brought us some of the honey his grandfather produced. I still can taste the difference between the springtime and fall batches. The Mikeskas were not rich, but that access to the country gave them an advantage not all the inhabitants of Vitkovice had. Riko understood the inequalities of opportunity even among those who were not at the bottom of the employees' ladder.

In the safety of Halina's home and company in Forest Hills, far from her unsettled times of childhood, she indulged me with continued recollections.

When Doman prevailed upon our father to let Riko stay to dinner, we noticed Papa directed Riko to a table where we kept art books. Riko repeatedly picked up a book of Matejko's paintings and lithographs and poured over these pictures, especially drawings of hands. If he found a painting wanting in some aspect, he would point out the flaws without hesitation, as if he had imbued centuries of art expertise.

At table, Halina recalled, Dr. Rogoisky further directed Riko to sit opposite Mrs. Rogoisky. He knew Riko found her beautiful, and it was only time that stood between that observation and Riko's committing it to paper. He sketched quickly and with a sure hand, and ended up making portraits of all the women of the family.

Riko's world was art, even as a young boy, Halina said. *And where from? No one taught him. His family had not the slightest idea what he was doing. They were down-to-earth people, very loving, trying to do the best for him and his younger sister, Julci, but about art, they knew nothing and didn't encourage him. Instead, they were keen to have them learn instruments to be properly bred. Julci chose the piano, Riko the violin—an instrument he admittedly played with 'resolute enthusiasm and bad counting'.*[3]

[3] See F. James Rybka, MD in notes on page 258

Halina sketched how the Rogoisky and Mikeska children filled their hours with rigorous schooling and childhood utopias. She recalled one muddy day seeing the boys when they were eleven or twelve standing in deep conversation with the blackened rain pouring on them, their shoes getting ruined. *Shoes? Impossible to replace during the War, but there they stood arguing the baffling injustices they felt in their worlds.*

Clear to me was that like Don Quixote, errant knight of skinny frame but of brave heart, Riko railed against real and imagined enemies and rallied to the underdog. He wanted to defend his father in the foundry, himself and his schoolmates over the German bullies in class. When he was seven, Halina said he started making artistic instruments of war. Riko's weapons were potentially quite harmful. He fashioned arrows and spears from umbrella struts, and then decorated them with shells, feathers, coins, any kind of bright thing he might pick up on the streets. He wanted them to resemble some of the African spears he had seen in books a friend of the family used to bring him. His shields were of thick protective leather, as if he had taken apart a saddle. Of course, he then etched swirly patterns into the leather, embedded the swirls with Vaseline and the plentiful coal dust around, or painted the shields with frightening faces or geometric patterns, as if they had been stolen from the Maasai or Zulus.

He made one truly lethal weapon, Doman added in a rare interview. *It was a mace to which he somehow glued or screwed in nail-heads so that the nails were sticking out. Of course, Riko decorated the handle in some artistic way, put raffia and ribbons on the end for a flourish. I felt he had every intention of using it, but the adversaries were smart enough to stay out of the way.* Doman smiled in memory of Riko's arsenal, his zeal, and his loyalty. *He was courageous and proper, ready to attack and defend as he felt necessary, like his father, in fact. He was fun to be with. His presence charged the air.*

I could imagine Riko puffed up as if he had fitted a suit of armor over feathers of a pouter pigeon. Remove his psychological mettle, however, and he was vulnerable to his fear of helplessness and subsequent rage. It would be four years after my encounter with the Rogoisky siblings that I understood to the marrow the terror they described, and Riko's gut need to avoid falling victim to oppression. In the meantime, a greater tyranny was closing in on the world.

7

World War One

Art to the Rescue

WHEN THE FIRST WORLD WAR BROKE OUT, Riko was eleven. By that time, he had incorporated four years of discovering and practicing the art of commerce. From age seven, he sat on door stoops fashioning saleable sculptures with his pocket knife. He added these to small paintings he had made and put the proceeds into marbles which he could then barter or sell again. Here were useful savings rather than contributions to the family coffers. His father looked askance at Riko's trade and would not accept his money. He was concerned with weightier matters.

Kazimir Mikeska knew that if his son were to advance in any way, he should align himself with the Germans. The first step was to move Riko out of his Czech school and into a German one. A normally mild, even gentle man, Kazimir took Riko by the shoulders and forced eye contact.

Learn German well. It is the language of power. It saved me, and it will save you, too. Master it!

Kazimir based his evaluation on years of rulers and ironies. Centuries before the Habsburgs, the peasantry of Bohemia and Moravia were considered German and spoke German, but each succession of seamless wars identified that *the Serbs, the Croats, . . . the Czechs of the Sudetenland (that is the Bohemians and Moravians and Czech Silesia)*, wanted to assert their own identities through indigenous languages. In the late 18th and through most of the 19th centuries, there were alternate relaxations and constrictions on the use of languages other than German, but the push for pan-Germanism came from people as diverse within the Monarchy as Karl Marx, whose works Kazimir had read. Marx derode *Pan-Slavist dreamers as agents in agitating a portion of the Bohemian and South Slavonian people.' '. . . can they expect that history would retrograde a thousand years in order to please a few phthisical bodies of men, who in every part of the territory are interspersed and surrounded by Germans, who from times almost immemorial have had for all purposes of civilization no other language but the German, and who lack the very first conditions of national existence, numbers and compactness of territory?*

Marx was speaking in 1852. Kazimir in 1912. A staunch Czech, Kazimir had seen the Czech civil servants, such as school teachers, station masters and himself, advance because of their German, but Czech nationalism, language and pride were in ascendance. Kazimir felt it and knew Riko's fiercely nationalistic generation felt it too. Kazimir rued they needed reminding of where real power held sway.

Kazimir's employment in the Austrian steel works and railroad helped him pull strings to transfer his son into the German curriculum, but Riko was the only Czech in class, and he was not welcomed.

His family belonged to the loose federation of ethnically mixed Austro-Hungarians who, after the Napoleonic Wars, had not been as well-trained as the purely German conscripts, nor had they been impressed with their expected length of service—up to the age of 45. Their lack of moral homogeneity as a nation-state meant kinsmen would not fight against kinsmen, and the Austrian-Magyars did not accept German directions gladly; nevertheless, the loose cloth of unnatural fibers that entangled them had to hold in combat.

While overt signs of anti-Semitism had not yet surfaced, the Germans singled out Riko and the two Jewish boys in class as 'different,' and it did not help that the different three were brighter than the other students. In Riko's case, Nature stepped in.

There came a time when Riko had a sudden growth spurt. He grew so much in two months, that he insisted the teachers didn't recognize him. His long pants began to look like the shorts he'd discarded the year before; his uncontrolled voice registers betrayed his adolescence; his Adam's apple looked enormous in his skinny neck; his blushes deepened over his physical chagrin.

His studies of history, art and literature kept earning him high standing in class, but in mathematics and physics, *I was an utter fool*. A crude teacher, who *would become a dedicated Nazi* twenty years later, would take hold of boys' heads and smash them against their desks or against the wall. He broke Riko's nose forcing him to lick off an equation he had written on the blackboard. Whenever he called on Riko, he beat him until Riko became *frightened like a lizard in front of a snake*.

Despite his formidable intellect, Riko admitted he began to do badly at the ever too-cold school. He was also hungry.

With the war, food had become scarce and expensive. He recalled evenings when his father came home after he and Julci had eaten supper—a thin potato soup with a bit of 'milch' in it, if the butcher had extra fat. Mr. Mikeska would make fingers of toast and sardines that he would feed alternately, first to Julci, then to Riko. *No meal ever tasted better.*

Riko's art deflected his hunger and saved his academic career. Two widely different art teachers at school began to notice this thin fellow and concentrated on his sketches. One teacher in particular, Karl Harrer, appealed to Riko's sensibilities.

Harrer was a very nervous and high-strung bachelor living with his mother. He was poor, talked too fast, smoked too much, got older and greyer, was despised and made jokes of, but he made the most beautiful drawings I have seen since Holbein's.

No sooner had Riko and Karl Harrer begun to appreciate each other's talents than Harrer disappeared, whether dismissed from school or because of poor health, Riko never found out. This was not a time to ask questions.

A second teacher, Anton Klinger, Riko described with the same, if opposing, minutiae. *He was jealous, vain, and a raté—a failure.* He hectored pupils on how to become draftsmen in order to fulfill the requirements of the curriculum by making them copy subjects he had picked out of art magazines. One student, Salo Salomonovič, would profit from this kind of style and would come to Riko's aid in a few years, but for now, Riko's concern was Klinger's bullying. Threatened by Riko's more creative abilities, Klinger pestered Riko and got angry with him for *my laziness, my wasted time creating war weapons and carvings*, yet acknowledged that in Riko's drawings, he 'had something there.' He then hounded Riko in another way—to join an inner artistic circle where Klinger held sway, and where Riko's talents would accrue to his teacher's benefit, but Riko estranged himself.

He learned to avoid Klinger's classes by hiding in the marbled school corridor filled with paintings and large plaster busts. He found an uncomfortable wrought iron bench painted white where he could squirrel behind a generically sculpted Roman with a dramatically protruding front covered in generous layers of a tunic. There he read a purloined school copy of the Decameron (which, along with other Romantic sagas he was not allowed to read at home), some 'sexy' novels (*What did we know about sex?*) of Hanns Heinz Ewers, and translations of Edgar Allen Poe's stories, both masters of sadistic horror fiction that fed Riko's adolescent fantasies.

Alone at home, or hidden in one of the crevices of the school halls, Riko started painting with oils he begged from his father. At age sixteen, he started to illustrate Poe's *The Adventures of Pym* and *Murder on the Rue Morgue*. He tried painting nudes, *this without ever having seen a nude woman*. He got hold of a weekly art journal published in Munich whose reproductions *had some color and wit*, and became acquainted with artists like Heinrich Kolbe, Feodor Dietz, and Alfred Kubin, artists who trended towards Jugenstil, a movement away from the increasingly unpopular Berlin Academicians. For now, Riko was copying their nudes.

Before the war came to an end, Riko was in badly undernourished physical and mental states. He collapsed with the Spanish flu and pneumonia. It took him a year to recover in a sanatorium whose name and place he buried in a psyche troubled by knowing he had yet to attain his 'Abitur,' the high school graduation. Once home, his ever-watchful parents fussed over him, see-sawed in their hopes as they saw him improve one day, droop the next. They propped him up with scarce calories and little by little exposed him to academic tutors. Once restored to health, with coaching in math, and with his precocity in the classics and literature, he won the Abitur *cum laude* by the age of eighteen.

And then, what? Riko wondered aloud to my own consternation.

If Riko's world seemed unstable, the larger world was also foundering. The four years of World War One's barbarous slaughter led to the overthrow of the mores, expectations, aspirations and social stratifications everyone, including Riko and his family, had accepted until then. These cultural and economic upheavals caused more lasting and incomprehensible damage than the bombs, strafings, mustard gas, mud, lice and dysentery had and, although the populace would be able to clean up from this last clutter of conditions, Riko's professional compass would teeter. He needed to stabilize his academic career.

Riko never thought he would be able to make his life as an artist, but the next thing to it, he figured, would be architecture. He proposed this to his father and together they considered possible schools for this discipline. The classes at the University of Prague seemed provincial to them, the German University had shut itself from the international currents of main life and, besides, was anathema to them after the War, so they looked to Vienna. He enrolled at the Akademie der Bildenden Kunste, the Fine Art Technical University of Vienna, whose head was Peter Behrens, already a celebrated architect who had designed many famous buildings in Europe and Russia, among them the German Embassy in St. Petersburg.

Riko began his studies in architectural drawing, copying three-dimensional plans, learning perspective. He was unsure of himself, especially when it was his doodles and not his academic class assignments of blue prints that attracted the attention of a set designer, Hofrat Alfred Roller. Roller, well-known for his productions at the Vienna Opera House, used to wander in and out of the various classes at the Akademie to search for new talent. He called Riko to his office about half way into the term and asked him to bring his portfolio. Riko was terrified, felt he would be dismissed from architectural classes as a fraud, and faltered into Roller's office. Roller introduced Riko to a *flamboyant, wonderful-looking, dignified, un-named gentleman*, who leafed through his work and doodles, then passed judgment:

You will never build homes, but you will paint them.

Riko was horrified. Did the Professor really mean that all Riko had to look forward to was painting the outsides of houses? He didn't dare ask. The Professor dismissed Riko who left unmindful that the Professor had kept his portfolio. When a few days later, the Professor sent for him again, Riko was convinced he would be expelled and imagined the humiliation of having to tell his parents, but he was in for a surprise. The Professor said:

I want to introduce you to Professor Ludwig Otto Haas Heye from the Berlin Academy. He is interested in your work and would like to meet with you and your father.

8.

Peripatetic Education

THE MEETING WITH PROFESSOR HEYE took place in Vienna at his home on Prinz Albrecht Strasse, 8. He pointed out the villas of the composer Richard Strauss and of Princess Pauline Metternich, a woman of such high social visibility and repute in Prague, Dresden, Paris and Vienna, that even Riko knew she had introduced cigar-smoking to Parisian ladies, and taught Czech women and men to ice skate. Riko applauded her promotion of the Czech composer, Bedřich Smetana but, as an ardent young Czech, he could not understand her equal enthusiasm over the works of the German composer, Richard Wagner. Many artists, including Edgar Degas and Eugène Boudin, fought to paint her. What about her caused painters to see her so differently, he wondered. Why did they choose such divergent palettes to show her off to their patrons, to history? With his head in the clouds of social history and artistic decisions bound to the opulence of the surroundings, Riko barely heard what Professor Heye was offering Riko through his father:

I would like to have Riko come to Berlin. He could live in my own home with my son and two daughters. I can arrange for him to receive a stipend from the government and to study to become a painter.

Riko never knew and, therefore, never explained, what it was about his art that Professor Heye liked enough to promise such a generous education. Riko's sketches, shapes, colors, shadings, and compositions may all have been fine, but it was the close relationship between Professor Heye and Riko's father, Kazimir, that cemented the offer. The two older men had taken an immediate liking to one another's courtly manners, probity, devotion to their progeny, and interest in culture. When Riko's father accepted this extraordinary offer on behalf of his son, Professor Heye proposed that before Mr. Mikeska return to Vitkovice, he accompany Riko and the Professor to Salzburg to the Festspiel Haus, where Heye was in the midst of designing the costumes and stage settings for Mozart's *Don Giovanni*, *The Marriage of Figaro*, and Franz Léhar's operetta, *The Yellow Jacket, Die Gelbe Jacke*, later changed to *Das Land Des Lachelns*.

And while there, why not drop in on the foremost theatre director of the day, Max Reinhardt and his éminence grise, Rudolph K. Kommer? Riko was meeting the artistic geniuses of the day and listening to music fit for the kings and princes who came to this hilly town of cultural renown and exhalted cuisine.

Professor Heye paid for every expense of the heady detour to Salzburg as well as for Riko's life and education in Berlin.

Berlin

Go on! Fifty yards into the street by yourself. I dare you!

The challenge from a fellow student at the Academy of Art lodged like a tick in Riko's ear and begged to be plucked. He tended to it on one of his first nights alone after his father's departure from Professor Heye's haven.

Yes, you must explore the city, go out and have a good time, the kindly Professor allowed, but the route Riko took to prowl the city detoured around the Professor's avenues of expectations.

The allure of the red light district overwhelmed. Seedy bars were on four corners of a street, and women with breasts exposed twined their legs around men against the walls between the saloons. Inside whirled a fug of smoke that once inhaled made you forget simple woes. Beer foaming in tankards were Riko's for a small dollop of his now relatively generous allowance. If he didn't like beer, he might try gin, transparent as scalding water, or liqueurs layered in intoxicating colors hiding the unwashed finger smudges on the oft-used glasses. Lift a finger and whatever illicit taste you wanted was yours. Best was this fresh comrade inviting Riko to prowl the city with him, encouraging him and giving direction.

Not yet a tom cat, Riko steeled himself for his voyage into the dark alley and heard, *Liebschen, wilst Du mit Mir Kommen?*

He realized from his reading of the Hanns Heinz Ewers erotic novels that he had run into his first proposition. He faced the voice, bowed stiffly, apologized with a lie that he had no money, and backed away both thrilled and horrified.

It's true! It's true! he remembered baying to his co-prowler. *Berlin came over me like a little boy*, Riko admitted to friends. He became a connoisseur.

The former and familiar Wilhelminian society so closely knit together for one hundred and fifty years, the one in which Riko's mother represented the paradigm of purity and inviolability, had unraveled into an enjoy-today-never-mind-tomorrow spirit of freedom and rebellion against the devouring inflation following World War I. For someone who had not even drawn a nude from real life, Riko plunged into a fleshy freedom he had not imagined.

His eyes raked over the women who came into the cafeteria at school, who were ready to sell themselves for a meal of white beans and brown bread, but he waited. He was living in luxury at the Professor's house with a room of his own, whatever meals he wished to eat there, and remarkable privacy within the Professor's larger family.

In the meantime, with his stipend, he could afford something new in his life, to host a few male students, for example, to a sauna, steam room and swimming. Here he showed off his athletic body and took diving lessons, and may have practiced the art of male seduction in his experiments in *fleshy freedom*, commonly accepted in the variations Berlin offered. All this is speculation, of course, but not unreasonable. It is equally probable that Riko, in the flush of confidence in his new station, felt that among the men he consorted with, he might find further promotion through his artistic talents and sexual magnetism. He felt, *rare, powerful and successful* for the first time in his life. He continued his entertainments by going to the *Schal und Rauh*—Noise and Smoke—Cabaret, ordering wine, playing grand. He learned which tailors fashioned the best double-breasted suits, silk shirts and ties, so that he might dress like a gentleman, *someone from a noble home.* Riko's push-pull between siding with the proletariat and aspiring to the rich had its first vigorous run.

There were among the students three girls, he said, and introduced what would become the constant grace in his life: women. With a flair for few revelatory words similar to his watercolor brushstrokes, Riko described the first trio he met in art class.

I remember them so vividly. They were lovely. One was rather voluptuous, red-haired, clever, spoke many languages. She was called Ellen May Keller. Another was Lottie Hammer. She had flat feet and hand-made shoes which intrigued me considerably, a wonderful complexion, handsome but not beautiful. The third girl had a receding chin on which she wore a brace to push it forward. She had dark hair, white milk and roses skin, a small heart-shaped mouth, lovely eyes, and was still rather a half-boy, not grown up. She was supervised by a governess. The young woman's name was Ilse Gruenfeld.

Trouble began when Ellen May Keller and Riko took a shine to each other. Even before Riko's departure to return home to Vitkovice for Christmas holidays *to show off my new wardrobe*, Ellen and Riko began exchanging letters. She had left him a watercolor he described as in her *flashingly brilliant* style, and this he had tucked into his desk at home in the Professor's house. He added some of the first letters flush with inquiry and undefined passion.

During his absence, the Finance Committee asked to review his work to judge whether or not they would extend Riko's stipend and scholarship. Professor Heye intervened, went into Riko's room, opened the drawer, saw Ellen's watercolor sketch and read the letters alongside.

Professor Heye interpreted these artifacts as a flagrant trespassing into his domain. He expelled both Ellen and Riko. *She is taking away from your artistic purity*, the Professor told Riko in Olympian misogyny.

Riko reported being furious, but on whose behalf is not clear. It is unlikely he would have leveled his anger at Professor Heye, the most ardent and financially helpful promoter he had experienced to date. And though his fondness for Ellen was genuine, Riko had not transgressed any sexual bounds in the home of his host; instead, he felt chagrin on his and Ellen's behalf, but despaired over only his own future.

Ellen's father pleaded with Professor Heye and with Riko. Had they but told him there was a friendly connection between these two students, Mr. Keller would have been happy to welcome Riko into their own house. Like Professor Heye, he took Riko's side, either not conscious of, or uncaring that Ellen was deeply hurt. Professor Heye publicly mocked her by showing both the offending painting and correspondence to her classmates.

Ellen was given no reprieve, and Riko stopped going to class. He packed his belongings in the wooden suitcase he had brought from his parent's house and found new lodgings on the first floor of a still fairly noble house. He had saved enough money to continue his diving lessons and to explore galleries and museums around town, but he saw no one. By Easter, he had eaten into his funds so dramatically, that the only place he inhabited was his own bed, where he might neglect caloric needs.

Ever the tender father, Kazimir Mikeska appeared at Riko's door the week after Easter. Professor Heye had spoken to him about the troubles, and admitted he reacted harshly. The two worked out an arrangement whereby Riko might return to the Academy long enough to put his works on display at the school's end-of-semester exhibition, and to sit for his exams. He had stellar results in both.

The next semester, Professor Heye suggested that Riko should have a separate studio in Berlin as a Meisterschuler. This would keep Riko out of the class before which he and Ellen had been humiliated, and entitled Riko to unhoped for largesse: to receive correction only once a week, to all the art materials he needed, and to a large room with illuminating windows in which he started to receive other artists, among them the great calligrapher for typography, E.A. Barber, whose alphabets are still in print, and whose dedication to Greek literature ensnared Riko. Of Ellen, nothing more was heard.

Another was Emil Orlik, painter, graphic designer and draftsman. His portraits of Rembrandt, Michelangelo, Bach,

Beethoven and Mahler continue to hang on walls of contemporary art and music schools. Orlik had traveled to Japan and returned to Europe to promote "Japonism" and photography. In Orlik, Riko found the catholic curiosity and god-given talents he craved. Orlik became Riko's teacher. He was the first to plant the idea that Riko would profit from spending substantial time in other art centers, starting with Paris.

Under Orlik's guidance, Riko experimented with the structural impressionism of Paul Cézanne vs. Seurat's pointillisme; the blatant German expressionism of Otto Dix and Ernst Ludwig Kirchner; Paul Klee's fey oddities; the Cubism of Fernand Léger and Pablo Picasso. Riko experimented but did not imitate until, two exiles later, he painted his homage to Pablo Picasso's 'Guernica,' a tribute itself to the Basque refugees bombed by the Germans and Italians during the Spanish Civil War.

Riko stayed in Berlin until 1923, the year of the most crushing economic collapse, when even his stipend was stretched thin, the sight of hopelessness beyond enduring. When school was dismissed for the summer, he returned home, where he met two young Dutch students specializing in mining from the University of Limburg. Riko's father had welcomed them into their home and helped them learn the coal-mining trade at their front door in Vitkovice. To show their gratitude to the Mikeskas, the students invited Riko to come stay with them in Amsterdam—*When you can find the time.*

Peripatetic Education

Amsterdam and Home Again

Riko accepted the students' invitation and arranged to arrive in time for the Koninginnedag in Amsterdam. The celebration of Queen Juliana's birth date on April 30th had become an annual event with thousands of devoted citizens cramming into the streets and taking advantage of the free open markets. Riko told me he pictured himself in the company of his friends, joining the crowd, sketching in his mind's eye the movement, color, atmosphere of this already emblazoned town, but the students were not there to greet him.

Whether intentionally or not, Riko did not telegraph the students who had invited him ahead of time, and forgot the address of the place he was meant to stay. This amnesia was suspect in a man with such an acute memory. Fine lines of a life-long pattern of arrogance and insecurity had etched themselves into his character. The arrogance showed in his belief he knew more than anyone else, but the self-doubt in monetary matters forever assailed his sense of social standing. He was embarrassed by the old and cumbersome wooden suitcase he still carried. He recognized the Dutch guilders were *powerful and stuffed with gold* compared to the Czech crowns in his pockets, and he did not know how to convert the values of the currencies well enough to take control.

Outside the railroad station, he stepped into the first tram in line. He had no destination or fare to offer, had no idea what to ask for in Dutch, but his apparent helplessness and good German mellowed his practical incompetence. The tram driver and passengers jockeyed for a chance to win his favor with suggestions. The result was that the conductor stepped down from the trolley, took Riko by the elbow, and pointed where he must go: 98 Braestrand Road, a butcher's shop.

Like all the other houses lining the canals, this one was four-storied, narrow, spotlessly clean and, in this case, very busy. Riko walked in to find the manager by the cash register, a wooden box in the far corner of the shop. He was a big aproned fellow with a large moustache who took in Riko's humble suitcase, his pantomime of putting his head on a pillow, and his *Ein zimmer, bitte.* The butcher put one of his enormous arms round Riko and led him up a narrow staircase where a small round, blond woman greeted him, took him to a pleasant room, and lodged him, Riko said, as if he had been expected.

In the next few days, Riko explored the many cobble-stoned streets that lined the canals in Amsterdam, took his sketch books into the Rijksmuseum, hardly moved from the Rembrandt portraits and Hobbema landscapes. He went past the tulip fields to Haarlem to see the house in which Frans Hals lived, and to the Hals Museum where he gawked at the sensuous paintings of the matrons (*some old and starched, some hard and bitter, some sloppy and sexy*) and of the Rabelaisian burghers swallowing sausages, dribbling wine and seducing the women. He visited Zundert in northern Brabant, where Van Gogh was born and spent his youth before going to The Hague, London and Paris—Riko's longed-for city. He wished Van Gogh had left behind more watercolors, tried sketching the outlines of his paintings, identified with Van Gogh's frustrations and melancholy, and studied him with obsession.

In The Hague, he witnessed the Dutch citizens swarm into the streets to cheer their beloved Queen Wilhelmina and her daughter, Juliana. The roads were covered in flowers, and horse-drawn carriages transported royalty and all higher-ups. Riko again suppressed his socialist tendencies to lap up the royal pomp and glory. He took in the rousing scenes, the clouds and their reflections in the water, and puzzled over how he might capture the unique northern light the Dutch painters already had mastered.

He lost no time in finding artistic circles and met the Dutch-Indonesian painter, Jan Toorop, who had painted a recent portrait of Queen Wilhelmina, and who was experimenting in Symbolism, Art Nouveau and Pointillism. Riko reported he managed to impress Toorop sufficiently with his pencil sketches of portraits to become his student for the fleeting time he had in the Netherlands. Time was going fast, and Riko had more to explore.

He traveled as far as Nordweg, where he saw the sea for the first time, swam in it, and became as one reliving his phylogeny from fish to human stages, but his trip was cut short by unexpected happenings at home.

Charges of theft against the company for which Riko's father had worked devotedly all his life were leveled against

Kazimir. That the charges were unfounded made no difference in the short run, and had more to do with the political levels of power between the Germans and the Czechs in the company, but Mr. Mikeska became the unwitting disposable fulcrum around which his family on one side, his work on the other, would collapse.

Riko discovered his father jobless, in disgrace and despair. In a little town like Vitkovice, Mr. Mikeska compared his condition to being buried alive. Riko's sister, Julci, had left for Poland taking on a job as a lady's companion, his mother engaged herself not at all in an imbroglio outside her ken and sensibilities, so Riko was left to look after both his parents. Characteristically, Riko rallied to the underdog, his own father in this case, but he churned with anger and disappointment in watching his dream of going to Paris evanesce. That his father had got him to this point in his remarkable education did not touch his conscience.

Riko returned home with the credentials of his prestigious schoolings, his first-hand visions and copies of the artists he admired for their colors, narratives and delicacy: Piero della Francesca, Mantegna, Masaccio, Giotto. From the Renaissance[4], he moved to Van Eyck and Rembrandt. Rembrandt as self portraitist, where he had to please no one, especially impressed Riko. But it was contemporary art that was pulling him. He didn't need to go as far as Paris, he kept telling himself. In Prague, at the Rudolfinium, he could visit first-hand the decorative designs of their own Alfons Mucha, Vienna's Gustav Klimt, stop before the strong distorted sculptures of France's Rodin, and

[4] See Leonardo di ser Pierro da Vinci in Notes on page 270

the cubism of Emil Filla and Otto Guttfreund, both from the Mánes school. But an impatient Riko knew Pablo Picasso and Georges Braque, Albert Gleizes and Jean Metzinger awaited him in Paris with their own different views. Every style was grist for the mill, but he had to be there to see first hand. He had to get to Paris, distinguish the scents of the Seine from the Moldau, note the different lights in the more northern city, pad about in what Art Nouveau—the French version of Jugenstil— had created in the architectural landscape.

To make this happen, Riko put his schooling and talents to work. He drew beautiful portraits that would please his clients in Vitkovice, and he was a keen social observer: landscapes were in vogue, so he painted them on commission.

His parents' friends and foundry colleagues, who had seen Riko's work when he was home during summer vacations, banded together. They admired Riko's talent and respected his father, so here was a way they could help redress a wrong and actually come off the winners by owning a painting by this accomplished young artist who came from their own town. Whether or not Riko was yet masterful was unknown beyond his own assurances. Surviving small paintings were certainly promising and, to them, Riko added his flourishes.

By foot and word of mouth, some of his paintings journeyed to Prague, Vienna and Berlin. To cope with high demand, Riko began to rely on the help of an artist he had known in his German High School, another pupil of the despised Mr. Klinger's, Salo Salomonovič.

Salo was, in Riko's words, *a gentle, nice, indolent person, whose artistic development had stopped under Klinger*. He could, however, put together backgrounds of Lago di Como and Lago di Garda, for example. Riko would later finish off the paintings with his *signature strokes*. There is no doubt both worked hard. Salo helped enlarge Riko's sales, and the commissions increased.

With none of the lures of Berlin to spend money on, Riko saved more than he ever had. What business arrangement he had with Salo remains a mystery, but the parting was friendly enough that they would reunite to share a room in Paris, their dream-come-true.

When Riko's father was reinstated within the year, Riko felt no need to remain with his parents. He left for Paris with a good conscience, a scholarship from the Witkowitzer Bergbau-und Hüttengewerkschaft for a year's study at the École des Beaux Arts, and . . . with Ilse Gruenfeld. How she managed to appear in Vitkovice, Riko said, was a mystery! The conjunction was fortuitous.

Paris

Riko's first exposure to art instruction at the École des Beaux-Arts was when students, who heard ahead of time there was a bright (and threatening) new talent coming to draw and paint with them, dumped a bucket of water on his head. They had balanced the bucket over the door they knew Riko must walk through, and enjoyed their savagery. Riko persevered to his ultimate and almost immediate benefit.

In the next week, he met the *only caricature of my life*, Jean Poleront, the director of the studio into which Riko had been crassly baptized. Academically recognized, a friend of Rodin's, gold medal winner at many of the salons, Riko nevertheless described Poleront as *ossified, jealous, vindictive, and a ham in art*. He came around correcting the pupils' work with a long stick, injurious to body and canvas.

Who made this? he asked the first time he saw Riko's charcoal of a female head.

To Riko's proud *I did*, Poleront shouted *Out! I never want to see you again.*

This was the second time Riko had been expelled, first from the Academy of Art in Berlin by the much more honorable and talented Professor Heye, and now from the École des Beaux-Arts by this *clown*. Secretly relieved at his speedy escape from an academic dungeon, Riko was nevertheless humiliated. He lost the scholarship, his French was primitive, he smoked only the Egyptian cigarettes his ever kind father sent him, munched on sausages he grew to hate for their over-abundance of garlic, and hid on Rue Dorcel on the fifth floor of a pension he shared with women who rented by the hour.

One day, the old concierge climbed the uneven wooden stairs to hand Riko a special-delivery letter from Ilse. The letter included a forwarded note from her brother who recommended

Riko visit a well-known Swiss-French art dealer, Georges Keller (no relation to Ellen). Keller was familiar with many of the artists painting and exhibiting through the Académie Moderne, the Académie Montparnasse, Académie Julien, Académie Scandinave—the panoply of the best art schools and movements in the most scintillating city of the times.

Would Mr. Keller be able to help? Riko has to rely on someone. He knows he is where he wants to be, and the present tense is the only one that exists even as every breath, scent, sound, sight and prowl through Paris reminds him of the tradition of art students who have come before. He boxes with the shadows of American artists who similarly thronged to Paris in the late 1800s, displayed their works in the early Salons, watched the Eiffel tower grow to completion in time for the Exposition of 1900—a mere three years before he was born! They saw Gustav Eiffel put together Lady Liberty, France's gift to America, shipped piecemeal once ready. Those same iron workers helped the American red-haired giant, Augustus Saint-Gaudens, forge his statues of two Civil War heroes, Admiral David Glasgow Farragut and General William Tecumseh Sherman. These masterpieces will stand respectively in Madison Square Park and the Grand Army Plaza on Fifth Avenue outside the Plaza Hotel—sites and art work Riko will come to know intimately in a portion of his life as yet unforeseen. He will appreciate their histories.

Riko hears stories of the very private Mary Cassatt who, able to paint only in Paris, nevertheless evades its outdoor beauty to paint exclusively the interiors of rooms with mothers bathing children, or her sister reclining on a divan reading a book, or writing letters at a desk—all indoor occupations. He admires the brilliance of John Singer Sargent, studies his dramatic master-pieces of the Spanish flamenco dancer in *El Jaleo*, daring portraits of the four Boit sisters, *The Daughters of Edward Darley Boit*, and of the audacious depiction of the pale, powdered Mme. Gautier in her black evening décolletage. He contrasts these depictions of interior light with the emergence of the Impressionists who cannot be torn from painting exterior light in the rippling waters of the Seine, on lily ponds and in oceans, and of dappled light in the Parisian parks and gardens. He becomes Derain's student, exults in brilliant colors, colors he missed in his childhood, and he experiments with Cubism, but the geometric constructs dismay him. He prefers painting landscapes in organic shapes.

Riko's recollections of these years for him speed up like a drum roll. In his L-shaped studio at the Académie Moderne with large spotlights, lots of easels, platforms, wash basins with big tubs and bars of green soap to clean off brushes, time gallops. Students come from Sweden, Norway, Denmark, France, Germany, America, Japan, South America, Central Europe. The teaching is informal, professors come round twice a week— once to demonstrate some technique or style, the second time to correct. He checks off the names of artists as if reading from a Who's Who: Fernand Léger, Amédée Ozenfant, Albert Gleizes. Archipenko, Giacometti, Bisièque and the Greek woodcarver, Galamis. All are there.

But the best are the comradeship, competitions and fights. *You think about art, painting, getting ideas, clarifying ideas, divesting them or digesting them, so you try and find new faith. If you work à la André Lhote, you'll be all right, but if you work à la Jean Metzinger, you are not so all right. If you work like Matisse, oh, no good! Or vice-versa. So it is alive, alive all the time. You don't stand still. At school or at the Louvre, or in cafés over a sandwich with not much ham but a lot of good bread, there is badinage, and you belong, you belong.*

At La Rotonde on the corner of the Boulevard Raspail and the Boulevard Montparnasse are mostly Russian students; across the Street at Café du Dôme, more Germans, and Nils von Dardel, who is Swedish. They see Man Ray sitting with his model and lover, the actress Kiki. The Swiss Alberto Giacometti, already a post-impressionist, hops in from his work in Bordeaux, always looking for his brother, Diego. On the Rue des Ombres near Montmartre, they fantasize about stepping into Gauguin's former studio. Riko is headily in love with the world of art—his own and that of others, and he is filling sketchbooks and canvases with sure-handed speed.

In the shuttlecock rhythms of Riko's life, however, he is smacked from paradisical artistic and intellectual rapture to the financial bathos of his carelessness. To help pay his rent, he has taken on roommates. The first is Salo Salomonovič, his old-time student friend and co-painter of landscapes in Vitkovice. Salo joins Riko in Paris and, under André Lhote, *gets even worse*. The second is the Swiss painter, Willy Guggenheim, who distances himself from his too-well-known family by adopting the name Varlin. At first, they go to the Jockey Club, to museums and cafés together, but two weeks after Varlin has moved in, he gets a telegram from Zürich saying his mother is ill and to come home at once. He leaves without paying the rent, but Riko hopes he will be back.

Then comes a letter from Salo's father saying he is bankrupt and can no longer support his son. Salo also leaves without paying the rent. Riko knows he will not be back. Riko's pattern of lending money generously and improvidently, playing le grand seigneur when he has funds, leaves him no margin to maintain himself when his sources run out. He begins to sneak by the concierge's station to avoid confrontations about paying up what he does not have.

His savior? Ilse. She sends him a huge bouquet of flowers to commiserate with his loss of roommates. With such a gift, the concierge thinks Monsieur must run in elegant circles and be financially sound. She gives him the benefit of the doubt during which time Ilse meets Riko as often as possible in costless museums or for walks in the parks. She convinces her father to treat Riko to dinner at a restaurant on the upper-crust Rue de la Paix.

For this, Riko has dusted off his tuxedo and ironed one of his dress shirts he acquired in Berlin. He self-consciously pretends to dismiss the elegance of the surroundings, the choreography of waiters, the dimmed voices, and candles quivering on tables making even the polished mahogany mullions reflect light. The table is set with a damask cloth and heavy silver service. The Villeroy and Boch plates are beautiful yet serviceable. Riko has a wonderful time seducing Ilse and her parents with his erudition, good manners and good prospects. He is anticipating Mr. and Mrs. Keller will become his in-laws.

As he accompanies Ilse and her parents to a horse-drawn carriage to take them home, he slips into the muddy gutter full of the leaves and detritus washed there by the rains of that day. He is disheveled, filthy, aghast and furious. Ilse puts her parents into one carriage and accompanies Riko in another. They go to his apartment where the truth of Riko's penury is apparent. She leaves him money, but Riko feels degraded, humiliated by his own arrogance and ambition. Apologize? How? There are no apologies for a life-style he would continue <u>if</u> he hadn't tripped, <u>if</u> he might have covered his withered finances a while longer, <u>if</u> he could start all over again, but he sees no resumption of his relationship either with Ilse, less so with her parents, and lets her money lie around until so-called friends steal it. He gets into artistic difficulties.

He loses interest in Lhote's curves, straights, cubes, and planes, feel they are dry, badly stolen from Cézanne. Riko is not drawing well, his sense of color has disappeared, his friends Giacometti and Varlin agree. Riko withdraws from the Académie Moderne and enrolls at the tuition-free Sorbonne to study Slavonic literature. He lasts the year until summer vacations, but does not hand in his thesis. In abject shame and depression, he abandons Ilse, but Riko's Fortuna hovers close as ever.

A school friend from the Sorbonne proposes a cockamamie scheme for Riko to pass his summer vacation with him in Brittany. The plan requires Riko to play a part as if in a bedroom farce by Feydeau. In exchange for having the use of his friend's house in Douarnenez, Riko will date the sister of his friend's mistress. Doors start to open and close on hidden intimacies and unintended consequences. Sister Erna and mistress Lenka both fall for Riko. And so does the landlady. There is a day when two of these, one on each side of Riko, get under the duvet of a chaise longue. *They begin to finger my usefulness, and I let them join hands over this precious thing they both seemed to covet. In the end, I feel rather friendly towards the whole world.*

Whether it was the women, the ocean (into which he plunged with love and competence *among the conger eels, mullets and lobsters*), the rugged seacoast, the history of the gigantic stone dolmens and menhirs, or the complete charm of the landscapes, Riko began to return to life. He took in everything: the crooked routes—*les chemins Bretons qui vont à travers au lieu d'aller droit*—the women in their high-hatted lace coifs; the wealthy inland farmers and the communistic, impoverished sardine fishermen; the role of the curate in the political arena.

He befriended the man who was secretary to the Bishop of Quimperle, a man who might have had a bright career in the Roman Catholic Church himself, but who took pride in the parish, who passionately believed in bringing the Gospel to the people, to be a simple curate, but who admitted to Riko he could not reach them. No doubt Riko appreciated the curé's vulnerability and his sense of insufficiency, and embraced qualities he saw in himself. He started attending church simply to add one more person to the congregation, but Riko's attendance was not entirely without ulterior motive.

There was a certain Aimée Richard who played the harmonium. She was young, pretty, devout, had a modicum of musical talent, and must have kindled the flame in Riko's fantasies about combining the pure woman with someone in whom he might hope for more passionate expression; in short, Riko developed a serious crush. She spoke Breton, his French was faulty. He solved the problem: *I pulled out the violin and added my music and my voice to the responses.*

Since neither his singing voice nor his violin playing figured as real talents, one wonders what Aimée's reactions to his gifts might have been. There is no record, but for Riko, she, too, helped revive him. He wrote his thesis on Slavonic philosophers to submit to the Sorbonne (it was accepted and honored), and painted in the different lights of dawn, noon and dusk.

Riko explored Brittany for over a year, wearing out, he said improbably, three pairs of wooden clogs. When he returned to Prague to set up a studio in 1927, he met Greta Schmied Passer.

9

Greta

OVER MORE BIKE RIDES, more teas, soups, teasings followed by panics that her story might be told by anyone other than herself, Greta fed me her history.

She was the fifth in line among eight sibling births, and the case of measles her younger brother, Max, brought home from elementary school changed her life more than the concurrent First World War did. Her brother shared the highly contagious disease successively with his five older and three younger sisters. All were flattened by it, and Greta's father was appalled when the quarantines of a month apiece added up to a full school year and turned his home into a hospital. His unscientific, if fortuitous, ultimatum:

No more school! You girls will have tutors at home.

While over the years her brother had to attend schule, fast on Yom Kippur, and prepare for his Bar Mitzvah, the girls avoided most religious traditions along with childhood bacteria, viruses and parasites. They stayed home surrounded by the elegance they took for granted: stained glass windows made in Bohemia, tapestries from Belgium, leather-bound books tooled in Florence, floors parqueted in different stains of white oak, crystal chandeliers from Venice, and a Bösendorfer piano her sisters and brother practiced on.

At meal times, and for the math and spelling lessons their governess drilled into them, the girls (her traditionally-schooled brother was exempt) sat at an extension of the dining room table covered in oil cloth to prevent spills and scratches from ruining the highly polished mahogany beneath. Six of the eight children survived to fend off scolds offered in German by their parents at the upper end of the table, and in Czech by the servants and helpers within the house. Similarly dressed in dark blue sailor suit collars and bows in their hair, the girls absorbed what they could or wanted to. Greta knew this was not how she would learn. The Guvernanta was not her friend.

You are so stupid, the Gypsies must have brought you, was the governess's favorite taunt.

Then why do I have to take lessons?

Greta was not cowed then, nor would she be in her entire life. It wasn't that she spoiled for a fight, but if slapped with a glove, she was ready either to draw her sword or, if she understood the advantage of avoiding a fight, to manipulate. In speech alone, she could change her address from *Guvernanta* to the more prestigious *Vychovatelka*—Tutor—when useful.

Greta's escape from lessons was to engage the peddlers, knife-grinders, fruit sellers, carpenters who came to the cobbled courtyard at their back door.

Where have you come from? Were they a nice family where you stopped before? Did they buy from you? Did their children speak to you?

Greta

Her deep set dark eyes bore into those of the trades people who tolerated her as much because she intrigued them, as because they hoped that by engaging her, they would make a sale.

What do you prefer to sell? Where did you learn to fix cabinets? Are the soldiers bothering you? Her questions prattled on, her curiosity boundless about the world outside the confines of her home. Her manners careered unchecked in what her parents would have considered prying and her governess detested.

Why do you spend so much time with these people? You should not speak to them at all, and it does you no good to speak in Czech.

They teach me things, and I speak in Czech because that's the language they know, Greta countered with understood insult and unimpeachable logic. Greta cared not at all that the governess spoke German to show she was on social par with the Schmieds; Greta recognized and despised Guvernanta's pretense.

Her sisters stood apart from Greta's fights with the governess, their reactions varying from resenting Greta as a trouble-maker to admiring her lack of fear. No one doubted she would get her way.

Mr. and Mrs. Schmied spoke French at table when they did not want their children or the governess to understand what they were saying. Greta determined to learn the language as soon as possible, and vowed to separate from the ignorance of Guvernanta. She would need to help her father find the tutors he had promised, but for that she needed a ploy. In the spring of her twelfth year, the weather offered some help.

In the slanted winter sunlight and in the present full force of summer, the Schmied's grand apartment house shone with mica embedded in outdoor concrete composite. It faced a small park with graveled pathways and trees pruned to knob-like shapes in the fall, pregnant with early foliage by spring. Best of all were the French windows, like doors, that opened onto narrow balconies. Greta used these as her observation deck to the outside world. These windows lined the large pearl-painted living room, the birch-paneled library, and the master bedroom whose repousséd wall silks played with the optimized northern light.

From her glassed-in post, Greta followed the course of three male friends who gathered for lunch on the same bench in the park across the street. One, though young, was very handsome, with thick black hair and aquiline features, but *slightly hunchback*, she reported. *The others sported moustaches and had cigars sticking out of their mouths.* They intrigued Greta by their constantly interrupted discussions, their shared laughter, and their apparent delight in one another's company. She traced their routes to and from the place as far as she might crane her neck and decided she wanted to meet them.

Please, Vychovatelka, may we go out? Greta asked on a particularly sunny morning. *It would be so useful to throw a ball— remember, the piano teacher has asked us to practice throwing and catching with each hand over and over? And we need to collect leaf samples for your art project/science diorama/colors.* It didn't matter what the project; Greta invented them as needed. *I'll not go to the courtyard, if you will take us to the park*, she wheedled.

When the ball strayed to the feet of where the three young men shared lunch, Greta apologized, but always added something:

Greta

Sorry. I'm trying to learn to catch, but I'm not very good at it. You, on the other hand, must be very good at conversation; the ball nearly hit you, and you didn't even notice it.

Sorry, again. We're taking a break from our lessons.

Oops! We'll soon be going so we don't disturb you. We live right across the street, where you see that open window on the first floor.

The building they would have seen was built in 1911 by Richard Klenka. It was an elegant, light-grey apartment house of five stories with Bedermeier ornamentation. Although it lay outside the boundaries of the ghetto, the address of the apartment house was 21 Maiselova Street, named after Mordecai Maisel, celebrated leader of the Jewish community in Prague in the 1600s. Two standing carved graces stood on either side of the entrance portal. Both held baskets of fruits and flowers like cornucopias of plenty. To the left of the front door at the level of what the Europeans consider to be the first floor (the second in the west), a Star of David was included. The three men would have known the building's history as they and the Schmieds had been living through the ending years of the ghetto's demolition.

From 1893 to 1913, the area was destroyed as an initiative to rebuild a model city along the lines of Paris. Only six synagogues, the Jewish cemetery, and the Old Town Hall remained. What prevented the area's further destruction was that the Nazis kept it to provide a site for a planned 'exotic' museum of an extinct race.

Sometimes, the three men weren't there, and Greta panicked. She could not know that they varied their encounters to meet after their part-time jobs, Kafka's in an insurance company,

Brod's at the post office, and Weltsch's at the German University Library. Inevitably, the men returned to the park.

Over the weeks, Greta eavesdropped on them. She caught their names: Franz, Max and Felix. She even got the governess to play ball and to engage in the *sorries* and *clumsy mes* so that the outings became more integral for all.

Felix Weltsch was the first to introduce himself. *Librarian,* he bowed. What need to add he was a philosopher, lawyer and journalist, and that he, his friends, Max Brod and Franz Kafka, seated beside him at the moment, were part of a literary circle of Jewish intellectuals? Or that he was a Zionist writing for a weekly magazine *Selbstwehr*—Self Defense—that had appeared in 1907 (and would go on with him as editor-in-chief until the Nazis took over in 1938)?

The 'stupid Gypsy' was no fool. Greta overheard her parents speaking about members of the Jewish intelligentsia in Prague, and the names of these three men figured prominently. Had she been following a hunch that these three were, indeed, the men her parents mentioned on and off during dinners? After all, Franz, Max and Felix sounded the same in French, German and Czech.

Guess whom we have met, Papa? Greta asked of her father. *Vychovatelka found them for us, and we think they would help her not be so tired giving us all our lessons.*

Ask them to come see me after their work, he suggested, showing pleasure over their names and no surprise at his daughter's wiles.

Felix Weltsch was the first to teach the girls German

literature. He was taken by how bright they were, Greta in particular.

Might I not come to teach them piano? Weltsch's wife asked.

They already have a piano teacher, but I'll ask Mr. Schmied. He is sympathetic to me.

As Felix and his wife shared the stories of their progressive lessons at the Schmieds', of Greta's amusing and intrusive questions (always off subject), Kafka and Brod also approached Mr. Schmied, a bank of fortune for them during the war years. Mr. Schmied hired Kafka to tutor the girls in Greek myths and history, and Brod to teach philosophy.

Remember, Greta remarked to my awe over her singularly illustrious teachers, *they weren't so famous then. Neither Brod nor Kafka had published his first book.*

While they taught, Greta observed, questioned and listened. She developed a crush on Kafka, delighted over his sketches, and asked him to tell her about Dora Diamant, his girl friend, an actress in the Czech-Jewish theatre.

She helped him get over a destructive relationship with another woman, Greta gossiped with her sisters, proud of her psychoanalytic know-how borrowed from her fascination with Freud and Adler, the latter in particular, whom she came to know through an older cousin, Charlotte. With Kafka, the subject of Dora was inexhaustible, but Greta could steer him to divulge other fantasies.

He wants to be on a warm island with just his toes in the water, she told her sisters on another day.

In fact, it didn't matter what the subject, Greta liked Kafka's *warm way of speaking.* She told me he calmed her by not seeming unduly troubled by the outbreak of war in 1914 and shared his journal entry: *Germany has declared war on Russia. Went swimming in the afternoon.*

I was not sure what journal Greta referred to then, and—as with her entire account of her time with her notable tutors—I ignorantly took her word for Gospel. Kafka's *Diaries* from 1910-1923 reveal nothing about his ever having taught her or her sisters, and though the entry in his Diaries on July 28, 1914, the day War was declared, is indeed relaxed to the point of sublimation, the exact entry Greta quoted appears *2 August. Germany has declared war on Russia—Swimming in the afternoon.*

It is doubtful Kafka shared his more troubled observations about the war with Greta; instead, she reported he spoke to her of the importance of Jewish and Zionist communities, and of his own depressions. Greta was smitten and, intellectually, he might have been, too.

According to Greta, the idyll of their lessons and company lasted beyond the war, although he no longer held her in thrall. At least, he was no longer a subject of conversation.

Before his death of cancer of the throat, Kafka gave me autographed copies of all his books—a fortunate decision since he had asked Brod, his literary executor, to burn all his writings after his death. I gave them my collection in 1938, which Brod took to Palestine in 1939.

Because Greta's recall was so keen, it is unlikely she would have intentionally misled. For example, her stating that Kafka died of 'cancer of the throat' is not too far amiss; in fact, it was tuberculosis of the larynx.

Greta

―――――

As Jews in Prague, the Schmieds were little affected by the war. Their wealth allowed them to circumvent food and fuel shortages, no one threatened to take them elsewhere, or demanded they live differently from the way in which they had carried on. The ones who suffered the most were the Jews in Galicia, near Poland, as well as those in the coal-mining industries found in Ostrava-Vitkovice where Riko was struggling against German professors keen to humiliate the Czechs as well as the Jews.

The closest fighting the Schmieds observed took place along the huge promenade leading from Wenceslas Square. Sheltered behind windows of a café, Greta and her sisters met with friends attending the university near the statue at the high end of the promenade, the traditional place to meet. They watched the police ride out from the manicured cavalry barracks on one side of the avenue to patrol the streets, sabers drawn. One side of the promenade was preferred by the German students, the other side by the Czech. At lunch time, when all the students were out of class, it did not take much provocation for the students to be at each other's throats. The German students wore colorful school uniforms and so were easily identified. The police sabers left many scars on the faces of the Czechs, who wore them as badges of honor to show their rebellion against Germanic rule.

Unbeknowst to Greta, Riko, in Prague by the early 20s, witnessed the same scenes. He reacted with nationalistic rancor, but did not engage; instead, he recorded the swirls of colors and motion in sketch books and on canvas.

Returning home, the Schmied girls put political fights out of mind. It was pure luck and timing that Mr. Schmied's Jewish home, and others like his, did not attract the German acquisitiveness instituted at the build-up to the Second World War. According to Greta, her father lived what, an ocean and decades away, came to be known as the all-American success story.

As an office boy in a brewery in Prague, he bought hops and experimented at home with his own recipe for fermentation. He concocted a mould that he presented to the brew meisters. The breweries took it up with great enthusiasm and gave him a percentage ad perpetuum of the business. He then designed machines for bottle washing, a result successful enough to require building a second factory, but Mr. Schmied's mind was restless. He left these inventions as a sideline and went into designing memorials in wrought iron to commemorate those who had died of the plague. Villages and cities all over Europe clamored for wrought iron fences surrounding wrought iron fountains, whether ornate or simple. Most cities had one. In Prague, Mr. Schmied was commissioned to fashion the head for the horse of the statue that sits at the high end of Wenceslas Square near the University, where Greta would meet her friends. And, of course, the balcony or fence railings in houses such as theirs were Schmied-produced.

When the First World War ended, there were many newly drawn lines of national identity apart from those on student faces. The Bohemians, Austro-Moravians, Slovaks, Silesian, and Ruthenians became Czechoslovakian. Their first president, Tomáš Masaryk, felt this was the time to repossess what they all had lost to the Germans, and while Greta and her friends cheered, her father grumbled prophetically: *You are crazy! To split up a huge Empire! Now we are all helpless and tiny and insignificant.* He had a lot to protect.

Seeing no irony between making his daughters as helpless, tiny and insignificant in their own eyes as he saw his nation becoming, Greta's father's believed that no daughter of his would ever have to have a job. He made enough to support everyone and, but for the undreamt-of Second World War, almost made good on his estimate.

In 1918, Greta brought the first contagious disease into the house since measles. She caught the flu. Ironically, she was the only one who became ill this time.

Until Greta was twenty, her father's voice ruled. When she expressed a desire to become a pediatrician, Mr. Schmied dismissed the idea out of hand. Then might she take some sketching and painting lessons with the artist to whom they had rented their top, light-filled floor? Those worked until Mr. Schmied asked to look at Greta's sketch pad and paintings. There he saw one rendering after another of a nude man—the top floor artist, for all he could divine from the always headless model—and the lessons ended, but Greta had spent enough time at these exercises that she knew she wanted to pursue art and design. What Greta wanted to do, her father insisted, was to get married.

Greta's father settled that she should marry Rolf Passer, a decent, hardworking, generous Doctor of Chemistry whose family passed muster in religious and economic terms, though Rolf was fifteen years older than Greta. Yes, Mr. Schmied was sure this was what Greta wanted. His argument gained urgency for Greta when her mother died and Mr. Schmied married Guvernanta.

———

My wedding ceremony was everything a girl could wish for, at home instead of in a Temple, since my father had excused us girls from ever attending one. They brought in a chuppah and a finely woven carpet. Rolf crushed the glass and the men carried me around on a chair whirling me through the sunlit room, so that I felt I was a white cloud flying through the prisms of the rainbow. My closest art friends from Prague were there, Lotte Radnitz and Richard Schroetter. Mimi LowBeer and her husband Fritz, and Mimi's cousin, whom I remember only as Miss Pollock, attended. They played vital parts in my life with both my husbands.

Greta's marriage to Rolf gave her all the freedoms her father had denied. Rolf was supposed to take over a sugar factory near Prague, but first needed tutoring on the refining processes. The training for this was in Berlin. Lotte Radnitz and Richard Schroetter, married shortly after Greta's and Rolf's wedding, decided they, too, should go to Berlin. Lotte and Richard enrolled at the Berlin Academy, and Greta enrolled in the Reimann School of Art and Design, which offered classes in textile painting, poster illustrations, crafts and plastic arts, something more than painting. Greta's love for her countryman Alfons Mucha's Art Nouveau, his theatrical posters, and his espousing Russian art made her search for teachers with similar tastes. When both Moritz Melzer and the Ukrainian Alexander Archipenko were assigned to her, she preferred Melzer's style: *closer to illustrations.*

Greta

Yearly there was a Bal Masqué when all the students got together to paint the backdrops.

Ornamentation was in the air, from Gustav Mahler's 'sound-mosaics' to the musically related descriptions of Klimt's 'cadences and colors'. Though Greta never detailed the costumes she wore, the reticules and fans she carried, the gloves she wore, the laces, pearls and stitchings on her dresses, the delicacy (and pain?) of satin dancing shoes she wore into the ballrooms fresh with the latest Jugendstil decorations, she left it to later art and music reviewers and to my imagination. She summed it up with, *It was fun.*

Greta's pleasure in her milieu was akin to hearing Riko delight in his own colleagues in Paris. She belonged!

Few periods of the Twentieth Century concentrated as many intellectuals, political theorists, and Jewish scholars as the interregnum between the First and Second World War in Berlin.[5] Five of the nine Nobel prize winners during this period of the Weimar Republic were Jews. Physicians and physicists (Einstein most prominently), commercial wizards and craftsmen, architects, film makers, artists, musicians and dancers were bold and exciting, and Berlin attracted all possibilities.

Those years in Berlin were terrific, somewhat the way New York became in the '60s with lots of drugs, homosexuality, wonderful theatres, movies, concerts, Greta recalled. *It was a wonderful town in a wonderful time, until inflation set in. To eat, one had to sell everything. Lots of fine paintings were sold then. We returned to Prague after two years, and Rolf never did take over the sugar factory.*

Unfulfilled by his work as a chemist, Rolf started his own

[5] See Kati Marton on page 281

publishing house in Vienna, and took on the job as the unpaid secretary to the Prague Secession, a newly formed group of diverse artists painting in the Jugendstil he knew appealed to Greta. He sensed her restlessness and tried to involve her.

All of us who were part of the Secession used to meet on a monthly basis at the Café Edison, where we would talk about art, exhibits, when and where to have them and, of course, to define styles and to gossip: Maxim Kopf and Marie Duras were lovers; Willy Novak was post-Impressionistic; Karl Wagner was a realist. Both were well-known professors, somewhat dispassionate about any of the art groups springing up around town, but supporting the Secession as the most daring. My friend, Schroetter, no definitive style yet, was part of us. We had exhibits once a year and after that, the exhibits were shown in various German cities. Essentially, we were against anything German, the art coming from the Berlin Academy, in particular. One firebrand was an artist called Riko Mikeska.

Rolf introduced me to him at one of our meetings during the following year. Riko, too, was a source of gossip since he and Maxim Kopf took a special interest in the Secession. They brought in Oskar Kokoschka and colleagues from Moravia, where Riko and Kopf had met. They ended up good friends, but when Kopf married Mary Duras, she became jealous of Kopf's attention to Riko, especially when he asked Riko to take over his studio and students while he and Marie went to Tahiti. She had all of Riko's things thrown out of the studio. Marie's jealousy was in vain; Riko took over another studio on the same floor, and the students kept coming.

Rolf asked me to have Riko over for dinner some night. I took one look at him and said no. My marriage was already shaky by then and I must have felt threatened. I started going to Paris on my own with the excuse I wanted to study more art. I had too much money and could do what I liked, and Rolf was compassionate. I think he would have done anything to keep me, even if it meant separations.

Although Greta would not be lured into conversations about Rolf, it is more than likely, given the broiling foment of artists, writers, composers of the time, that Rolf's circle in the artistic community in Prague was extensive. For example, he most probably was at least acquainted with Greta's three tutors, Franz Kafka, Maxim Brod and Felix Weltsch, as well as Jan and Vilma Löwenbach. The Löwenbachs were from Prague's German-Jewish section and made a particular effort to befriend and promote Czech writers and musicians. Jan Löwenbach[6] was Bohuslav *Martinů's librettist* in the 20s. When Greta was elsewhere, it is unlikely that Rolf was idle.

During one of Greta's partings from Rolf, she ended up working in Paris with gratifying success. She illustrated a book of Colette's called *The Cat*, which Rolf published. She also illustrated the book *Mozart in Böhmen* by Paul Nettl published by Verlag Neumann and Co., Prag-Karlin. She sometimes signed her art as G. Schmied, her maiden name, then sometimes, G. Passer. The Modern Gallery in Prague bought one of her paintings, which bore no signature at all.

I had both Cubists, Fernand Léger and Amédée Ozenfant, as teachers. Léger I liked. He was out-going, gregarious, a good teacher. In the morning he would put together a still life, encourage us to be

---

[6] See Jan Löwenbach in notes on page 283

modern and do with it what we wanted, freely. In the afternoon, Ozenfant would come in and remind us that it wasn't shameful to learn from Nature before developing a style of one's own. 'Don't be afraid of practicing a conservative style.' The next morning Léger would come in and ask: 'Why did you do that?' I found them very humorous and both were important to me. I admired how Ozenfant tried to keep the artists who were fighting in the War connected to those who stayed in Paris. He, Max Jacob and Guillaume Apollinaire published 'L'Élan', a review to keep everyone abreast of the Cubism they were painting then.

Greta lived in a British pension close to the Cloiserie des Lilacs near the Café du Dome, where so many artists spent their days. Lotte Radnitz and her husband, Schroetter, Bram and Geer Van Velde, were all good friends of hers. They shared their successes and failures over apéritifs and Gauloises.

I was having such a good time, that they wrote Rolf to encourage me to come back to Prague, but he knew the bit was in my teeth and let me have my head. But I did go back, and if I didn't invite Riko to our house for dinner, Rolf did.

Every fortnight Rolf's parents gave a dinner, which they almost always followed with a musicale. It was a given that I would accompany the artists on the piano. Riko was present as much because Rolf wanted to introduce this new talent to Prague society as because Riko told him he played the violin, so Rolf generously asked him to bring it along. Riko did not keep good time and was touchy on the subject, but it allowed him to hover over me.

One night, Albert Schweitzer was there. He was a good friend of the Passers' and was talking about his hospital in Labaréné. I asked him if I could come to visit.

Riko, who had been following me around possessively all evening exploded.

'You are not going to Africa. You are going to marry me.'

His words carried around the room designed for fine acoustics. Rolf, his parents, their guests, Albert Schweitzer fell silent and Riko won Greta.

What Rolf's reactions to this thunderclap might have been, I did not press, and Greta did not broach. She never so much as granted Rolf a physical description. I learned over our many interviews that there were other subjects that were completely taboo. I can only speculate that in each case, her guilt and sense of self-preservation demanded silence.

In 1929, Greta did go off with Riko. She asked Rolf for a divorce he did not contest. It may be that Rolf's acceptances of Riko-the-artist, a key part of the Prague Secession Rolf so passionately promoted, and of Greta as individuals seemed to squash any actions of reprisals.

For the sixth time in as many years, Greta headed back to Paris, her city of refuge. When Riko came to pick her up there, he was shocked to realize how many friends she had, and not a little jealous of what surely must have included sexual liaisons during her forays there.

What did he think? she asked me. *That I was alone all the time pining for him? As it was, he kept me waiting four months. He had to finish a portrait of a little girl in Prague—a commission that would*

*bring him a generous payment, he said. For him it was generous, but
he had no idea about money.*

Greta started to laugh, so that the next words came out in
a guffaw: *Do you know he wanted to become my financial advisor?*

Not for the first time, I wondered who Riko was, so full of
fantasy and contradictions. What convinced Greta to abandon
the honorable, steadfast Rolf? A scientist, he nevertheless allowed her free rein to pursue and promote her artistic career, to
live the Bohemian life he saw her enjoy in Berlin and Paris, to
give her, as she said, 'her head.' Riko, a true Bohemian artist,
was the autocrat. He was the one who had the nerve to an-
nounce to her, in the home of her in-laws no less, that she would
abandon her wish to go to Labaréné to marry Riko instead. He
was the one who put an end to flirting, would ruffle up in indig-
nation if a man so much as kissed her on the hand, and when her
brother—disguised as a frog at one of the masked balls so prev-
alent at the time and which Greta so delighted in—kiddingly
paid court to her, Riko exploded.

Was Greta feeling *shaky* not so much in her marriage to
Rolf, but in abandoning what was familiar to her: an authoritar-
ian father and a dictating Guvernanta? Did Greta need Riko's
flint (like theirs) to spar against?

Was she doubting her own talent? Riko was demanding and
needy, Rolf was neither. Did some motherly instinct kick in to
care for this insecure artist? Greta was not a traditional beauty,
and knew it was not her looks that wooed. At some level, Greta
was comforted and flattered.

What had Riko seen in her? Courage, surely. Money? No doubt. Greta footed the bills thenceforth.

We went to Marseilles and Juan les Pins, where we found a house in Golfe Juan. We were going to stay there a few months, but Riko came down with typhoid fever. He was critically ill for one month, and it took him a year to recover. A country doctor came every other day to give him camphor injections. It terrified me to see that sometimes the needle would separate from the syringe. I was glad I did not become infected; I'm sure I had become immune to it in my youth from swimming in the Moldau, which was full of bacilli. The doctor told Riko his intestines were as thin as cigarette paper.

Riko's mother came to help and fed him orange juice and milk. She and I got along well. Maybe we were happy to spell one another, though I did not see it that way then. When he was well enough to travel, his mother, he and I went to Vitkovice, where I met all his old friends. They told me what a wonderful man and what a genius and fine artist he was, but how anyone could marry him, they just couldn't understand.

And yet she did just that in a civil ceremony in 1931, during a vacation in Ischia.

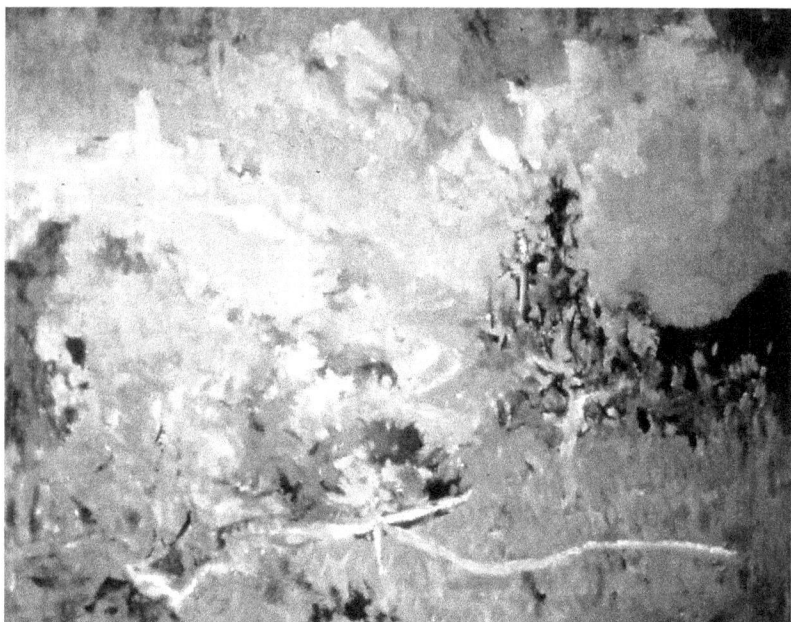

Casa Anticha, Ischia

10

Friends and Flight

Collected Voices

IN BOTH 1906 AND 1907, Oskar Kokoschka and Adolph Hitler applied for candidacy at Vienna's Academy of Fine Arts. The Academy accepted the former, but rejected Hitler as *unfit for painting*.

Too bad he was not judged unfit for governing, Kokoschka lamented. Among Riko's and Greta's artist friends, he more than others sensed Hitler's insanity, but all joined together in cringing when he was named Chancellor of the Reich in 1933.

In Berlin, they attended movies as much to watch Movietone newsreels as to enjoy Mae West, Clara Bow or Charlie Chaplin, recent American imports, early talkies that were light and fun, whereas F. W. Murnau's *The Cabinet of Dr. Caligari* and Fritz Lang's *Metropolis* were dark, disturbing, silent, almost hallucinogenic and prophetic of the controlling horrors to come. The friends wondered at newsreels showing Nazi party rallies full of pomp and pageantry, but the one they saw in September of 1935, seared them with Hitler's unmistakable intent and reach.

Hitler commissioned Leni Riefenstahl, a heretofore modest cinematographer, to choreograph the ultimate rally to brand in people's minds the Führer's iron-clad view of Germany's future. She had shown promise in previous small films in knowing how to sway a crowd. In this movie, they would pull no punches to impress upon the German people—no, upon the World!—the intractable power Hitler now exerted with his vision of law, order, purity and restored economic power. And so the world gaped as 800,000 arms saluting *Heil Hitler* rose as one, and the frenzied cries of the precisely placed Aryan crowd and Hitler Youth pierced the air until it was time for the Führer to speak. All fell silent until he filled the vacuum with his raucous spiel of hate towards anything and anyone not supportive of his image for the new Germany.

In 1936, Hitler again called on Riefenstahl to film a spectacle the whole world would be watching: the Berlin Olympics. Here, Hitler's artistic talent was finally on view. The Nazi banner he designed—a black swastika in a white circle against a red background—flew over the stands.

What the world also viewed was Hitler's hostility to *inferior races*. He despised blacks, turned his back on races in which they competed, and walked out on each of "Jesse" (J.C.) Owen's triumphs. A grandson of slaves, a sickly boy, and carrier of 100-pound cotton sacks by the age of seven, Jesse developed athletic skills to win four gold medals in the 100 meter, the long jump, the 200 meter and 400 meter relay. His black teammates brought home to the United States another eight. Hitler rued the making of the film, Leni feared his wrath, and most of the West was aghast over this new ruler.

By 1937, Hitler's cries for Lebensraum and Racial Purity, and Goebbel's use of the radio transmitting Hitler's jarring messages mortared together all who had no will of their own, and made propaganda against Jews easy. He blamed them for the economic disaster following the Treaty of Versailles, and as agents for the communists, Roman Catholics, homosexuals, gypsies, and international capitalists. The list was flexible and growing. Riko and Greta figured in at least two groups.

Newsreels now showed posters that caricatured Jews as rats, or as greedy financiers opening up grotesque mouths to swallow the world. The audience saw JUDEN and stars of David splash-painted on German storefronts, repetitions of beatings, round-ups, humiliations already in view by 1933, and precursors of much worse to come, but the West looked on in silence.

Denying, or at any rate not immediately touched by the political toxins, Riko and Greta optimized their time in Vitkovice and Prague. In Vitkovice Greta got to know and love Riko's father, Kazimir, an old-style gentleman devoted to his son's health and welfare. He knew the agonizing year's care Mrs. Mikeska and Greta collaborated on to restore Riko's health after his year-long battle with typhoid fever, and rejoiced that Greta and Mother had established an understanding friendship; after all, it was to their mutual advantage to save the man they both loved in different ways. And he understood on a very basic level that Riko's future rested in Greta's hands alone. Kazimir trusted her. It worked both ways.

With uncharacteristic patience, Greta enjoyed Kazimir's recapitulating the pluses and minuses of growing up in an agricultural village. From him she learned of the linguistic and cultural divisions between the Bohemians, Moravians, Silesians,

Ruthenians—*Oh, such a complex of small nations the Austro-Hungarian Empire clung to!*—and of allegiances split between Czech and German forces. Kazimir's fascination with Greta's own father's iron business made Greta understand that despite Mr. Schmied's more decorative than industrial foundry, both manufacturers advanced with similar lucrative demands for production during the First World War.

She met Riko's childhood friends: Doman and Helena Rogoisky, Eve Korner and Erica Kalmer, school chums who had shared trams, studies and stories, and who would continue to serve her and Riko through the Second World War. The best Greta could do was listen and memorize. At this she was phenomenal.

Eve introduced Greta to her father, Professor Emil Korner. *He and Mum are about to leave for Fort William, Scotland, where the University has asked him to teach economics.* In fact, Dr. Korner's specialty was physics, but he was a devoted communist with feelers all over Europe, and especially in Czechoslovakia. The university appointment afforded good cover for keeping an eye on the Nazi forces fulminating since 1927. Their subversion was his intent.

Come visit us, Greta, he said prophetically. *And bring that daughter of mine, even if she wishes we were moving to London instead of Scotland!*

Eve and Erica went on to Prague as students at the Charles University, and Eve started taking classes with Riko. *I felt his art lessons were a continuation of my majors in philosophy and languages.* Eve's admission that Riko was such fun to be with met

Greta's approbation, not jealousy. She understood Riko's allure. It may be that Greta felt lonely, overshadowed by the ever-scintillating Riko, and that she warmed to a female companion, or simply that Eve offered the unbroken thread to Riko's early life. Possibly, Greta sought in Eve the clues to how she would survive her marriage to Riko, a union all others regarded as impossible. The three bonded in friendship.

In the summers, Greta paid for not-so-expensive vacations in Yugoslavia: Kotor, Belgrade, Ischia and Hvar. In 1937, Eve travelled with the Mikeskas to Hvar, the largest of several islands off the coast of Croatia. Riko fantasized about buying a house and land on Hvar, envisioned putting Greta on a donkey to climb the precipitous hills to their imagined house, and giving her a trumpet to call him in case of need. Why he did not picture himself at her side in the protective reverie never arose.

Whether it was the rocky hills and the sparkling ocean that appealed to his eye, or accidental contact with famous vacationing dignitaries, including the Viennese economist, General Friedrich Hayek, and the Duke of Windsor, is unknown but—as ever with Riko—his reasons were conflicted, if not suspect. No more than a moth can resist its attraction to light, Riko would bat against wealth and notoriety and woo them to his detriment.

General Hayek's defense of classic liberalism, his studies on the economic fluctuations of money were magnets of interest to Riko who continued to imagine that he would regulate Greta's finances—a ludicrous project for those who knew him, but Riko's fantasies were protean. It was not for General Hayek's formidable intellect (rewarded in 1974 when he shared the Nobel

Prize for Economics with Gunnar Myrdal) that he became a particular favorite on the island, but for the great bowls of caviar he would order from the Russian Embassy in Belgrade for his parties, open to all.

We enjoyed these, Greta said simply.

While Riko felt at home spinning tales about Hvar's Greek-then-Roman history, Eve entertained Greta with stories of Riko's school days in Vitkovice, but both fretted over what was happening on the German political front. Sitting on the terra-cotta tiled terrace canopied by purple bougainvillea scrawled across the trellis, the two women smoked, sipped coffees or young white wines in the warmth of the sun, and prayed these days might last. Riko, shaded in his Panama hat, painted nearby al fresco, eavesdropped and corrected if he thought Eve's stories exaggerated, or if he disagreed with their political misgivings.

You know nothing!

The summer vacation of 1937 vaporized into fall and an increasingly turbulent winter. Riko and Greta denied any urgency to leave their meetings at the Café Edison, or to cease their promotion of the Secession, or to stop painting in their respective places—she at home, Riko in his studio. Students kept coming from the university and by word of mouth. He guided when to choose charcoal vs. sepia, watercolors vs. gouaches, and what adhesives to use with oils on canvas.

What works best? Rabbit skin glue or egg yolks? Why? Why not? Try! Fail! Are there other adhesives? Sap? Try it. Did it work? No? Why not? Might you have thinned it with turpentine? Would the result be worth it? What fixing of paints did not fade in the sunlight?

If a new student shied at where to begin on a blank page, he recommended starting at a corner. And if this did not work, he'd suggest going back to basics.

Draw using only straight lines/cross hatches/ a continuous line to include body, head and one extra object. What object? I don't know! Try an umbrella or a chair—you're the artist!

Never loathe to show his displeasure when someone was slow on the pick-up, students varied in their reactions to him. Some tolerated his vituperative, mercurial moods and threatening tone of voice (which grew softer rather than louder), and stuck with him because they understood the education he imparted was rich and multi-disciplined; others quit in fury.

Greta watched the comings and goings with curious dispassion. Her passivity then seemed vexing especially when, as a result of their painting and exhibiting together, he prohibited her from signing the name Mikeska.

There will be only one Mikeska, and that is me.

 He would not agree to her returning to Passer, the name of her first husband, and thought her maiden name of Schmied sounded too German, so he gave her the name Gill which she used for the rest of her life.

What had happened to Greta, the feisty girl who stood up to her father, the courageous teenager who manipulated her governess into letting her speak to the trades people, the stalwart who found her own tutors? Perhaps deteriorating health had something to do with a nascent fear that she would not be able to paint again. Palsy, a sign of Parkinson's brought on by the Spanish flu of 1918, began to affect her dominant right hand.

Practical to the core, she may have understood her days of independence as an artist were in jeopardy. Quarreling with Riko and standing her ground would not have been productive. Here, I thought, was an example of Greta's immense adaptability to the accidents of history and health. It may not have worked to her advantage as an artist, but it reconciled her to carry on wherever she was.

As the year segued into 1938, the Nationalist Social Democratic Workers' Party set in motion one horror after another. On March 12, the Czechs watched Vienna welcome the Nazi troops, heard them cheer while the Austrian police joined the Germans in stripping Jews of humanity and property by a relentless orchestration of psychological intimidation, physical brutalization, and personal humiliation. The pace and disintegration of civilized life showed up in dire communications.

A realistic Cassandra, Riko's father penned his son a succinct note the following day: *We will be next.*

And three days later: *Greta, you are in danger staying on in Prague. What is your family planning? And you? Love, Father*

When in May the Nuremberg Laws defined Jews as non-citizens and dictated they must not enter parks, restaurants, movies or theatres (the Nazis did allow them to attend puppet shows), the Czechs saw the Jews crowded into ever narrowing perimeters. By June, the Statute of Jews defined what professions and businesses and enterprises were open to Jews: none.

During the First World War, I saw despairing Czech citizens pushing wheelbarrows full of worthless Czech crowns in exchange for loaves of bread and tins of sardines. *Now,* said Greta, *I saw de-feated Jews straining against wheelbarrows overflowing with their furnishings, treasured books, silver candelabra, and clothing. I had to pay attention.*

11

First Exile

Collected voices

IN SEPTEMBER OF 1938, Greta escaped to London. That same month, the British had welcomed Edvard Beneš as the recognized head of the Czechoslovakian provisional government in exile. Greta felt sorry for Emil Hacha, who had been left behind as the ineffectual working president of the dismembered post-Munich Czechs. Small in stature and with a bad heart, Hacha vainly tried to stand up to Hitler's Hobson's choice: *Surrender your country without a fight, or we will take it with armed forces. All you have to do is sign here.*

The story quickly got around that when Hacha appeared in Hitler's office for the third time, German photographers were poised to record the moment and, for better propaganda, to capture the disparity in height between the two men; Hacha had no choice but to look up to Hitler. Three times he refused to sign the document, and then he fainted. Hitler became terrified he'd killed him in front of so many witnesses, but when Hacha revived, Hitler annulled his fears and forced Hacha to surrender Moravia, Bohemia and Slovakia.

Along with all fervent Czechs, Kazimir and his family were appalled by and fearful of the ease with which the Nazis had capitalized on the historic and linguistic Germanic base to take over the Sudetenland at the start of World War II. When the Germans marched into Prague, they did so to empty streets.

Greta's flight was made possible by Mimi and Fritz LowBeer, friends from Prague. As with all things Mikeska, little was straightforward. The differences in Riko's and Greta's backgrounds and attitudes colored their responses to places, property and people, the LowBeers being no exception.

Greta met the LowBeers through her niece, Charlotte, first child of Greta's eldest sister, Lotte. *Charlotte went to school with a girl called Mimi Pollock*, Greta explained. *After Mimi married Fritz LowBeer, Charlotte, Mimi and I remained in close touch. My niece, who was one of Riko's pupils, constantly praised Riko for his paintings and for his finely-honed faculties, so Fritz became curious and suggested she invite Riko along with me, her Aunt Greta, for supper one night.*

It would have been no shock for the well-heeled Greta to walk into the LowBeer's home full of Chinese porcelains and East Asian art, but for Riko, Fritz represented the attribute that both attracted and threatened Riko the most: enormous visible wealth. Riko had, of course, seen this in both the Schmied and Passer family homes, but that exposure may have heightened his financial insecurities, not allayed them. On the other hand, Fritz was bright, quick-witted, and well-educated in the classics, history, language, geography, the arts; in short, the subjects

Riko was fluent in, and needed in others, the better to engage his intellectual prowess.

Mimi was charming. *Some of it was put on*, Greta insisted in her always cool appraisals. *She had no choice. She was intelligent and knew charm saved her with Fritz, who was demanding and considered her one of his slaves.* Mimi pursued her passion in art, for which Fritz patted her on the back. As long as he did not derail her, she put up with his condescension, something Riko dismissed and Greta then viewed sardonically, but the pattern of submissiveness in the face of a tyrant was one Greta would revisit firsthand.

Fritz was old-fashioned, wore a neat moustache, dressed in three-piece suits of silks, linens, and cashmere, and drove expensive Daimlers and Mercedes. He came from a rich textile family that draped themselves and their homes in the opulent fabrics they or others produced. French jacquard weavings covered the infrequently used piano, and Persian carpets of tightly-woven silk threads changed color depending from which direction one crossed them. The paintings on his walls favored landscapes and still lifes of the Dutch and Flemish genre. Not surprisingly, Fritz mistrusted whatever was termed modern.

He accepted Riko's art when he saw that the distortion of shapes and explosion of non-representative colors of the Expressionists, the Blaue Reiter Group and of the Fauves were not yet on his canvases—or at least the ones Riko showed him. In fact, Riko's love for André Derain and Maurice de Vlaminck, both leaders of the Fauves movement, was as intense as their colors—pigments unseen (but yearned for) in the chiaroscuro of Riko's coal-scrimmed youth.

Unsentimental as ever, Greta noted of the budding friendship, *Fritz was the kind of Jew who was proud to be friends with an Aryan painter.*

Equally as dispassionate as Greta, and with a great fortune to lose, Fritz recognized the times called for making decisions. Mimi and Fritz both filed papers to immigrate to the United States. *Follow us*, they entreated Riko and Greta. *We'll help.* The waiting list was enormous, but all four were offered a propitious alternative to use England as a stepping stone. The next challenge was affording their communal escape.

It was becoming more difficult for Jews to get their money out of Czechoslovakia, so Fritz started by arranging to exhibit the family china in Holland, where he hoped it would sell for a deservedly high price. He had to trust agents in Prague to arrange for the transfers of the china and to supply, up-front, the money needed to mount the exhibits. There were payments to the bureaucrats en route, dues for the bills of lading, and contracts drawn up at each step. Every succeeding transfer of goods produced more middle men, and with each new link came a fresh financial expenditure and an exponential risk of discovery. Capture by the Germans meant internment (if not yet death) in a concentration camp, but Fritz's foresight and daring paid off; the still significant transactional left-overs were deposited into the personal bank accounts of the LowBeers in England. Fritz moved Mimi there forthwith and set her up in a house in London.

In the meantime, Fritz and the Mikeskas remained in Prague. Fritz hired a young British student, remembered only as Jeffrey, to give them English lessons in preparation for their departure. *Let him be Greta's escort*, Fritz suggested.

Jeffrey might give Greta some pointers in English on their passage over, they thought, and he certainly could cope with, or at least understand, the red tape they chanced. And while he was at it, Jeffrey could carry a new camera and some watches Fritz entrusted to him.

Let's see how he does, Fritz said, his concern split equally between the delivery of his goods and of Greta.

Greta's and Jeffrey's trip to London required a stop in Nuremberg, where a big Nazi rally had assembled at the railroad station. Greta was terrified, the newsreels of the rallies and random beating of Jews on the streets fixed in her mind.

We had to stay there three hours, which seemed to me like three years, especially since Jeffrey got drunk with the Nazis and we missed our connection.

Like Jeffrey, Greta was hiding some jewelry and watches, commodities that might help bribe her way to safety or, to the contrary, incriminate her further as a smuggling Jew. Here they were, not even off the continent, her young protector becoming a potentially lethal liability. Jeffrey's alcoholic solidarity with the Nazis, however, must have played to his and Greta's advantage as they were not detained and finally crossed to Dover. It was here they met their challenge; the Dover Customs officer made them open their luggage.

Is this a new camera? he asked Jeffrey of the one Fritz gave him to smuggle. Greta recalled that Jeffrey told a stupid lie and the officer threatened him with arrest, but Greta recalled: *We were such a funny looking couple—I so much older than he, my hand already palsied, and not even able to speak decent English—that they didn't delay us beyond their threat to Jeffrey. And so I safely entered England.* Fritz's pre-sent money cushioned her arrival.

Fritz was not only immensely rich, he was practical. He started to send money to England in the days of huge inflation when those without great money in Czechoslovakia bartered a bicycle for cigarettes, or rolled up a wheelbarrow of worthless bills for a small sack of potatoes. Until the Statute on Jews limited their movement out of a city, never mind country, Fritz traveled a great deal, delivered the beautiful dress shirts from his family's enterprise to France, Austria and Hungary. With him, he carried envelopes stuffed with 1,000 Czech crowns he brought in from his Moravian estate.

Fritz pursued his long-established practice of delivering shirts. He made longer trips and crossed the borders where he had come to know the guards. They admired the rich young scion in his beautiful Mercedes, and Fritz took care to make the border crossings become social events. He established personal intimacies, routinely gave them bottles of plum brandy or robust red wines, fine cigars and even chocolates for their wives or mistresses, whose names he committed to memory.

Here, for Adelaïde tonight.

If a new guard were on duty, an experienced one accompanied him for a cursory inspection of the boot of the car. Times were hard enough without having an eager young pup cancel an opportunity to gain favors where they might be found. A wink and a nod, and Fritz was off.

In anticipation of his arrival, Fritz began to hide money among the shirts as another means of transferring as much of his family's fortune as possible to England.

If Riko had no money to send, he helped Fritz move his own fortune. One time Riko and Fritz drove in one of Fritz's racing cars, a Mercedes convertible which made calamitous noise.

Is this your way of not being noticed? Riko asked Fritz.

They won't imagine we would dare bring in contraband being this obvious, Fritz answered.

The contraband on that particular trip was a suitcase full of Czech crowns and two of Riko's rolled-up canvasses.

Once en route, the convertible had a flat tire. *You have to help me,* Fritz told him. It was nighttime. Without the benefit of a flashlight, they had to unpack the boot of the car, discard the suitcase, the canvasses, unlatch the emergency tire, find the jack, put it under the car, jack the car up, and remove the old tire. Fortunately, they had a replacement tire and did not have to patch the old one. With the new tire fully blown up with a hand pump, they started repacking the boot.

A couple of hours after the incident, Fritz asked Riko if he remembered packing the suitcase full of bills back into the car.

I thought you did.

I left it to you.

You must have packed it!

I assure you I did not.

In which case, it's still by the side of the road.

By the time they turned back to where they had changed the tire, the sun was rising. The locks on the suitcase had broken in its pitch from the boot. Czech crowns blew into the air with pastel green and mauve swirls that contrasted with the gold and mustard leaves of the oak trees around them. This vision might have appealed to Riko's artist's eye at any other time, but the suitcase full of bills was all they had to get them across several borders from Prague to London.

They did not find the rolled up paintings, and the wind unpacked the suitcase more effectively than the men had packed their few belongings. The bills flew into the forest by the side of the road, caught in the upper branches of the trees, joined the tumult of drying leaves on the verge of the road, and left Riko sitting on the ground holding his head in his hands. So far, they still were not out of Czechoslovakia.

What are we going to sell now?

Never mind sell, how are we going to establish who you say you are?

Neither man thought the effort of catching up with the playful money was worth it. They closed the suitcase with the few crowns that were left, revised routes to avoid the immense dangers of crossing Germany and Poland, and chose southern routes via Austria, Switzerland, France—only slightly less perilous, but ultimately successful.

12

Keeping Contact

WITH AUSTRIA'S CAPITULATION TO THE NAZIS on March 12, 1938, the Czechs knew Hitler had their country in his cross-hairs and conscripted every able-bodied man.

Thank God we are in it. We have been called to arm, Riko wrote Greta from Prague. He added, with unrevealed feelings, that her former husband, Rolf Passer, had joined the Czech 11th Infantry Battalion. What neither Riko nor Greta could have known at that time was that the Battalion was being organized in Tel Aviv, Palestine, and trained in the Judean desert, so that the soldiers might become acclimatized to similar conditions to fight alongside a Polish regiment and the British in Egypt and Libya. News reached Greta after November of 1941 to say their contingent was soundly beaten in Tobruk, with 14 soldiers killed and 81 wounded. They had no word as to Rolf's state of being.

Whether or not Rolf stayed with the Battalion until 1943 when the British recalled the troops to disband, I never learned. Greta reported she wasn't sure if it was an American or British ship that brought them to England, but that's where Rolf landed with only his uniform.

He became a chemist in England and visited with me and Riko years later there. Riko illustrated a book on Tobruk, but not until after the War. No doubt he was influenced by Rolf's part in it, and the book may have been a way of apologizing for taking me away from Rolf, she said.

And that was the end of the story as far as Greta was concerned. There was no record if Rolf had been wounded, no recollection of stories he might have told them, no sense of collaboration on a future book, no sense at all of any emotional interaction among the three people. It is possible their survival through the War meant more than revisiting the split Riko had caused. Greta's emotions were occult.

The contrast between the careers of her two husbands in the war could not have been greater. Against Rolf's active enlistment and service under fire, Riko's tour of duty in the Army was defined by his carelessness. When asked to write down his occupation after his conscription, he wrote 'painter.' The recruits assumed he was a house painter, so he served with the common people, whom he liked anyway. His bumblings as a foot soldier resembled those of the *Good Soldier Schweik*, leg puttees unraveling while on parade and a general lethargy while obeying rules.

The Army transferred him to the veterinarian corps where the cavalry was still important, the accelerated birth of horses crucial. Riko was left in charge of taking the temperatures of the mares to establish their times in the oestrus cycle. On his first attempt to take a horse's temperature by rectum, he lost the thermometer. With difficulty, and more than a little disgust to see his full arm disappear into the animal, Riko rid the mare of her incumbrance, and was transferred again.

This time the change came through the revelation that in his family there was one Bishop and one Military General. The Bishop Riko dredged up was from his maternal family, one of the descendants from those who helped establish the iron foundry in Olomouc. Riko smiled at the improbable justice.

I have no idea who the General was, but the military found him, and so much the better for me. Perhaps he was the be-ribboned fellow who gave me my first set of colored pencils. Perhaps he was making up for a bad conscience when he came to paint Mother and made advances to her. My father caught him in media res.

In fact, it was more likely that General Hayek, from the Mikeskas' summer in Hvar, interceded on his young friend's behalf. The Army put him in charge of drawing maps, which is how he ended his abbreviated military career. Riko's skein of help from others remained unbroken, and while he read maps in Prague, Greta coped across the Channel.

On October 17, 1938, Greta opened a letter addressed to her at the first home she had in London, that of the same niece, Charlotte, who had introduced her to the LowBeers, and yet another person Fritz helped escape. Greta recognized Kazimir's fine penmanship.

Riko is still in the Army, but we expect him home on leave soon. Mother and I find the project Riko proposed of having you both move to Australia very disturbing. I will nevertheless write to Marianne (never defined as a relative or friend) in Australia to ask her for an affidavit to sponsor you. We understand that the living conditions in Czechoslovakia are not inviting and that both of you would be better off there. Love, Father

If Greta was aware of the ravages and degradations of Kristallnacht in Vienna in November 8-9th, the same year she found refuge in England, or if she feared what might happen to her own family when the Nazis marched into Prague, she never mentioned it. Might her helplessness in the face of such monstrosity have purged her of thought, or was she simply struck dumb by her luck in being safe from such threats? The mechanisms for her adaptability lay so deeply hidden, I doubt she guessed at them herself. I certainly did not. What prevailed were the generosity and equal adaptability of exiled friends in wartime.

Within a month of receiving Kazimir's letter, Greta fought with her hostess and was looking for a new place to live in London. Eve Korner and her mother invited Greta to move into their home in Hampstead. Kazimir tracked her down, and Greta received her second letter from Vitkovice, this time from Riko's mother.

November 23, 1938. We are sad that you did not visit us before you left Prague. We love our son greatly and hope you will take good care of him. Our daughter, Julci, hopes to have us come to visit her and her husband in Poland for Christmas.

And then came 1939.

Until March, when the Germans marched into the Sudetenland, Eve returned frequently to Prague. Her role as a carrier of gossipy news and goods for her friends hid her deeper spying and code-breaking for the Czech government now in exile in London. She accompanied Riko on the last trip he would take out of Prague. He carried with him a few frivolities—fine soaps, dress shirts and chocolates.

The Channel crossing was relatively calm, though Riko, who prided himself on having sea legs, would have scoffed at the idea of getting seasick. Four days before he was due to go back for a final farewell to his parents still in Vitkovice, Hitler marched into Prague, and Riko never returned.

Eve intercepted a short letter from Kazimir to his wife, Anna, dated March 2nd, in which he spoke of his efforts to remain in Prague to try to clear Riko's and Greta's belongings from their apartment (address unspecified), and to clear Riko's studio before the Nazis moved in. He was able to take away some of Riko's paintings, but he questioned where to send them. It must have been a horrifying irony for this caring and dedicated man, so capable in the ways of postings, to remain ignorant of the hopscotching addresses where his son and Greta were finding shelter. A week later, the Nazis destroyed Riko's studio.

The frenzy to connect with his son during these fractured months shows up in subsequent letters. What price did Riko want to put to the pictures Kazimir had saved? He now needed permission from the Narodni Bank or the Ministry of Education (this ministry may have been misnamed in the letter) to sell the pictures as all works of art had to be checked and evaluated. *Who is Fritz?* he asks. Kazimir sends birthday greetings to Greta for her April Fool's birthday. *And what has happened to the three parcels Mother sent you? Did they arrive unbroken?* In an anguished cry denying reality, Kazimir passes on that Mother proposes Riko should return to Vitkovice and bring Greta with him. *Since Greta is your wife, she should have no trouble.*

But for a single postcard Riko sent to his father in April asking about his personal belongings, there is no evidence either Greta or Riko kept their side of the correspondence. As to Greta's family, she uttered no word in all the years I knew her. I had to assume by now that the Mikeskas' impecunious status was the price she paid for running off with Riko. Although Rolf Passer might have continued his generosity towards his wayward wife, it is doubtful Greta's father would have done so, and it may be she held that against him. We know she cared not a whit for the Guvernanta stepmother, but what about her siblings?

And still Kazimir writes. In June to Riko: *Greta has a few remaining funds, but I am having difficulty sending foreign drafts. Apparently, people who leave Czechoslovakia cannot ask for money to be mailed abroad.*

Until he has a firmer idea of where Riko and Greta are living, he tells them, he is mailing boxes to Vitkovice with whatever belongings he can organize from Prague. *Mother and I will keep things for you. I have enclosed the prices of some of the furniture that might be sold, but the market is bad as many people in the same position as you have left their things behind. No Czech wants your art books because they are in German. The truth is that no one has money to buy them, and I do not propose to offer them to the enemy. Regrettably, you should know that the border guards pierced the few canvasses I was able to bring home with me from your studio. They were checking to see I had hidden nothing inside.*

Keeping Contact

Through August of 1939, Kazimir writes of the suicide of a friend, someone else who has the flu, his sadness in learning Riko and Julci are no longer on speaking terms. *I know you are of different characters, but what has caused this? She, too, is having trouble: her husband is in the hospital* (reason unspecified) *and they are hoping to leave Poznan.* In increasing panic, Mother suggests the name of a friend of a friend she has heard of, someone who might help show Riko's future work. Where would Riko like his watch mailed to? What about his citizenship and marriage certificates?

The last letter from them during the war is dated August 1st to wish Riko a happy 36th birthday.

13

England During the War

At 4:00 pm on September 7, 1940, the Germans loosed the Blitz on London, Birmingham, Southampton, Bristol, Plymouth and Liverpool. Nowhere was the bombing as constant, intense and destructive as in London, where it would continue with only slight abatement until May 11th, 1941. By then, Hitler needed to move his bombers to the Russian Front.

Greta, too, moved. She left her niece's house in central London to the relative safety of Eve Korner's parents' home in the more removed area of Hampstead. When Riko arrived, their house was filled with transient exiles, and Eve could not take him in immediately; instead, she welcomed him into her shattered apartment in London.

There's a cot and a chair for each of us and a table on which I can't lay out much food or drink, but what I have, you are welcome to. You'll have to get used to having no windows. They were blown out long ago. Now the mice and rats come in at night looking for food. You'll have to get used to them, too. Nice company, really.

Don't you go down to the bomb shelters? Riko asked.

Her answer was elliptical. *The hardships are not terrible unless you lose someone and, of course, many have. They see their men come back maimed in head or body or both. I keep myself busy,* she said in oceanic understatement of her de-coding and spy work for the Home Office. And then, understandably frustrated, grieving and furious, she added: *Imagine! We all were present at the birth of our country. Twenty years later, it has been swallowed up, and we are refugees.*

With Eve, Riko witnessed how the high whine and percussion of incendiary bombs and their endless fires unnerved some, but by no means all, of the population. Apart from Eve, he saw that many others avoided the crowded shelters in favor of taking their chances above ground. *Nothing you can do about it anyway,* seemed to be the by-word of the taxi drivers who kept up their trade, chose new routes around the nightly ravaged landscapes. Similarly, *Hop on,* was the invitation to discover which of alternate pathways the bus drivers would take to get from point A to point B.

Riko discovered a population he found unperturbable, tough-minded, and 'plucky'—one of his favorite words. The Churchillian we-shall-prevail attitude was pervasive. Riko had come from Prague with nothing, and here were attractive, educated people who didn't mind showing they had patches on their sleeves, who didn't complain because they found no luxuries and frequently had too little to eat. He found them valiant, resilient and helpful, and tried to copy their virtues. He skirted the different areas of London, made quick sketches of the rubble, the firefighters with their spraying hoses (*No more efficient than spit, but the firemen were indomitable!*), doffed his cap to people whose language he did not share sufficiently to open a conversation with them, to tell them how much he admired them. His optimism was fed through his contacts, Czech refugees in London, friends from Vitkovice and Prague who never let him down: Eve Korner, Erica Kalmer—women I met in London years later—and Mimi and Fritz LowBeer. And if he was not together with Greta, he knew she was safe, realized the dangers she had escaped.

Perhaps to mitigate Britain's acquiescence in initially ceding the Sudetenland to Hitler, the British government was generous to the Czechs who reached her shores. They found funds so that the exiles might take over the greater part of the bottom flats on George Street in Putney for various Czech ministries and their enterprises. The President's nephew, Bohuš Beneš, was there, too, and with a large and growing Czech community, he helped establish a fortnightly newspaper, *The Czechoslovak*, edited by Dr. Cisaz, a scientist in his former life. Bohuš was searching for someone who spoke and wrote English decently. Erica Kalmer did both.

I, of course, had learned English in the prestigious German-run school in Prague. Such irony! England was being pounded, and my Czech friends kept telling me it was my duty to write for the paper. I did mainly advertising—can you imagine finding advertising in time of war?

Unlike Eve, who could not share her clandestine work with anyone, Erica readily informed Riko of the work that found her in London and that kept her involved in the Czech community. She invited him to become involved. *I tried to get some circles interested in Riko's art. Bohuš made stabs to arrange an exhibition of Riko's few paintings, but it never came off.*

One day, a woman came to the Putney offices where—thanks to the efficacy of Erica's collecting advertising funds—*The Czechoslovak* was producing various other publications. The woman introduced herself as the personal secretary of Jan Masaryk. She expressed interest in looking through some of *The Czechoslovak's* more recent publications. Would Erica show her these? In fact, Mr. Masaryk was casting about for a real secretary and had sent a mole to get to know who Erica was. The mole approved.

She introduced Erica to Jan Masaryk, *our new Foreign Minister in London.* From 1923 to 1938, Masaryk had served as Czechoslovakia's Ambassador to England, but resigned after the signing of the Munich Agreement in March. He was furious that Britain, France, Germany and Italy had pared and parceled Czechoslovakia. *It is the terrible tragedy of my little country that it had to be crucified to redeem the sins of others.*

Erica was reluctant to leave because she enjoyed her first encounter with journalism. *I even liked the smell of the ink and the printing. 'The Czechoslovak' was like family. The editors were fun, and Bohuš was lively, amusing. 'I'm happy where I am,' I told the woman from Jan's office, but my friends insisted it was an honor and an obligation to be offered such a position, so once again—under duress—I changed jobs.*

Alone in her dark office where electricity was at a premium, Erica ruined her eyes. She was given all the confidential papers to sort for Masaryk's weekly BBC radio broadcasts to the Czech community in London and in Prague, all the while staving off visitors who clamored to see him.

Listening to his broadcasts in Prague was punishable by death, but there were lots of listeners, and he became closer to the Czechs. He had to make encouraging radio broadcasts every week, hard work as the war was going badly.

I had little time to connect with Riko unless Masaryk was out of the office and I took time off. It was almost impossible as I really was always on call.

While Erica lay buried in visible work, Eve Korner remained above ground spying. During the Blitz, she understood Riko was not thriving where the whining bombs and their thundering percussions were incessant. As she had done with Greta, Eve moved Riko to the Hampstead house where her mother was the matriarch.

Greta confided to me years later that in an obtuse decision, Riko suggested he would rent a room in the same house, but separate from Greta's. She let that interior bombshell explode without further comment to my *What do you mean?*

How ever had he thought such an act would be perceived? Could Greta have seen it as anything but a cruel rejection and profound humiliation, especially in their friend Eve's home? Was he mad at Greta for having made him move from Prague? How could he be when they all had heard and read about its fall to the Germans, bullies he had resented all his life? Besides, all his friends were in London, too. Was he blind to the current housing crisis? Or did he want a separate room so he might, at any time, carry on an affair? All was conjecture, and practicality reigned. The number of Czech refugees Eve welcomed did not allow for separate rooms, so Riko moved in with Greta, and they all shared a severely taxed bathroom.

One of the frequent visitors, and even sometime tenant, was Oskar Kokoschka, whom Greta liked enormously, welcomed as a touch from home and from past artists' circles. Riko, on the other hand, was threatened by him—everything from his art to his endearment to Mrs. Korner for her cooking. Riko enjoyed co-opting the role of the spoiled child; in Kokoschka, he met his match. Kokoschka discovered Mrs. Korner's oatmeal and insisted she put it in cookies, cereal, soup. Before he tasted something, he would ask: *Is there oatmeal in it? Don't laugh; it's good for me. I can feel it.*

If Riko was chafing, Greta was, too. In the midst of the rubble which lay at their feet, Fritz and Mimi LowBeer entertained them as often as possible. *Tomorrow night I have a surprise for you both. Come!*

There stood Riko's former art professor from Berlin, the courtly Haas Heye, now also an emigré. Greta fell under the spell of his erudition and manners. She recognized traits Riko appropriated and learned to use in his own seductions, but one month after the Blitz started, not even Professor Heye's charm distracted Greta from their communal danger and from her growing dislike of the crowded and only slightly safer conditions of the house in Hampstead.

The LowBeers suggested both she and Riko move with them into a house they managed to secure in West Runton, in

Norfolk. It was a summer home proscribed to owners during the war. Only the Bishop of Ely might grant permission to live in it, and the LowBeers met with their customary success. The town was tiny, beautiful and old, full of cottages with slate roofs and small surrounding gardens where they would see roses blooming in February, and from which they had a commanding view of the North Sea and the chalk and sandstone cliffs.

Professionally, things looked up for Riko. An animal lover in Aylsham, not far from West Runton, commissioned him to paint her cocker spaniel. He did not let pride stand in his way. *And by the way*, she added, *I think you should get to know the Headmistress of the Runton Hill School. Her name is Janet Vernon-Harcourt. Don't let her advanced age dissuade you. She is a remarkable person and might have a position for you.*

She did. In his typical fantasy world, however, and with his overwhelming love for the British, Riko was sure they would call him up for war duty, so he suggested Mrs. VH, as he came to call her, offer the job to Greta instead. The Headmistress gave them an irreproachable offer: Riko would be free from teaching at the school in case he were 'called,' (as she knew he would not be), but she would allow him to use the studio at school. After all, she was simply being pragmatic: she had started taking private art lessons from him and wanted him near-by. She readily accepted Greta as the school's art teacher, especially as Greta was prepared to give valuable lessons in German conversation, *In case we ever get caught*, the Headmistress said in another bow to accommodation.

Accommodation to survival was entirely what those firestorm times were about. Riko's and Greta's independent adaptabilities to constantly changing circumstances became apparent.

In that first year of war, they were considered 'friendly aliens.' Greta, as ever, saw the irony of the proper English manners. *They thought I could not be a spy. I could drive with my friends anywhere, whereas Riko had to walk two miles to register every day. When the policeman was not on duty at the moment Riko arrived to sign in, the policeman's wife would simply tell Riko to go and sign in anyway since he was privy to the routine. Riko knew that in one of the drawers there was a gun anyone could have taken, but no one did. Riko had a 9 pm curfew, but I had none.*

Riko, to the English, was a painter of unknown talent with scant art work to show. Only his friends' assurances of Riko's associations with the painters of the Prague Secession stood in his favor. The British did not care whether or not he sided with a rebellion against the traditional styles of any kind of painting. There were so many teachers away at war, they eagerly embraced him. He was not declared a war artist, however, so it was difficult for him and for the school to get materials, but Riko was innovative, a real artist, and a true 'Mr. Chips.' He would have gotten his pupils to paint on shoe soles, if necessary, and he began to paint in earnest. Their idyll lasted short of one year.

As early as May of 1940, Hitler's armies invaded the Netherlands, Belgium, Luxemburg and northern France. As the war progressed, the parents of the children attending school in West Runton feared the students risked being in the line of intended or capricious fire across the Northern Sea. Riko and

Greta kept their Bishop Ely home for school vacations, but they, the Headmistress, the students and staff left the grey seas and sandstone cliffs to move to Ilmington in the Cotswald Hills of the Midlands, near Stratford-upon-Avon.

Foxcote Manor, set in a ring of five farms, was their new academic home. At one end over the stables of the Manor, Mrs. VH assigned Riko a studio. At the other end, lived a single, young and handsome woman, Miss Roberts, who had a piano and invited Riko to play duets. She said she would teach him to count. Their other musical arrangement consisted of his keeping up the bellows for the organ she played every Sunday at church. The students noticed he frequently forgot to pump.

The Mikeskas' living arrangements were less well-defined, but accounts indicate that whereas Riko kept close to the school grounds most times, Greta was left in one room of the farmer's guest house where she had access to an unusable rusted tub. To commute between the farm and school in the dark of early mornings and late evenings of their winter move, she had to climb stiles and cross fields that were full of cows. She was terrified of them and announced, *If the bombs don't get me, the cows will, so I quit.*

She suggested another of the do-si-do steps in her increasingly isolated life from Riko: since the British had not called him up for duty, Greta would cede her art teaching back to him. Eve Korner, who seemed to manage keeping in touch with everyone, came to liken this move to *putting the fox in the chicken coop.* Once again she became realtor to the Mikeskas. She got her father to ask Greta to come do some secretarial work for him in Fort William, in Scotland.

He offered me a huge room and bathroom all to myself, which is why I took the job. I was so tired of primitive life, but I exchanged one difficulty for another: Professor Korner would interrupt me any time of day or night 'Excuse me, Frau Greta. Would you mind taking notes? I just had a good idea for my book.' In nine months, I was completely run down. I had to exert myself to look for another teaching job somewhere without hurting Professor Korner's feelings. All the Korners had been good to me and to Riko. I started putting ads in the papers.

It is impossible to guess at the bases of Greta's psychic exhaustion. For all the time I knew her, she never referred to her life and family in Prague, nor did she speak of missing her married life with Riko, or express jealousy over stories she admitted reached her about the students, teachers, and even the seventy-two year-old Headmistress fighting over him.

Greta accepted the statement from one of the students who told her, *We thanked you for your visits to him as it kept us all honest*, and she was able to laugh about the seven hot water bottles found in his bed one morning after seven different devotees came up at night to give him comfort. She heard the story the Headmistress told on herself when she admitted to Riko that she had bad rheumatism. He said he did, too, so she knit knee warmers for him. After some weeks she asked him how his knees were feeling.

Wonderful, he told her, *no more pain.*

I'm glad, but you have left the knee warmers here.

Ms. Vernon-Harcourt viewed with humor the relationships that criss-crossed at her school. She was aware that Riko was older than the young staff and that it must have been hard on him to have no male company with whom to bounce intellectual discussions. The only other true intellect at the school was, in fact, the Headmistress herself. *We got along very well*, he admitted to me with an enigmatic smile.

The account one of Riko's students gave me from this period is worth quoting in its entirety. It is from Mary Marquardt, whom I met when she moved to the United States.

As art students we dreaded his coming to correct our pictures with his thick black pencil. He had a dark saturnine face. He was shy, brusque and irritable, and if he did not like our work, there would be an explosion of dismay. He was always 'Mr. Mikeska'; we never gave him a nick-name. We held him in awe and recognized that there was something mysterious about him. He was so totally different from anyone else we knew. I'll always remember seeing him silhouetted against the gateway into the walled garden on the grounds of the school. He was plunged into a letter and his face was very serious. When he finished reading, he burned the letter with his lighter. There was a singular isolation about him, whether by accident or intent.

And yet, he loved to communicate. We had a French table and Riko was always there. On the whole, he spoke English well. He would only confuse the sounds of the 'v's and 'w's. While Riko was primarily an art teacher, he also taught German to those girls over fifteen years of age. There were only three or four girls in the class, which ended up being an education in language, literature and world politics. The classes were often a monologue. He was intolerant of mistakes, insisted on accurate grammar, and gave drills. We read Schiller, Heine, the Lorelei folk stories, and Goethe's 'Götz von Berlichingen', a story about a maverick who succumbs to the laws of an imperial unjust society. I'm sure he used it as a metaphor for what was happening all over Europe under Hitler. He was purposeful, but not heavy-handed. He had a passion for poetry he made us memorize, and my German still is good today, thanks to him.

In art, he taught me the magic of 'Chinese white' to take the wateriness out of watercolor. He used the out-of-doors as his studio. We would take stools out onto the grass and paint from there, perhaps the flower beds with their low-lying alyssum and tall delphinia and hollyhocks, or the brown and white Hereford steer in the fields.

Another review I found among Riko's papers was a single page of an assignment in which a younger student had been asked to interview him. The page begins with Riko's answers for advice.

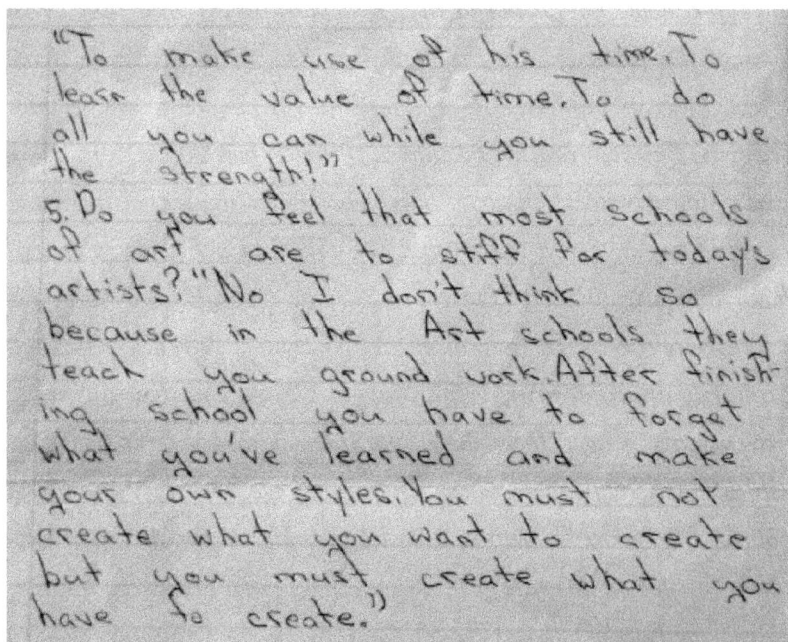

"To make use of his time. To learn the value of time. To do all you can while you still have the strength!"

5. Do you feel that most schools of art are to stiff for today's artists? "No I don't think so because in the Art schools they teach you ground work. After finishing school you have to forget what you've learned and make your own styles. You must not create what you want to create but you must create what you have to create."

While Riko was taking advantage of every minute teaching art and history to his besotted male-starved pupils, he set up a tea shop with a woman in town, kept in touch with friends and goings-on in London, and encouraged Erica Kalmer to come visit when she could get away from her work with Jan Masaryk.

He arranged for me to stay at a charming thatched cottage belonging to a friend of his. Weather was absolutely marvelous, and Riko insisted we go to market to buy or barter vegetables for the school. We were both on bikes. Eggs were scarce during war, he needed them for his tea shop, and while we were looking around, he spied a box with 2-day-old chicks in it. No one wanted them, so he brought them to the school figuring they would grow and be the logical source of eggs. Most ended up being cockerels. He would call them by name: 'Gonner', 'Palest', all signifying the physical states of the chicks at one time or another. Chicks would follow him back to school where neighbors, mostly women, would leave meager scraps. After the war, Riko kept a pig. He would cook up a mash made up of all leavings except tea leaves. The mash smelled terrible, but the pig smelled so sweet, Riko named her 'Violet'. We valued keeping animals during the war as we learned from them; they heard bombers before we did.

About the time that Greta was putting ads to teach in the newspapers, Riko received an invitation from the sister of the woman with whom he was running the tea shop. *I would like you to come teach at Longstow Hall near Cambridge.*

Riko did not want to leave. He suggested Greta accept the offer. Greta, recovering from her work with Professor Korner, was reluctant, but submitted to the interview with the Headmistress of Longstow Hall. She recalled it went like this:

Greta: *I never went to school. I was brought up by a governess and tutors.*

Headmistress: *Wonderful.*

Greta: *I'm married.*

Headmistress: *That's wonderful. All the female teachers here are spinsters.*

Greta: *I only have learned to paint, play the piano and I know French, German and Czech.*

Headmistress: *You'll fit right in.*

For many reasons (and one felling secret), Greta was feeling frail. Prematurely white-haired by now, she looked a lot older than her forty years. She knew what energy was required in teaching and wanted to try her skills at a local church school first. The duties she came to appreciate had little to do with academics. She learned how to sing hymns, take children to church, make sure pennies and not buttons were placed in the collection dish, and insist all the children wear Red Cross arm bands. Perhaps out of empathy with non-stars, she was particularly good at encouraging children who were frightened to perform in school concerts. The children liked this odd lady who often turned a blind eye to their mischief, and proved she was tough under real fire.

The Americans had an airfield next to the school. Those at school watched the planes take off and land, prayed that when the pilots returned, there would be no German plane following on a suicide mission to destroy either the fleet or the airstrip. Greta described a direct hit once that had shattered the walls and windows of the school, sent bricks and stones flying like added missiles. Greta had scrambled and dug through the mess to search for students and teachers to make sure no one was buried, hurt or even—heaven forbid—dead. Miraculously, no one suffered so much as a scratch, but she had needed to hold a heavy hose to put out small fires that kept springing up. *'See,' I told the Headmaster's husband, who had put us through drills as firefighters, 'I learned how.'*

Greta stayed one term training for the school near Cambridge, and was pleased with Riko's praise of her: *You are a tapferle!* With that short affirmation of her courage, she felt she was ready for Longstow Hall.

She stayed there for six years, from 1941 to 1947, her most difficult task was getting used to the smell of peanut butter the Americans gave the school children. *The children were so hungry. They would spread it on horrible yellow bread. When you came into the meal room, you were overwhelmed by the smell of peanut butter. The girls were delighted with these gifts, but to this day, I can neither smell nor eat peanut butter.*

When, in 1947, Greta learned by letter from her niece, Charlotte, that all but one sister in her family had been killed in Auschwitz, she left what had been her longest and most consistent work. She moved back to the Bishop Ely home in West Runton. She still gave private lessons in piano and French conversation, but never again taught in a school. Riko resigned from his teaching to join her.

Where early in the war they had ceded their places to immigrate to the United States to those in more urgent need, the Mikeskas now had no excuse to stay on in England. Riko, however, did not want to leave. He had come to love and value the people and his experiences with them more than he thought possible. He had skirted true danger, and because he had not been witness to people punctured by shrapnel, deprived of their senses, or buried in rubble, the few deprivations he suffered acquired a romantic sense for him. On the other hand, Greta's losses were real and numerous: her family, her independence, her money, the use of her dominant right hand, and her career as an artist along with that. Her long separations from Riko found little solace when they were together. Their encounters were often strange, surrounded by on-looking pupils, his bevy of admirers.

Greta felt deeply isolated, inundated by news that overpowered. After the war, her niece, Charlotte—the one who introduced Riko to the LowBeers, oh, so many lives ago!—traced Greta through the Czech community in London. Charlotte's correspondence revealed horrors Greta did not know how to process, and thanks she was dumfounded to receive.

I have been able to return to Prague because your and Riko's art lessons kept me alive in Terezin, she wrote. *I had to paint lampshades for the German officers.*

Whether or not Charlotte knew the lampshades had been cured from human skin, or, indeed, if Greta was aware of that fact at the time of Charlotte's letters is unknown.

I can tell you that your sister, Anna, survived by walking to the Swiss border, but I heard her journey was dreadful and her mind suffered from the adventure. She has been able to go to the United States where she lives with her young son, Jacques.

Greta wanted to reunite with her.

Riko's and Greta's immigration papers were in order, and the LowBeers, who had left for New York the year before, sent letters urging Riko and Greta not to delay further. We will help you, came the familiar and reassuring refrain.

Days before they left England, two letters reached them in West Runton. They came enclosed in the same envelope and were postmarked September, 1947, from Poznan, Poland. Both were written in Czech. One was from Riko's parents, the other from his sister, Julci. Unlike Greta's parents, they had survived the War.

Dear Children,

We finally decided to write to you. We are here since July 4th to-gether with Julci, her children and Mrs. W. (Julci's mother-in-law) who all are well. We only miss you both. Stanko (Julci's son) got two free days from his school so that he could be with (us) his grandparents. He leaves today for Gostyn where he studies in a convent school (St. Phillips) and is now in the third class of gymnasium. He is a big boy and we are glad that he is in an institution where he is well taken care of. We do not know how long we are going to stay here but I think another two weeks. Ania (Julci's daughter) was delighted with the parcel from Czechoslovakia with the things the lady from England sent and which we brought. All clothes fit her so well as if made to order. Forgive us the poor paper, but there is no other. We shall write to you from home how things are there. A great difference between here and Czechoslovakia.

We kiss you and wait for news from you,
Father and Mother

My dear Brother and dear Greta,

Our parents arrival convinced me that I may write to you. What a pity that so much time elapsed during which we could have written to each other. I hope that from now on we shall write much more often. We did not see each other ten years, which is a lot. During those years I went through a lot, the whole German occupation, the murdering of my Julek (husband). I was left alone to take care of my children. The mother of Julek is my third child. The estate of my children being mortgaged on Kurzany (another estate in another part of Poland) is gone. Happily a part of my apartment and furniture although damaged has been rescued. We grew indifferent to these things, to live is the most important thing. What we went through with the children during the battle for Poznan is impossible to describe. Four weeks—we stayed in a cellar without light and water which was the worst. We only ate raw beets and potatoes. The coffee house which I had before the war was damaged, only the furniture was rescued. But I rebuilt it and if I had no debts—life would not be so bad. The most important thing is that the children recovered from all they went through. Stanko is as tall as I am and they say he is very good looking. I am glad that he is a serious and honest young man. He is a good student. Ania is delicate, very intelligent and pretty. Both children are physically graceful. I have aged greatly but that is not important. I am so happy to have the parents here they look well. Rikerle and Greta when shall we see each other, when will you meet my children? They constantly ask me about you. Thank you very much for the things which our parents brought, they were gifts from heaven. The navy blue dress looks so well on Ania she does not want to take it off and the coat is very useful. Once again-thank you. Greta, I have a favor to ask you. I think Riko-as he did before-hates to write letters. Please write about everything, how you live, what you do and if you can–please send us your photographs, I beg you.

And now, Rikerle, I kiss and hug you from all my heart, my darling brother, kiss and hug Greta on my behalf. (Greta please write me if he has done it and does he know how). Please write as soon as you can I shall be waiting impatiently for news from you and our parents, too.

Once more kisses and love to you both from

Yours old

Jula

Eight years had gone by since Riko and Greta had received a letter from his parents. At that time, they were sending their love and good wishes for Riko's 36th birthday. By then, his father made clear his and Mother's dismay that Riko and Julci had had a falling out (for reasons I never learned), and hoped they might make up. In these post-war letters, there is little doubt that, bolstered by the presence of their parents with her in Poznan, Julci took the first step to restore her relationship with Riko. It helped her to know Riko and Greta had thought of Julci's daughter by sending clothes after the war in care of Kazimir and Mother. The stalwart who insured that the perfectly-fitting navy blue dress and coat reached Ania most probably was Eve Korner. Julci's pleas to have Greta be the continuing responsible intermediary correspondent and general fixer-upper was not lost on her. Riko would be Greta's responsibility, her child to guide through their next exile.

On September 7, 1948, Riko and Greta boarded the S.S. Mauritania in Southampton heading for New York City. They carried in their motley possessions a packet of as yet unanswered letters from Riko's parents and from Julci, three cartons containing some of Riko's sketch books, his paintings and watercolors from his time in England, and some watercolors Oskar Kokoschka had given to Greta. Left behind were several paintings Riko made for Eve and Erica in thanks for all they had done for them. It was time to go.

Studio Study, while in England

The Washerwomen

Rebuilding Houses

War Bombed Houses

14

Second Exile

Welcome to the United States

Let's go back! Greta cried.

The ambient clamor of traffic and foul air advanced the terror Greta felt from the moment they docked. First there had been the physician examining the disembarking passengers. Would he pick up on her increasingly palsied hand, view her as irremediably diseased, send her back alone? Where would he send her? Back to London? Prague? She could not have stood the latter. In London she still had friends, but in Prague, ghosts. Then came Customs. The Mikeskas had thirteen pieces of luggage. Would thirteen be unlucky, even if filled with threadbare clothes and paltry contents? Would the inspectors go through each piece, eye Riko's paintings with suspicion and, like the German border guards, pierce the canvases to see if they hid contraband?

The veneer of five days of good weather, a fine room, abundant and guaranteed food aboard the reputable Cunard White Star line had not layered sufficient coating to protect Greta from the gnawing conscience of her destroyed family's past, the exhaustion of her peripatetic moves in the past ten years, plus the recent epistolary demands placed on her by Riko's family. Nor was she ready to face the unknowable present. She was physically and emotionally spent.

The redoutable LowBeers came to greet the Mikeskas in Hoboken, where the Cunard Line berthed. Mimi and Fritz organized most of the Mikeskas' luggage into a taxi, then sat the couple in their convertible to give unobstructed views of the wonders of the City. The most immediate view, however, started with their passage through the Holland Tunnel—smelly, polluted, loud, dark and terrifying. Greta disliked feeling uncovered, vulnerable, and far from the 'plucky' self both she and Riko were used to. She thought of the anecdote among émigrés of that time: two are crossing the Atlantic, one headed for America, one headed back to Europe. As their ships pass, the old friends shout simultaneously: *Are you crazy?*

But there was something far deeper bothering Greta. It may be that the impending re-connection to her sister, Anna, and to meeting Anna's son, Jacques, piqued the images of an irrevocable act Greta had taken, a step that submerged her in unresolvable guilt.

During one of her rare escapes from Fort William to visit Riko at Foxcote Manor, she became pregnant. In secret, she carried the child past the first trimester, sought help for a 'good doctor' through the unwitting Dr. Korner, then had an abortion. Only after she found out her parents and siblings had been annihilated in Auschwitz, after there was any question she could become pregnant again, did she reveal to Riko what she had done.

She offered me the story almost as an aside during one of my bicycle visits to their home, after Riko died. While I was taken aback by her story and full of questions, none seemed relevant or right to ask at a moment she sought for expiation. It was all too late. She reported Riko's only question: *Was it a boy?*

For years, I had known of Riko's fantasy to have a son, a desire he openly shared with Greta and with their friends in Hvar, Ischia, London and New York. In his imagination, he named him Rudolf, his *luftkind*—air child—and painted him with Riko's own blue eyes and blond hair, but the budding reality had been mashed up and disposed of somewhere in Scotland.

Had the horrors of war convinced Greta it was better not to bring a child into the world, or was this her revenge for Riko's infidelities? Was she punishing herself and, if so, for what? For not insisting her family escape from Czechoslovakia when she had? Was she doing penance, sacrificing the unique life she carried in payment for the insensate murder of millions of others? Or was so much killing around that one more carried no charge? Her excuse? *Riko would have been an awful father.* It occurred to me too late to ask what she thought she might have been like as a mother, but by this time in her 80s, the question seemed moot as well as inappropriate.

One confession led to another in a pattern of delays she established to cope with moral problems. She delayed telling Riko about her pregnancy and abortion until after both were accomplished. She postponed confessing the story to anyone until after Riko had died. She put off marrying Riko in a religious ceremony for forty years until Rolf Passer, her first husband, was deceased. Her convolutions dealt with matters of conflicted loyalty, even to herself.

Just as Riko's father, Kazimir, had to convert to Roman Catholicism to marry Riko's mother, so I converted to Roman Catholicism to marry Riko, but it made me feel traitorous, as if I were getting rid of my Jewish heritage, or hiding it in case of some other pogrom or Holocaust.

Those disclosures came later; currently, she was suffering through the initial steps of her second exile, the vehicle for it: Fritz's and Mimi's car. If the car trip offered her a penance for her past, the arrival at the LowBeer's home in Astoria, Queens, gave her another.

Fritz and Mimi had a small flat. When we got there, it was obvious there was an extra bed for only one person, and that the bed had been assigned to Riko. (Had he confided to them about my abortion? Were they mad at me? Was he still?) With directions, I had to take a subway to Harlem where my sister and her small son, Jacques, were living in a much smaller flat with a communal bathroom. So the first night in America, I spent separated from Riko in conditions I had known in England. Perhaps it made me feel better to see America wasn't so different.

The next day, Riko and Greta looked for a Bed and Breakfast arrangement across from the LowBeers', who were consistently decent and helpful. In short breaths, Greta acknowledged she had let panic get the better of her. All these new realities bordered on hallucination. She was safe. She wouldn't dwell on why only she and Anna had survived the war. They had been able to reconnect. Greta would repair attenuated familial threads, but feared it would take another lifetime. For that, she needed to trust, and to trust, she needed experience in this new country. That experience would come with work and friends.[7]

Fritz, as ever, supplied the latter. He introduced them to Win Sands, a friend he, himself, had met recently at a social gathering. They had found much in common, and Fritz thought those connecting threads would stitch in the Mikeskas.

George Winthrop ("Win") Sands was the grandson of Anne Harriman Sands Rutherford Vanderbilt, a name Riko would come to appreciate for the wealth and prestige it conferred on Win. By 1950, when the men met, Win had suffered a poor-little-rich boy's life. Orphaned as a child, he had traveled and lived in his grandmother's houses in Poissy and Deauville in France, been brought up by an uncle, Ogden Mills, in affluent Woodbury, Long Island, graduated from Harvard as an undergraduate, but failed to finish his Business degree from the same University. He had married, divorced, lost a son and failed at several attempts to make a living in banking and private enterprise. In 1939, while the War was accelerating in Europe (and the Mikeskas were in London), Win enrolled in the New York University Medical School, graduated, and finished his internship at Bellevue. He interrupted his medical residency to enlist in the Army in 1944, landing on June 26 as the Allies were invading France. He served with distinction as the surgeon in the 359th Regiment in northern France, then later as Troop Transport surgeon. He returned stateside in June of 1949, nine months after Riko and Greta landed in Hoboken.

[7] See F. James Rybka, MD in notes on page 291

Fritz, Riko and Win shared a great deal of common ground, not the least being the war they experienced to different degrees in Europe. They all hit it off. Riko related to the disappointments and tragedies of Win's life—being a young orphan, too many moves, trying but failing at various enterprises, including marriage, and—worst of all—losing a son. On the other hand, he was titillated, as ever, by Win's family's wealth and renown.

While Riko and Greta were settling in, Win finished his residency at the Goldwater Memorial, one of the beautiful stone hospitals on Roosevelt Island affiliated with Bellevue. There he worked with and befriended Edward Schechman, a psychiatrist who also had served overseas in a medical unit, and had been in London at the same time as the Mikeskas. Win correctly assumed Ed and the Mikeskas would enjoy one another, so he arranged for a meeting at the LowBeers'.

Ed and Riko immediately got along. Ed's admiration for the Londoners matched Riko's. *I remember stepping my way across craters and mounds of ruined homes and businesses to a place across from Harrod's. A bomb had blown out the windows and the previously elegant display of oranges—oranges, for heavens sakes! Fruit the British hardly saw, never mind bought—had spilled into the street. Everyone saw this treasure that had rolled onto the sidewalk, yet no one touched the oranges or tried to steal one. Everyone was hungry, yet the sense of propriety and respect for the store owners held.*

If Ed's reaction to Riko and to the British was unalloyed appreciation, Ed's reaction to Fritz was equally pure but opposite: *He was the ultimate arrogant European Jewish snob. He came from a rich family and had no adaptability whatsoever. He had a great collection of Oriental art and seemed to live off that collection. He was highly intellectual and a scholar. If you listened to Fritz, there was nothing he didn't know. I came to observe that Fritz was one of the few people in the world who bulldozed Riko. They were constantly at one another's throats. There would be absolutely violent separations and ecstatic reunions, which was typical of Riko anyway. It had to be intense one way or another.*

They all found ways to mesh, however, in their shared quest to establish the Mikeskas in their new country. Ed, Fritz and Win found and settled the Mikeskas into the charming brownstone apartment 414 West 20th Street in a quiet and shaded section of Chelsea in Manhattan. Four sets of stairs (including the outside ones) were manageable then, and the third floor was full of the light Riko and Greta craved.

Next they secured Riko's first studio at Lincoln Square. It was soon to be torn down for the establishment of Lincoln Centre, but it was roomy and serviceable for starters. Ed enrolled at once and brought in others, notably Bernie Gurevitz who would become Riko's framer and another devoted friend. As a student, Ed noted: *Most of us were not particularly gifted, but Riko brought a transference which allowed his students to reach higher levels than we ever felt possible.*

Riko intuited that the pace and aggressive curiosity of American lives might be too rushed to accept the intellectual contributions he had to offer, and he knew he was not alone in this. So many others from torn backgrounds were keen to contribute their talents, thoughts and culture in exchange for acceptance. He saw how many had come before, during and immediately after the war. America now was full of them: the Einsteins and Tellers of the scientific world, but closer to Riko, were the musicians, writers, film-makers, architects he had met or heard about in Berlin and Paris: Arnold Schönberg, Berthold Brecht, Otto Preminger, Fritz Lang, Mies van der Rohe, Walter Gropius. In Paris, he had met André Breton, who was not only making his mark in America, but promoting that of other Europeans. In New York, he re-met the theatrical genius Max Reinhardt, now lionized in public. Riko fantasized accosting him, saying *I knew-you-when.*

Hello, Mr. Reinhardt. You don't remember me, but I remember you well. Professor Haas Heye insisted I take a detour with him and my father to Salzburg so I might see your productions. Professor Heye was taking me to Berlin to study…

But Riko hardly dared recall these long-gone times for their unencumbered pleasures. He knew Reinhardt was en route to Hollywood himself, where old-world culture was transforming itself and American innocence into uncontainably vibrant new forms. Riko, Greta and the world watched those bounce back to Europe and transform dance, music, movies, jazz, and change the lingua Franca into American English forever. New York had the same energy Greta and Riko encountered in Berlin. Then, they had the vigor to match. Now, Riko had to hope he might enter the competitive fray. Greta thought she was beyond that expenditure of energy, and adapted by smaller steps instead.

Greta found work in a textile industry where her fey graphic designs were used to make wall coverings. She made friends immediately, fit right in, listened to their stories, and showed no reluctance to speak in her distinctive European accent. Her co-workers acknowledged she was someone special and accessible. As soon as they realized she could sing French and Czech operas in German, they would command, *Sing us 'Carmen,'* for example, and away she would go with Don Jose's *La rose que tu m'avais jetée*, his song of yearning about the rose Carmen threw him through his prison window, or *Carmen's* brazen *Prends-garde a toi!* when she tells her suitors to beware of falling in love with her. Greta imbued the arias with acting, and her colleagues loved her.

Stop your work. She's going to sing again!

Do Papageno! All the pa-pa-pa-pa-pa-pas are the same in any language.

No, go back to 'Carmen'. We haven't much time. If we hear the bosses coming, at least we'll remember the last interpretation.

They delighted in her daring for interrupting work to command center stage in the middle of their workplace, for dancing gracefully even as she moved her palsied hand and slow steps. Greta looked older than her 48 years. Her hair had turned completely white during the War, and she wore it in a severe style parted in the middle and hanging straight on both sides, but her spirit was young. She had chutzpah!

Her co-workers might have guessed, but never asked, about the privileges in which she had grown up. They assumed she spoke French because she was European, not because of the importance the Czechs gave to all things French since before the First World War. When the Germans appropriated art from Czechoslovakia during the Second World War, they chose the

French over the Czech artists, and denuded her father's walls of his extensive collection of French Impressionists. Only in the opera she attended frequently with her father, did French not predominate. In Czechoslovakia, German continued to be the language of culture, of the elite. All opera, whether Smetana's, Rossini's, Gounod's or Tschaikowsky's, were sung in German. Greta sang what she had learned.

When I asked her if Riko took pleasure in her success, she replied, *He never entered my working world; if he had, he would have been jealous of my friendships.* And how often did she go to Riko's studio? *I was not allowed to go to the studio because I criticized too much. He allowed me to come if I would keep quiet, but when I did, he said my silence terrified him more than ever.* If, however, she reminded me, he was commissioned to paint the portrait of a child, he would bank on Greta's presence and her abilities to keep the child engaged so that Riko might produce the result he liked.

Riko's manner of involvement differed. He did not seek work, but counted on others to bring it to him.

15

Perilous Steps

He could have been a money machine. He was a superb portrait artist and could have knocked them out like potato pancakes at $500 to $1,000 for a fine pastel done in fifteen minutes. He was unwilling to compromise with commercial reality, and he was afraid of money. He was given lots of invitations and backing to show his works, but after the first experience with a very wealthy patron in the USA, he equated the art world with the world of money and hype. He saw that big dollars in the art world could make or break an artist. He became paranoid about what success would mean in this country.

ARTHUR BEECHER, friend

IN THE SUMMER OF 1950, Ed invited the Mikeskas to come to Martha's Vineyard, where he and his wife had a big house that was always full of people. Next to the house was a barn-like structure designed as a sort of dormitory with twelve or thirteen bedrooms on the upper level. Ed housed the Mikeskas here and left the full space for themselves. They loved it. Riko had his own expansive studio and painted feverishly in every medium.

Riko and Ed quickly established a ritual; typically, they would take off in the car early in the morning to go to different sites on the island. Ed was interested in photography, and Riko came with his water colors and pastels.

The clay cliffs of Gay Head were full of crags, grasses and pigments whose shadows and intensities changed with the time of day. Riko would sit on the beach watching the transformations of light, making one watercolor after another, producing sketches *fast and quick* he said, as if one synonym were not sufficient to keep up with his pace. Ed, who loved to watch him in this state, described it as 'hot,' the flood of sunlight on his paintings radiating that heat. Riko was enchanted. He worked from these watercolors for years, and though some of the resultant oils were effective, Ed said he rarely considered them finished.

He reworked them to move a figure in relationship to another, to change color, to reorganize. He stymied himself, but could no more leave the oils alone than paint another from scratch. If he had treated the oils with the same spontaneity as his watercolors, and he was quite capable of doing so, he would have produced a great deal more and better than he did. It was a reflection partly of his perfectionism, partly of his masochism. He could be persuaded only with difficulty, to sign his watercolors, even though retrospectively he would say, 'They were rather good.'

Ed never detailed what Greta did with her time on the island, nor did she or Riko. If she sketched or painted a bit, I never saw evidence of, or heard any reference to her art work from that summer. She might have socialized with the other guests that swamped around the Scheckmans—she was a good listener and raconteuse, after all—but my guess is that she spent her time recuperating. After the war and her second emigration, her traumatic first night in New York, her reunion with a sister she thought slaughtered along with the rest of her family, her meeting with her only young nephew, Jacques, she never mentioned any interaction with others. It was as though she were flensed of feeling. She knew she had to recover, but it is doubtful she responded to the scent of sun on her arms, the salt spray she could lick off her lips, the blinding light alternating with gauzy fogs that struck her eyes, or the kindly invitations to join other guests at the Scheckmans. Attention to Riko, eventually and as ever, provided that impetus.

Ed, perhaps more than most, understood that in America, Riko had little to be excited about. He lived marginally and adapted poorly to his new environment. He felt threatened by age, he missed his European culture and the *badinage* he'd had with his fellow artists. He didn't know how to fit in.

From Riko's eyes, America was at once an extraordinary place because of its energy, its ferment, but it was not quite civilized. He thought Americans in general were not well educated or well-mannered and, in some ways, rather primitive. It wasn't the Europe he'd grown up in.

Nor was it Britain, where the equalizer of war pitched everyone together to get through one minute after the next, or one day after another. Cooperation trumped competition. Lords' hands mixed in with those of lorry drivers'. Housewives, air raid wardens, code breakers, proper nurses, whoever was available, grubbed through recently bombed debris, held fire hoses after incendiary bomb attacks, held their mouths and noses as they piled dismembered limbs and bodies onto litters bound for what should have been a morgue, but was a holding shelter instead. They kept track of the dead until the bodies might be identified, tagged, or written on with lipstick. There were instant infant orphans to be dealt with ("But which body was her mother?"), holes to cram themselves through—flashlights held in teeth—to see if life beat on the unseen side of a cave-in. Riko had been protected from these dangers and sights, but he knew from friends and their families what was going on. He and Greta saw planes crashing in flames as they tried to clear their ice-caked wings over the make-shift runway of the airport close to their school, or watched preying German planes follow them home to put paid to exhausted airmen and machines.

Greta had directed her pupils away from collapsing walls and falling plaster and windows, covered their mouths and noses from the scorching, stinking burning fuels, held the unwieldy fire hoses, had hung on after the smoke filled her own eyes and lungs, but there was no sense of heroism here. Everyone was getting on with it. This was bonding as intimate, immediate and heady as what they had encountered in the cafés of their art school years.

For the first time in his life, in peacetime America, Riko felt lonely and terrified. He stewed, became depressed, drank a lot and became mean on drink. He relied more than ever on others to lift him from his dark moods. His insecurities, envies, and resentments pushed him away from interacting with other Czech emigrés whose center was around 72nd Street and First

Avenue. They might have helped, but Riko did not wish to identify himself as a *Czech* artist, simply *an artist*. He knew he was
good, knew he had to engage in the American arena, but how?

Riko taught, but he didn't charge enough. He sold, but he
didn't charge enough there, either. He was contemptuous of the
entrepreneurial nature of the American success story, which
took doing and self promotion, the last talent Riko dared ask of
himself even as he knew the entrepreneurial spirit wasn't only in
America. In Prague, he'd heard Greta describe her father living
out *the American success story*, first as a creative maverick in the
beer and bottling business, and then as the head of the wrought
iron works that made him money through the First World War
and up to the beginning of the Second. The formidable anti-Jew-
ish avalanche of the Second World War eliminated for him and
millions of others the physical possibility of undertaking any
kind of enterprise, but not its spirit; Riko saw it in Greta. *What
does one do? One goes on*, she said. He attributed her resolve to her
undeniable grit, but it was as if so much had happened to her,
that new pitfalls held little threat. It was time for him to take a
chance. As ever, he had help.

In the fall of 1950, following Riko's intense productivity
while on Martha's Vineyard, and after two years of work since
the Mikeskas's arrival on American soil, Ed and Win decided
to organize a vernissage of Riko's drawings, watercolors, pastels
and oils. Both men agreed he had collected a representative body
of work and felt his first official exhibit in New York would bring
him much-needed money.

Ed's wife at the time had access to her family's apartment at the Ambassador Hotel, and the family allowed Ed and Win to take the spaces apart, put fluorescent lighting around the periphery and hang as many paintings as they could get Riko to frame. They enlisted Bernie Gurevitz to frame the works Riko chose, but this did not prove to be easy.

The pressure to be publicly visible, subject to scrutiny and criticism brought out the worst in Riko. For the first, but not the last time, his supporters would witness a streak of self-destruction that verged on the pathological.

Ed—*We have room for lots of your work, so don't stint. We'll hang them at your directions.*

Riko—*I haven't finished some of the oils.*

Ed—*What do you mean you haven't finished? I thought I saw the whole collection in fine order.*

Riko—*You don't understand; the light's not right in the portrait, and the figures on the beach are so small in the big oil, you'd think they were all shore birds.*

Ed—*I can tell the difference.*

Riko—*It's not ready.*

Or the arguments would be with Bernie over the kind of frame: wider vs. thinner; gilded to enhance the light on the beach or woody like the beach fence posts? Matting for the watercolors? If so, even width at the top and bottom? What about the sides? Contrasting color matting, or complementary? And once decided, there was no guarantee Riko would not change his mind at the last minute, insist on a new frame, or take the picture out of the exhibit altogether.

Bernie admitted, *there were times I would love him and times I would hate him. I never met a personality like him. He was his own worst enemy. I was limited by what I could do for him, and he was not responsible enough for his own life. I felt he was a contradictory genius in constant anger.*

Or the battle would be over money. All right, he would tell them, he would show, but only for the prices he insisted on, which was to say, distressingly low. If his friends suggested he augment the price, he resisted or threatened to scuttle the exhibit. Ed understood that Riko's conflicting attitude towards his work and his own worth was a critical part of his character and, as time went on, the habit drove a splinter, if not a wedge between the two men, but Ed, Win, and Bernie persisted, and the exhibit took place.

Riko was clearly pleased to be the center of attention, spoke volubly when addressed on the subject of each work, engaged his audience with charm and erudition, moved from room to room with his characteristic small smile on his face, smoked and drank a fair amount. Greta snaked her way slowly through the crowd, stopped if she thought there was something worth over-hearing about Riko's art work, moved on. Those who didn't know her never considered she might be his wife. She looked a good deal older and seemed as dispassionate about the paintings as the spectators. In fact, the concept of 'wife' was missing. In those days, Riko wore no wedding band.

The exhibit sold two or three thousand dollars' worth of pictures, a significant help in those days, but unequal to its potential gain. I thought of a passage from C. M. Bowra's *The Greek Experience*, a book Riko prized for Bowra's research and insights into the philosophy of artists and their aesthetics around the time of Socrates, Greek history in which Riko steeped himself. One quotation stood out from Riko's bold underlining: ". . . the Greeks saw no virtue in poverty and regarded it as a condition which degrades those whose lot it is . . . it is worse than old age." Riko faced both. It was not only this juncture that made him panic, but his alternating fears of success and failure, and his push-pull about the allure and need for money that tripped him up. And then, chance did not favor him at the time of his arrival in New York.

Unsigned watercolor of Gay Head in Martha's Vineyard

16

The Caprices of War

IN A BIZARRE POLITICAL SCENARIO put in place one year before the Mikeska's arrival, I discovered a ploy that neither Riko nor any artist of that time could have imagined. Ironically, it addressed Greta's plea for subsidization of the artist—<u>her</u> artist—but the supportive Renaissance Prince she longed for had turned into a frog.

In 1947, the American government was emerging from the Second World War with as much readjusting as the foreigners seeking refuge. The Soviets had replaced the Germans as fierce occupiers in Eastern Europe, and the threat of communism spreading to the United States colored its foreign policy. One of the ideas to combat the alleged allure of communism was to fight it on a cultural front, to contrast the intellectual freedom and artistic creativity of American artists with the rigid ideology of cultural programs emerging from the Soviet Union.

In a *Mad Magazine* kind of lunacy, the CIA[8] undertook to promote American artists, writers, film makers, magazines, newspapers, travel guides they listed in a Propaganda Assets Inventory. They appointed Tom Braden, former OSS agent, as the first Chief

[8] See Frances Stonor Saunders in Notes on page 296

of the CIA's International Organisations Division. It would subsidize everything from opera recitals to sending the all-black cast of George Gershwin's *Porgy and Bess* on a railroad tour through the Soviet Union. Borrowing from a Russian proverb, *When the Cannons are Silent, the Muses are Heard*, Truman Capote took the second part of the proverb for his title and wrote a branding account of the effect the sassy, talented, fearless cast had on the slack-jawed Soviet citizenry. There was no doubt of the cast's artistic and personal freedom, and the players did, indeed, cast glitter on the creative genius flourishing in the USA.

In terms of artists and painters, who were the CIA's unwitting Chosen? Artists such as Jackson Pollock, Mark Rothko, Willem de Kooning and Robert Motherwell, proponents of the then often disliked but pervasive American Abstract Expressionism. How to sell their style? Soviet artists, like those during the Franco régime after the Spanish Civil War, were painting their own brands of abstracts hiding political messages visible only to other artists. How might the CIA globally market the American artists, proclaim their more overt worth and dynamism?

They found their foil and propagandist in Stephen Spender, poet and co-editor with Irving Kristol of the intellectual and cultural Anglo-American journal *Encounter*, launched in 1953. Originally associated with the anti-Stalinist left, the magazine soon received covert funding from both the CIA and Britain's MI6. How Spender and Kristol rationalized the magazine's financial success I have not found out any more that they did then. They were glad enough of its success and didn't think to question the reinforcement in their choice of artists.

The ironies piled on. While the conservative Dulles brothers, Allen as Secretary of State and John Foster as Head of the CIA, joined forces with anti-communist sentiments and policies, the subversive cultural arm of the CIA was covertly recruiting the rich, powerful and liberal philanthropists to promote the very artists Joseph McCarthy's witchhunts were digging up and exposing as "communist infiltrators" in the House of Un-American Activities Committee.

The long and short of it was that the ruling cultural elite fell into place. It consisted of people such as Nelson and David Rockefeller connected to the Museum of Modern Art (MoMA), along with William Paley, MoMa Board member; John Hay Whitney, Chairman of the MoMA Board; and, of course, Tom Braden as executive secretary. The three latter had served in the CIA or in the agency's predecessor, the OSS. Under their purely administrative jurisdiction at MoMA, they organized an influential show called *The New American Painting*, which toured every big European city in 1958-59 at about the same time the cast of *Porgy and Bess* was up-ending Soviet cultural sensibilities. And how did they raise the money? They would go to millionaires with developed interests in art and ask them to contribute to the apolitical Fairfield Foundation to promote these artists. Julius Fleischmann, gin and yeast 'baron', for example, was a generous unsuspecting contributor.

At the height of Riko's paranoia, he could not have guessed at the games being played out by the CIA, nor at their marketing skills. None of this came to light until 1995, well after both Greta and Riko had died, but during Riko's artistic life in the United States, the unintended consequence of this covert program was to victimize him and others outside the 'long leash' circle of preference.

Against this unimaginable background, Riko and Greta adapted their art in the United States the way they could.

17

Adaptations

His was the world of the savant. Riko took you out of the mundane and made you feel special because his interests and concerns were on a different plane from those of most people.

Pat Budziak-Beecher, daughter-in-law of Bill Beecher, Greta's 'baby lawyer' and longtime friend, NYC.

Just as surely as there had been a change in mainstream art in Berlin in the 1920s and 30s, American art in the 50s and 60s experienced a sea change after the Second World War. The painting styles Riko and Greta had grown up with in Europe displayed thick paint, wild colors, effulgent gold leaf, the romantic curves of Jugenstil, the shimmers of Impressionism, the rigors of Cubism. The sometimes grotesque, surreal or explicitly sensual 'degenerate' art Hitler and Co. despised (but stole from anyway) was replaced in America by the minimalists, anodyne extremes to the flamboyance and rebellion of Grosz, Kandinsky, van Dongen, Klimt, Schiele, Breton and Magritte.

Since the '40s, Riko had been versed in the art of American Abstract Expressionism, a movement he saw segue into Pop Art, the comic book diversions of Roy Lichtenstein, the soup cans of

Andy Warhol, and the *non-portraits* Larry Rivers was painting. What Riko tried to grasp, but could not, was Minimalism.

He saw the flat, monochromatic surfaces that looked as if the artist had applied paint with a roller. They weren't pictures at all, in his estimation, and he was convinced they would not survive. They had no narrative, and human nature looked for stories in whatever medium. Hadn't the cave drawings of Lascaux taught the need to transmit stories? What about the wealth of architecture, art, and illuminated manuscripts derived from the lives and teachings of the Buddha and Christ? And hadn't the Greeks taught these popular artists anything? Surely they knew about the Greeks! How could one escape the galleries upon galleries of narrative art at the Metropolitan Museum where, by the way, he caught up with the paintings by Edgar Degas and Eugène Boudin of Princess Metternich, that grande dame of European influence he came to learn about in Berlin. *So long ago, her stories! Ach, ja! Now those were admirable paintings!*

Riko appreciated what each portrait revealed about the character through the brushstrokes, the nuances of lighting, the background textures, the objects that surrounded the model and illuminated her mood, but of this new art, he was skeptical.

He wondered aloud if the annihilation caused by the A bombs hadn't leveled all future art, along with life. That, at least, he might understand, but why then would people pay over a million dollars for a Jackson Pollock painting? Well, at least, Riko admitted, he'd dribbled paint of different colors on an overly large canvas. Riko thought the end product didn't reflect what the artists wanted to do or, if so, it was of no significance. He was talking about a personal language. *It's almost like the uselessness of a dream. It's your associations that matter, not the thing itself.*

Riko was fascinated when his confidant and student, Ed Scheckman, told him about going to I.M. Pei's new wing of the National Gallery in Washington, D.C., where they were exhibiting six American artists of the '50s and '60s. Among them was Barnett Newman, with his Stations of the Cross. The fourteen canvases, six feet high and maybe four feet wide, took up a special gallery. Each canvas had a white background, and on each Barnett had painted one to three vertical lines, some thick, others thin, some close together, some wide apart, the position of the lines different in each painting.

Ed recalled standing in a corner of the gallery from which he could observe the public's reactions to the series. People entered the room, had a cursory look at the uncluttered paintings in the relegated space, read the explanations on the wall, and exited. They did not risk looking at the pictures without reading the words, and since there was nothing much to search for on each canvas, it was the explanation that mattered. The gift was in the written promotion. It was what Tom Wolfe described in his book called *The Painted Word*.

Riko was thrilled when I sent the book to him.

Riko did try to see what was going on, and the '60s influenced him to some extent. The one contemporary master who transcended all forms was Picasso, whom he admired artistically and politically, whose portrayal of Guernica he copied in an homage. Even Picasso's warped faces or whimsical statue of a goat made up of found parts told something to viewers. They were not abstractions that said look-at-me just to *épater la bour-geoisie*. They told stories and delineated character as clearly as the rearranged features of his faces did, whether in painting or sculpture. His art informed about the past and future, with the emphasis on the power of the present.

Whether a cause of age, experience or experiment, Riko's paintings became more abstract, too. He began to concentrate on subjects such as the circus, which he felt represented life in a mythological way, and made studies of Marcel Marceau. His attachment to the mime was no mystery. Riko felt as alienated and voiceless as the white-faced fellow in a striped sailor's shirt and tight black pants, whose hands fluttered like the delicate butterfly that stuck out on a filament from his flat black hat—an antenna hoping to capture a code? Or Marceau's hands moved blindly, one following the other along the length of an unseen perpendicular barrier to measure how far he had to travel to find the break in the wall. Riko made many paintings of Marcel Marceau, sold one to Lars Björling, the fellow who had intro-duced Riko to us. Riko was tempted to offer one of his paintings to Marcel Marceau himself, but lost his nerve. Riko felt old, over-the-hill, out of balance, and caged in his new world at the same time that others became mesmerized by him as an artist and savant.

As ever, Ed's observations rang true.

Riko knew he was bright. He knew he was charming and could enchant a woman or man in two seconds but, after all, that was not what his profession was about. His life work was a relationship between him and an inanimate object. He was relating to a canvas, alone, in a studio. I think that beyond anything else, the characteristic that ran through Riko was his sense of isolation.

The art world moved away from him, the entrepreneurial system of this country separated him, he was increasingly removed from his friends because of his bitterness and because of the demands he put upon his friends. It became increasingly difficult to be one.

Ed spoke for all who had fallen captive to the Mikeskas' allure, to their obvious erudition, story-telling talents, artistic outputs, and historical backgrounds. Their invitation of inclusion into their refined world made us feel special. In addition, I daresay the challenge of relieving their economic neediness flattered and goaded us. Who amongst us would find the magic key to fit the marketing lock, open the door for Riko (specifically and finally) to achieve financial independence for them both? Greta's repeated plea was, like her, straightforward.

In Europe, artists were lionized, supported. Here Riko has to promote himself. He doesn't know how to do this. It is not his talent. People must help him!

Greta demanded with the nostalgia for dynastic patronage of artists that dated from Pharaonic times. In the USA, the Mikeskas needed the Borgias and Medicis or, had they known how to get to them, the more contemporary Rockefellers.

Had the Mikeskas' requirements been simply for funds, however, it might have frightened a lot of us away. The equation was more subtle. Their needs as two middle-aged artists in a second exile were also—perhaps even primarily—emotional and basic. Those we understood. After all, who amongst us had not experienced feelings of insecurity and vulnerability in our own lives, then been both relieved and flattered by those who bolstered us? How did one hang onto that support?

Repeatedly, Riko had proved his ability to seduce both men and women. Greta understood this better than anyone. Her life with his inconstancies prepared her to capitalize on a way to satisfy both artist and patron. Greta offered that gateway with a simple transactional equation: access to Riko was not primarily that you would get the art education of your life, but that you would get Riko himself. He would be your best and, if need be, your most intimate friend. Seduction came in various forms: artistic, intellectual and sexual. Riko shone in all three, and Greta exercised dispassion because her practical experience taught her neither she nor Riko could live without the other.

A significant event took place in January of 1963. Greta slid on the ice coming out of her working place on her lunch hour. A co-worker who was with her called the ambulance, and she was taken to a hospital near Carnegie Hall not far from her employer's office. She had fractured her left hip. She was placed in traction for five days, then operated on to pin the hip in place. A negative reaction to the anaesthesia left her in a coma for three days, and when she emerged, her immediate and urgent reaction was to speak in each of the languages she knew. This, to her, would have been a sign of complete control, but two days later, she sank back into a coma and when she emerged, she was blind except for shadow perception. She had impaired speech and was partially paralyzed.

Suddenly, Greta was not there for Riko, who alternated between denial and a fury born of terror—for him, for her. While Greta concentrated all her energy into re-mobilizing herself, he came to the hospital almost daily, ineffectually, as lovingly as his basic narcissitic nature allowed. He could do nothing for her, but feared not being seen at her side. He did not live easily under the censure of others.

At the end of March, with the intervention and constancy of Ed Scheckman, Greta was moved to the Neurological Institute at Columbia-Presbyterian Hospital for rehabilitation. Her doctor there was Hans Heller, a surgeon she trusted as he shared a familiar middle European culture and religious history. To boot, he spoke with a sophistication and interest in art the Mikeskas looked for.

Thanks to him and to Greta's determination, she was the first one in the gym in the morning and the last one to leave at night. Greta's discipline left little time for visitors, but the parade of co-workers, students and friends the Mikeskas collected could not fail to impress her doctors, nurses, and rehabilitation staff. In June, six months after her fall, Greta walked out with clear sight, fluent speech, and two arm canes.

The Mikeskas' coterie of friends and students bought a lot of paintings from Riko during the months Greta was in the hospital. It was a sensitive way to help him with payments without having him trip over his pride, and reminded me of the time his friends had supported him in Vitkovice after the mysterious and vicious firing of his father from the Witkowitzer Bergbau-und-Hüttengewerkschaft.

Now, in New York, forty years later, he did not give himself to deep reflection on the sudden increased sale of his artwork. He was grateful enough for the money to put aside his chagrin. It may be he even expected the help of his friends. His dependence on others to get him out of fixes was deeply etched.

Up to this point, the vision friends had of Riko was of him pacing with a cigarette and a drink in hand. They knew he drank liberally in his youth, and during the summers in Ischia when he and Greta were together with the LowBeers, the Björlings, the Bozzis. They knew that when he drank, he became loud and aggressive. After Greta had the hip accident, Riko cut down on drinking. He also wore his wedding ring from that time on.

Greta's playful wallpaper design, NYC, 1950s

18

Riko as a Teacher and Painter

WHILE GRETA PIECED HERSELF BACK TOGETHER, Riko's student roster was steady and gratifying. Ed, in particular, responded quickly to Riko as a teacher and person.

Most of us were not particularly gifted, but Riko brought a transference which allowed his students to reach higher levels than we ever felt possible.

Bernie recalled that in his framing studio, Riko would set up a still life, then work on two or three representations of his composition at the time.

Everything he did, he did in depth. He would make numerous drawings, collages, pastels and oil sketches of trapeze artists, for example. He left at least a dozen little masterpieces before he finished the painting. It gave me pleasure to see what I might be framing!

When he came to my studio and he wasn't painting, conversation with him was an adventure. He would see a shipment from Leonidas, Texas, for example, and the name Leonidas would start him off on something Greek.

In the early days when Riko was still teaching in his first studio in Lincoln Square, Ed introduced Riko to the woman who would become his prize student, the wife of another medical doctor Ed met in his unit overseas during the war. Her name was June Singer.

As with any relationship that counted, their times were stormy. June had started as a casual painter in the summers in Wilton, Connecticut, to become a student at Parsons School of Design, the first American school to initiate a satellite campus in Paris in 1921. Whether or not Riko encountered anyone from Parsons while he himself was there in the '20s I never learned, but in New York, he certainly became aware of the Parsons table that had been designed in Manhattan in 1930. With its legs as thick as the top, it became the iconic table in American homes and offices. Riko acknowledged June came with credentials.

As far as she was concerned, however, *I knew nothing until I came to him in his studio at Lincoln Square. It could accommodate nine or ten students. His lessons were an education in fine arts, in techniques of stretching canvases, of making and mixing your own pigments, of layering paints such as the Old Masters must have taught. You had to be very serious about class. He gave morning and afternoon classes that lasted three hours each, and he didn't like anyone coming less than twice a week. I wound up going five times per week, and then I was sneaking into the Saturday classes he gave to men who couldn't come during the week or at night. It was a privilege.*

Part of the class was a discussion of the great painters, how one influenced the other in different periods. He gave insights into how to look at a painting, how to appreciate the layering of paints, the thinning glazes, the adherents, the materials and crafts used in sculptures, and how to appreciate art so that when you were in a museum, you could look critically. He insisted on knowing the histories of the times in which the painters were working. What happened to the depiction of fabrics in paintings once shipping between the Orient and Venice, for example, that made safe the delivery of exquisite silks? He would take the whole class to museums, this large class of mostly women trailing after him. Others would gather round, and he loved every minute.

There was a time when Riko took his class to the Frick to have them see how Rembrandt *painted the characters from the inside out*, to admire the differences between the two eyes in all his portraits, and to admire the Holbeins. Here they could see the chunky solidity of Thomas Cromwell in three-quarter profile, as if to suggest that full view of this austere man's face alone would chastise the viewer too harshly. The eyes are small, piggish. His fingers are fat and on the forefinger of his left hand is a ring with a stone of opaque blue—a moonstone (and what would be its meaning?) or a star sapphire (wouldn't the star show up better)? There is a dented semi-opened gold box from which papers have been extracted. They lie on the green cloth-covered table like homework still to be attended to. What judgment would he give to their contents? The hue of the worked gold of the box matches that of the simple wood of the bench on which he sits. Might it be chestnut rather than oak? Chestnut has a more yellowy-green pigment and highlights the splendidly rich green cloth covering the table on which he rests his arm. Green, such a welcoming color, the color of spring and summer, yet here, there are no complements in the yellow and green he used. What complexities lie here? Did Holbein hide a warning behind the magnificent portrait? In real time, Thomas Cromwell was suspect. And it was to these times that Riko alluded, though he would embellish with spoken details what the viewer could not help but notice.

What an emotional contrast with Holbein's portrait of Sir Thomas More! Riko did not need to point out the lush red velvet sleeves, so rich and resplendent in pigment, light and texture, it made one want to bite down on them. Nor did he need to indicate More's fine facial features and very human five o'clock shadow. As for the prominent medallion depending from the substantial chain around his sable-covered shoulders, it seemed a decoration more than a political commentary. What was its history? And there, just at the collar line, lay a small triangular swatch of white, an undershirt perhaps, a touch of purity next to his skin. Here was the saint, canonized not long after his execution, a beheading that had been viewed unjustly by all of Europe, as outrage by the Dutch humanist, Erasmus.

As his pupils devoured the banquet of the paintings, Riko detailed the times of Henry the Eighth; the implications of his marriage to, then beheading of, Anne Boleyn to move onto Jane Seymour; his insistence on keeping the divine right of Kings, and why, when Sir Thomas More could not consent to that hubris, the King, in an act of relative grace, had him beheaded. After all, the punishment for treason in those days was to be drawn, hanged and quartered.

Joan Berkowitz, one of his pupils and daughter of Fritz and Mimi LowBeer recalled his stopping that day in front of both Bronzino's *Portrait of a Man* and of Velasquez's portrait of Philip IV. She watched Riko pace back and forth in front of the latter painting while giving a dissertation on Spain, the Siege of Lerida, which King Philip had invited Velasquez to portray, and history of the King, himself. He skipped from point to point.

He may have been a weak King, but he was a great patron of the arts, and, in this quite humble; in fact, he had Velasquez paint him in a rude shelter in Fraga—the painting came to be known as the Fraga Portrait—but you notice his pink and silver clothing is anything but rustic. 1644, it was, he continued, not having to look at any of the Frick's notations etched on a copper plate below the portrait. *Rembrandt paints the soul; Velasquez paints like an editorialist*, he added with utter confidence.

Some twenty minutes later, Joan said, *he paused long enough to realize he had attracted the whole group of visitors to the Frick that day. He turned around, executed a hat-tipping gesture, smiled and said: 'That will be a nickel a head, please.'*

The general auditors no doubt heard it as charming modesty and self-irony, but his friends and devoted coterie of students who were present understood his acknowledgement at a deeper level. They all knew he was totally unrealistic about the prices he charged both for lessons and for his paintings but, as Bernie said, *If a group had gathered, and the conversation didn't center around Riko, he would show his resentment in a child-like manner. He wanted adulation and, in many ways, deserved it. He gave unconditionally in his teachings on any subject, and loved seeing the ladies respond.*

Most students gave Riko unqualified praise as a teacher, but with time, in June Singer's case, another dynamic appeared.

As a teacher, he was totally dedicated, very inspiring and he never spared himself. I think he squeezed every drop of talent out of whichever student he was working with. He could be very tactful for an untactful man, tried to criticize kindly if he had a student with limited abilities. But the more talent you had, the harder he was on you; in fact, he was merciless. Many times he reduced me to tears. What made me go back? I would suffer a greater loss by not returning.

I think that sometimes he was jealous of my work. He would get angry, say 'this isn't right' and without asking, take a brush and make corrections which I felt very strongly ruined the painting I was working on. And yet, he was a good judge of character and could tell things about you. This was often infuriating because he was right. He made me a better artist, so I have to think he knew I could take it. I couldn't be a total artist and Riko couldn't accept less from me. He, himself, was a total artist: self-centered, super critical, mistrustful, complicated. He was possessive and jealous by nature. It wasn't limited to art. It was in friendships. He required a total oath of allegiance and dedication well beyond the call of duty.

I could leave the studio and he would be in a wonderful mood. 'Give me a call. Let me hear from you.' You could call three hours or twenty-four hours later and he would be hideous on the phone—rude, discourteous. It was like a schizophrenic change, so you never knew; this is one of the things that made it difficult to get along with him. You wanted to be attendant and kind, but you couldn't face it.

Little by little, Riko made friends with a few of the artists on the floor of his studio. A young couple, Nava Atlas and Chaim Tabak, were gentle and deferential to him. When they met in the corridor, Riko would greet Nava with,

Good morning, Madame. You look very charming.

She appreciated his European gentlemanly manner, the way he doffed his Panama in summers, removed his beret in winters. Nava was working on compiling and illustrating a cookbook. As a chef manqué and artist-illustrator, Riko was genuinely interested in the merits of Nava's book.

What stage have you reached? he would ask.

He liked the humor of her drawings, the same way he reacted with a smile every time he went past a fey drawing Chaim made in which he included the figure of the Buddha. Not all people would have seen the humor in it, but it remained one of Riko's favorites.

Yes, yes, that's very nice, he would say.

Nava also appreciated his use of different languages—Yiddish, German, French—and when he asked *Do you know what that means?* it was genuine, unlike Greta's linguistic snobbery with her expectation that everyone should know at least those languages she spoke.

Chaim was experimenting. More than that, however, Chaim took on organizing the Union Square Open House. Riko did not understand this. *You must paint!* he would hector, though once he got to know Chaim, he felt more at ease in commenting on Chaim's involvement with the other artists, and Chaim with his.

As I began going to his studio, I saw only his most recent attempts with the circus series, the other stuff buried at the back and inaccessible. I had little with which to judge his art, but as we began talking, I realized I was sitting with someone quite exceptional, someone who had been around many different art movements and had a sound foundation. I offered to help him sort out his work. That was slow but wonderfully revealing to me of the different art styles he practiced, and his talent in different media.

He loved to experiment, felt that was really the duty of an artist, to find the right mode of expression. He would invite me to doodle (as Riko had done in Vienna when Haas Heye picked up on his talent) and we started discussing forms and problems. He would demonstrate with just a few lines. He spoke highly of Braque and liked Modigliani as a person; he was touched by him in a way, and insisted Nava read the book he had given her on Modigliani. He hated Marcel Duchamp, called him a 'schnorrer,' someone who is a scrounger.

He spoke with painful longing for his days with his peers at the cafés in Europe, of the constant debates they had about art, different artists, different schools of art, fights and reconciliations. I made one attempt to include him in a small group of artists who took turns posing, but Riko felt uneasy, thought it was too close to an academic setting he had long since outgrown. I suggested another project: I had arranged for the artists to visit other studios in the building. He started getting very nice responses from his colleagues, so that gave him a boost; it was as if I had opened a new world for him.

It was difficult for Riko to integrate with the community of artists and intellectuals in America. He didn't see that other artists might have obstacles, and resented that everything seemed easy here—for the likes of Dorothy Dehner, for example. He passed her studio every day, and Chaim noticed the wound never scabbed over.

We didn't discuss art at first, just neighbors. He and Dorothy Dehner had shared the same floor for 25 years when I came along.

They bickered about each other, she about him and vice-versa, but neither revealed the specifics. They were very insightful about each other and their personalities clashed, but towards the end, they both mellowed and respected each other.

I daresay Riko was jealous, not of Dehner's considerable talent, but of the apparent ease she had for promotion. Her sculptures and paintings were already in the Museum of Modern Art, the National Museum of Women in the Arts in New York, and at the Hirschorn Museum and Sculpture Garden in Washington, DC. She had been married to the deservedly lionized artist and sculptor, David Smith.

Riko felt she thus had a double dose of renown and opportunity. He was missing contact with people who could create a market for his work. His friends were doing their best, but they were not professionals. The more he recognized he needed promotion, the more he involuted, became pathologically shy of artistic and social exposure, and shunned chances to be discovered. Chaim's frustration echoed that of many.

Why someone as gifted and talented as Riko never made it in New York is quite extraordinary. Everything he has done has shown special skill far beyond the average. There is absolutely no doubt, when one sees his work, of a great concept behind every painting, and of remarkable technique and execution. What was missing was a contact with people who could create a market for his work. Today, artists have to be marketers as well as artists, and that is something that wasn't in Riko's background. He never learned how to sell his own work, and he remained very isolated.

Nevertheless, Chaim persisted in encouraging Riko to participate in the Open House Riko had been dismissive of. He agreed, *but even up to the day of the event, he was having second thoughts. He didn't feel he should expose his studio to the public. It was something very personal, and he didn't want to join the 'carnival' of artists—an irony for someone haunted by the theme of a circus! Finally, as I started to bring his work into the open, he started giving it an appreciative look, started smiling and acknowledging with what he considered was the ultimate compliment: 'there was something there.'*

———

Thanks to Chaim's organization and display of Riko's art work, I noticed an arc that brought together the manner in which Riko had coped with the tangible calamities in his life. I had learned how Riko, as a youth, fashioned lethal weapons so his friends and family might fight the oppressors, but his arsenal went unused, and he had to swallow the bile of resentment. It lasted through his student years, rife with experimentation and invention, but even these fell within the confines of traditional drawings, portraits, still lifes, and landscapes. During the War, his artwork was limited by his time and materials, and few examples crossed the Atlantic. As clever as many of these pieces may have been, none came through with the emotional impact, personal stamp and anger visible either in youth, or in his mature years in New York.

Riko's interests, his education and artistic preferences, his philosophy were steeped in Greek myths, stories that condensed the fears and frustrations, sexual desires, ambitions and hubris of the human soul. They were complicated, interwoven, used many names for the same demi-gods and gods, called upon soothsayers, courted superstitions. They invited the creation of extraordinary temples, frescoes, Gorgon heads, fertility symbols. They achieved in verbal and marble narrative a grace and perfection that enslaved Riko in his lectures to his students and in the working out of his own art. In the portrayal of some of these myths, he sought catharsis.

He did various studies of Clytemnestra dancing after she murders her second husband, Agamemnon. Riko based the story on Aeschylus's version, more dramatically brutal than Homer's, and the paintings he developed from the sketches show Clytemnestra in disfigured transports of joy as she avenges Agamemnon's crimes: his murder of her first husband, his raping her to enforce her marriage to him, and then the ultimate horror, his killing of their daughter, Iphygenia, as a sacrifice to the goddess Artemis. The reason for this particular carnage? To gain favorable winds from the gods so that Agamemnon might sail to Troy to save Helen, abducted from Sparta. Here Riko found the raw emotions of vicarious revenge with each dip and sweep of the paint brush. He painted Clytemnestra balanced on one dancing foot, her pale arm extended in crazed accusal against a background of actual purple passion. Riko knew the classics, savoured the different readings of the myths, and painted his vicarious vengeance with unerring strokes.

As the freedom his advanced years and I-have-no-more-popularity-to-lose attitude emerged, his painting became increasingly abstract and definitively his own. The circus series gave him more drama, color, daring, unspoken risk-taking and talents than real life did. The role of the clown alone was the supreme example of occult energy, carrying on powers established in Greek myths and Shakespeare, literary and artistic portrayals that resonated in his marrow. Riko's identification with the mute Marcel Marceau did not ask for deep analysis. I found his depictions of these themes and variations far more original than his previous paintings and wondered why these had not made his name in America. His personality answered that question.

No more in full control of his life than most people are, Riko nevertheless hung on to the fantasy that he could be. He grew to doubt, and resent as unasked-for intrusions, the multiple attempts of others to guide him with their own suggestions of art shows to mount, which Galleries to accept, whose favors to curry, what prices to affix to his paintings. With only word of mouth publicity for his shows (*Why is it so easy for others to get promoted?*), more openings went unreviewed; with fewer reviews, and those in secondary publications, his public either stayed the same or shrank; with a lesser number of viewers, fewer paintings sold. Riko's reaction? *What did we know!* It echoed his dismissive conduct towards Greta when he demanded to hear a re-run of material she had been giving me of his life. *You know nothing!* Indeed, in this case, none of us knew anything, and would remain in the dark until an equally unanticipated tool emerged: the Internet.

19

The Dream Birds Take a Long Time before they Reach the Blue Yonder.

BY EARLY 1981, RIKO WAS UNWELL. There were no specific symptoms, but his appetite—always put on hold if there were conversations to attend to—had decreased. His sessions at the studio required more time to do less in, and he no longer went to museums, places that animated him, temples where he collected audiences as he stopped to rediscover out loud the wonders of narratives in, for example, Van Gogh.

I imagined him challenging his students: *Van Gogh placed a peasant walking along a path by an orchard, his back to the painter. What difference would it have made if the peasant were walking towards the viewer? Was he walking up or downhill? Why an orchard in winter? Where was the light source? What time of day? What had happened to his normally vibrant colors? What time was it in that peasant's life? What time was it in the painter's?* I knew these questions fed him, informed his own work, but there was no nourishment coming in now, no audience or energy to share his mentoring with.

His appointments with doctors were at Beth Israel Hospital, which encompassed the blocks between 16th and 18th Streets, and First and Second Avenues. The trip meant walking from their 20th Street house to 14th Street, waiting for and then boarding a crosstown bus all the way to First Avenue and, once again, walking two blocks to the front entrance on 16th Street. In fair weather it already taxed the energies of two frail people. Eventually, they started taking ill-afforded taxis. Greta most frequently accompanied him; when she could not, I alternated with a few other friends of theirs.

Riko was diagnosed with cancer of the bowel and given chemotherapy—palliative at best in 1981—that sloughed the inner linings of his alimentary canal from his mouth to his anus. He shed it like a snake molting an inside skin. He could not swallow; it was too painful. Intravenous feedings punctured his tissue-like skin and left enormous bruises. For most of the late fall of 1981, Riko was in and out of the hospital.

Over two days starting on January 13th in 1982, more than nine inches of snow fell on New York City. It takes no more than three inches to snarl traffic or bring the City to a halt. Normally, tobogganers, big-dog owners and cross-country ski-ers dash to Central Park to cavort in the snow, but this storm was too cold and windy to afford them much pleasure. The few delivery trucks or pedestrians leaning into the winds and push-ing through heaping snows were people on a mission. On the second day of the storm, I was one of them. Greta had called me to say Beth Israel Hospital had alerted her that Riko was not doing well. He was asking for her.

I can't go in this storm. Go for me!

My mind raced with how to postpone the tasks she had

interrupted. In pre-cell phone days, I had to leave word for our children (no snow day for them) and for Tom why I would be gone for an unknown length of time. A note and snacks on the kitchen table would assuage the kids, and with luck, I would get hold of the miraculous Mrs. Troiano, Roosevelt Hospital's telephone operator who liked chatting with Tom and would give him a full message instead of leaving *Wife gone to tend to Riko until 7? 8?* on his beeper. I felt it would take hours to get to Beth Israel, and just as I was about to voice these reservations to Greta, she added, *Please.*

Perhaps it was the 'please' that did it, or the fact that our children would neither need me nor reject the adventure of lingering in the snow for the short distance they had to get from school to home. Or, perhaps it was the constant over-riding sense of attending to the Mikeskas' more acute privations that propelled me out the door.

The subways were slow and packed to accommodate those having to travel no matter what the conditions were above ground. I boarded the express at 86th and Lexington and when we reached 42nd Street, the laconic announcement of the subway's intercom said *End of the line.* The crowds on the platform had trebled from other interrupted service, and I thought I might better cover the remaining distance by foot.

I had dressed in L.L. Bean boots, warm slacks and storm jacket, and when I emerged into the white scene, I reveled in its silence. I dared look up into the maelstrom and was reminded of the irony of snowflakes looking black against the background of a light grey sky. Hood up, hands in mitts, I sank knee deep into drifts and arrived two hours after Greta's call.

When I approached Riko in his hospital bed, he was wild with agitation and fury over a tall male nurse who came at him spraying a deodorizer from an aerosol can to dull the acrid smell of acute diarrhea and poisoned mucosa Riko was passing with every bowel movement. To ask *how are you?* seemed an insult. I could not imagine he would be able to leave the hospital, yet he wanted nothing more. When the nurse left, rolling his eyes in disgust at both of us, I simply held Riko's hand in mine and was quiet for a while.

Tell me about the snow, he said finally, in a weak voice. And so, in the small, foul, hospital-green room, we spoke of snow, of the contrast it made with the black coal dust that constantly fell around his shoulders in Vitkovice, of the chiaroscuro that characterized so much of his life. I asked if he ever had wanted to go back to Prague.

Never, he said with strength, but his continued speech was interrupted by bouts of exhaustion, or violent evacuations that necessitated calling for a bedpan from, in ultimate ignominy, the hateful nurse.

I did go back to Europe . . . In 1957 . . . My mother's sister . . . celebrating her 80th birthday . . . The party . . . in Berlin . . . not Prague . . . I went alone . . . My mother was there.

And that was that. No what were the reactions on everyone's—or anyone's—part, no how did his mother's family make out during the war, and not a notation about his father, Kazimir. There was nothing about where exactly they had met, how they looked, about their health, about what they asked him, or what their prospects were. If Julci was mentioned, she, too fell into the vacuumed report. Riko's own feelings about the trip were a cipher. I took it as a given that Greta would not return to either Prague or Berlin since the murder of her family, whereas the insult to Riko had been the Nazi's destruction of his work. It had left him with a profound and lasting embitterment. In Berlin, Riko performed a duty, nothing more. What mattered practically was that he had mustered the money and discipline to attend the family party. He could not have felt like a returning hero; in the nine years in America, he had not made a publicly acknowledged artistic success of himself. I imagined he no more wanted to answer questions than ask them.

As I sat by him at the hospital, he was too weak and ill for me to press for any information, so we were silent, but the tempests in our respective minds howled.

The walk had allowed me to revisit what I had learned concerning the lives of the Mikeskas. Everything I had put together was episodic, hardly chronological, and a good deal of it second-hand. Whether from my own or Bernie's recorded interviews (which he gave to me with unguarded generosity), the anecdotes, letters, exhibit reviews, the roles of chance and transformations that kept Riko and Greta together through two exiles, one political, the second of hope, settled soddenly like leaves over winter.

The '50s and '60s for the Mikeskas had been protean. As they adjusted to New York, to new friends, living quarters, foods, hotter summers and colder winters, teaching and exhibits, they saved money to return to Ischia for infrequent summer holidays. Airplane passage was impossibly expensive, over $3,000 one-way between New York City and Rome, but $500 bought a crossing by ship for the couple. The trip was relaxing and the return to a one of the islands off the Croatian coast, a recognized place of beauty, peace, and happy memories, restored them enough to forget their most recent displacements and to gird for the re-entrance into bold and noisy New York City.

Riko painted, Greta sketched, and they reunited with their island friends, the Bozzi family—Aldo, Rudolfina and their child, Claudia. Lars and Veronica Björling were at the Casa Antica for a while, as were Ernestine Shargool (about whom more later) and Horst Winkelman, who completed their group of close friends from the past there. I had not heard Horst's name until Greta put in my hands some letters Riko wrote to him over the course of seven years, from 1973-1980, a revealing up-date.

Middle of May, '73

As I feel only 'so-so', I have become very slow, and work timidly and hesitantly. I unearthed old sketches and half-painted pictures. Some I found fresh and original, and so I finish them now. In former years where I worked a lot with pupils there were plenty of interruptions, and so my paintings were put aside (unfortunately often—much too often—destroyed) and not 'warmed up'. Today I find many of them adventurous and exciting, and work on them with joy. When I get tired—never mind—to-morrow I am going to continue.

The unearthed sketches and paintings were, no doubt, the result of the work Chaim Tabak had put into cleaning up and reorganizing Riko's studio. As to the destroyed canvases, I can only guess that happened by Riko's own hand, his mixture of insecurity, despair and self-loathing smothering the infrequent times of self-admiration.

1974

My dear Horst,

To begin with, I am glad that you call me Riko and Friend, the same goes for Greta. Your letter was good to receive and helped no end to cheer me up.

Now I started to write in English. The older you get, the more difficult it is to keep the brain flexible. One gets more and more satisfied to make do with something customary. When I was young I had to go to political cocktail parties and I could jump easily from one language into another. That is over with.

Also in painting one gets inflexible. The dream-birds take a long time before they reach the blue yonder. When I see sometimes little thrown-away sketches, I am seized by envy. In our lives there is no 'Permanence'. Money matters, talent, everything has to be renewed and freshly gained permanently. I have not been really drawing for many months. Now I wanted to do again something with the line. The beginning was so miserable. I thought: 'I am finished.' Now it's beginning again to breathe. I mean the lines.

Dec. 11th, 1976

Dear Horst,

We did not hear from you for quite sometime. May-be because of the delay of sending the paintings, or because of the paintings themselves. If I had less doubts and self-criticism, the pictures would have arrived a long time ago.

No wonder that I work so slowly. I scrape off more than I put on the canvas.

1977

Dear Horst,

It was good to hear from you. These last months we had to live through many disagreeable and sad happenings. So your silence upset us too. Nowadays we are easily given to doubts and renunciation (resignation) and we always wait for the worst. So it was good to hear from you.

Thank you for your report about Derain's exhibit. At last Paris realized that the tragedy of Derain deserves an explanation. Every artist, even the biggest ones, have lived through periods of anguish (to become void?). Loneliness and misjudgement were the bitterest and worst misfortunes for Derain. Cause and Effect? Or the other way around. I don't know the answer. Blind idolization and global success did not prevent Picasso of constant decline. I don't know whether I told you of my relation with Derain. For better or worse, I was his only pupil [in Paris]. When we see each other again, as I hope, I will tell you more about Derain, the painter and the human being.

The Dream Birds Take a Long Time before they Reach the Blue Yonder.

1980

> *Dear Horst,*
>
> *That I did not send your sister the long-promised painting has to do with our situation here, my age, and our increasing loneliness, and therefore I was influenced by all this to doubt that I could paint a good and lasting picture. I worked for two years on the circus problem. I made about 150 sketches, pastels, drawings, etc. Heaven and earth. Down there these unbelievable artistic tricks, and up there the aerialists. And the LIGHT! The light that makes everything possible. Only now I had to make the decision. Either one or the other. Now there are two versions finished and I am satisfied (for the moment). So you see, artists also have their problems, to which daily problems are added.*

Overwhelming loss and longing pervade these letters. The rage is gone. Riko has lost ease in using his German, the language of his oppressors, yet the language he spoke well, the language of poetry he loved and taught. His and Greta's health are deteriorating, so-so as he states. He has lost his sense of self-confidence in friendships. He has a hard time deciding which of two paintings he might mail to Horst, ends up abandoning the plan to send any at all. He misses their camaraderie. He misses his youth and energy. And yet the intellectual spark ignites at the mention of Derain, the artistry of the circus acrobats and aerialists, the light he must capture in painting. Most memorable in describing his slowed production:

'The dream birds take a long time before they reach the blue yonder.'

I hear his self-irony in those words, picture his closed smile and raised cheekbones, and then hear the exhalation that came to capture so many resigned end points of recollection: *Ach, ja!* And perhaps there was resonance with Albert Einstein's thought, which Riko surely knew: Einstein felt that as exiles, as opposed to being mere strangers in a different land, was like being *a bird of passage . . . for life.*

Their circle of friends held fast, though there had been a break with the sterling Ed Scheckman, and that was a loss of huge significance. The problem arose after Ed's second marriage. Whereas the first wife loved living in an apartment to receive 'Mikeskas' (meaning Riko only), Ed's new spouse did not like his paintings.

She was tolerant for a while, but the apartment over the next seventeen years was transformed from a kind of non-descript modern place which showed off Riko's work, to an 18th century French apartment with no Mikeska's. We kept a sanguine of Greta, a couple of sketches of my daughter, and a charming pastel still life, a bouquet of flowers which he had brought to my daughter when she had the measles.

When things started going rather badly for Riko and he was not very productive, and the paintings I had of his were still in storage, I said 'Riko, if you think the paintings are saleable, I'll give them back to you and you can resell them.' He accepted the offer very well, on the face of it, and said it was very generous. And he did sell some of them but, underneath, he was deeply hurt and furious at my wife for taking down his pictures.

Ever the analyst, Ed may have known that Riko was furious with Ed, too, for having acquiesced to his wife's wishes. In fact, both Riko and Ed felt grief.

For the first couple of years after my second marriage, we kept up our relations with the Mikeskas, but being friends with them was not always easy. My wife resented their demanding natures, the amount of time one spent with them. For me, it wasn't so hard. I got much more out of the relationship with Mikeska than I gave him. He was an inspiration and I think turned things around for me during the most difficult time in my life, after my first wife's suicide. His friendship was very valuable. I could talk to him about anything and he also talked to me about everything, as to a physician, almost. He talked to me about his relationship with Greta.

Riko loved Greta in a special way, different from all other women. He adored women and knew exactly how to enchant them, but with Greta, it was different. He admired her enormously. He respected her strength—much of which he didn't have—her optimism, her resilience recovering from the Spanish flu and then coping with the Parkinson's. She suffered her hip operation, her strokes, one thing after another, [yet she] coped with the most horrifying circumstances. He spoke of her as the pillar of his strength in his life. 'She is a very plucky girl!' were the words he used all the time about her. Greta had great character.

When I heard Ed relate Riko's measure of Greta as being a *very plucky girl*, I was embarrassed by Riko's limited appraisal. Was that all she was in his estimation?

In Greta's recollections, Riko's tender side shone. Ed admitted that he once tried to commiserate with Greta concerning Riko's treatment of her, but Greta confessed to me how she had felt.

I was upset when Ed took my hand and said how hard Riko had been on me. I came home and quickly dug up all the cards and

Valentines he wrote me to show how kind and loving he could be. I didn't want or need any condolences. The happy times were more than the sad.

In my perusal of Greta's papers, I found only one of these personal cards to her. It showed a pen and ink sketch of some of Riko's circus horses and acrobats. At the bottom he had added a poem, translated for me by Catherine A. Lillie, a Viennese friend, author and historian. Riko's poem read:

Wenn ich einst gestorben bin
Musst du um mich gar nicht traue
Meine Liebe wird mich überdauern
Wird im Traume did begegnen
Und dich segnen

When I am dead and gone
There'll be no need to mourn
My love for you will outlast me
It will meet you in your reverie
And bless thee.

What struck Catherine about the poem was its similarity to one by Joachin Ringelnatz[9], a popular cabaret performer in Berlin during the '20s, when Riko and Greta studied there. Devotées of cabarets, they surely would have attended Ringelnatz's acts full of word play. Ringelnatz was a pseudonym for his real one: Hans Bötticher, a gifted painter who, along with Otto Dix

[9] See Ringelnatz's poem in notes on page 306

A card from Riko to Greta

and George Grosz, showed his works in Berlin's Akademie der Künste. It is virtually impossible that Riko and Greta did not know his art and his satirical writings from that period.

The question remains, therefore, why Riko's Valentine poem to Greta bore such resemblance to Ringelnatz's. Had the three of them shared a relationship that would have allowed an inside joke between Riko and Greta? Would that joke have been interpreted as funny or unintentionally cruel? Was Riko so bereft of writing talent that he had to crib from an artist-poet? Was his hope that Greta would not make a connections between the sentiments in the two poems? This last is highly unlikely given Greta's tenacious and educated mind.

Regardless of the reasons for the similarities, what Greta recalled was Riko's love for her, this proof she offered sufficient. What does an outsider know?

20

Discoveries and Farewells

I LOOKED BACK AT THE CHANCES Riko had to exhibit. There were many, and his paintings showed at fine galleries. From 1962 on, his bandwagon of friends matched him up with the Argus Gallery in New Jersey, the Burgos Gallery, the Stenfner Gallery, Hirschl and Adler, Bernard Danenburg—all in New York City—then watched in repeated horror as Riko chose his canvases and told the organizers and gallery owners to wait a bit. *I need to add (change or subtract) something.* There were no reviews.

By the early '70s, Riko had turned down an invitation to exhibit in Bonn. There was a lot of correspondence with a German diplomat, but nothing came of the exhibit. Similarly in Prague, the Czech government wanted Riko to return to speak on the radio and to show his work. He refused, he said, for unspecified political reasons.

Other invitations to mount exhibits for him continued. The Bronfmans, owners of the Seagrams liquor company, wanted to arrange one. Bella Fishko, the director of the Forum Gallery, had made a visit to his studio, loved his paintings, but as she got to know him, she was afraid to show his work. He was too temperamental, too disruptive. Bernie, among others, despaired.

I suppose the reason he had such difficulty with relationships was the same he had difficulties in exposing his art. He was unsure of himself. And he was a masochist. He was quite systematic about the destruction of his work and his opportunities.

Greta watched Riko getting weaker, more dispirited and knew he needed to be the center of attention once again. The chance came when the Dorsky Galleries on 58th Street between Fifth and Sixth Avenues agreed to Greta's proposal to show a retrospective of his work. Mr. Dorsky was sympathetic to many of the European artists who had immigrated to the United States after the War. He had included Riko's works in previous exhibits ranging from the Cubist and Expressionist artists' works to their new American representatives in Abstract Expressionism and Modernism. He chose among Riko's sketches, watercolors, portraits and paintings from his summers in Ischia and Martha's Vineyard to his most recent portrayals of circus life and of Marcel Marceau's clown, 'Bip'.

Greta, who foresaw Riko would not be recovering fully, if at all, worked diligently and aggressively with their lawyer to ensure the exhibit would take place. When I went over to see her, she often excused herself to be on the phone with the Dorsky staff and with Mr. Dorsky himself, to agree to the terms of which paintings would go up, and what would happen to the paintings not sold.

Discoveries and Farewells

The invitation printed on ecru-colored vellum read:

"EXPLORATIONS"
RIKO MIKESKA

*A selection of figurative and
landscape studies from the past
three decades–representing
stages towards abstraction.*

COCKTAIL RECEPTION:
Tuesday, November 30, 5-7:30
GALLERY HOURS
MONDAY-SATURDAY, 10-5

The claque of the faithful organized and helped support the show which ran through December 18, 1982.

The weather was cold, and Riko, by then, never warmed up. Greta dressed herself in the best classical elegance she owned, a grey mohair cloak over her shoulders, a matching cloche on her straight coif of white hair, and left home for the Gallery independently in a cab.

The Tabaks stayed with Riko hoping they might stave off the inevitable last-minute botch, but that was like telling Riko not to breathe. They were to meet at his studio with a couple of hours to spare. Most of the work had been transported to the Gallery the previous days to be hung, special dispensation given to two paintings Riko insisted be left for delivery the day of the exhibit.

But friends did not arrive in time to stop Riko's meddling. In the studio that had seen little activity in the past year, the counters were covered with cloths wet with turpentine, small and larger sable brushes on two different palettes conforming to the pigments of each of the two paintings Riko was 'fixing' at the last minute. Riko's smock was as full of splashes as if he suddenly had been cooking in the foodless atelier. The paint could not dry in time for transport from 17th Street to 58th. Riko knew it. They all did.

These must be there, he said in a voice muted with alarm and dismay at the reality they faced. They did their best to place the paintings—paint side up—in the trunk and to tuck Riko, more gently even than the paintings, inside cab.

The show was wondrous, surprisingly good despite the inclusion of the two altered paintings. Because of the last-minute hangings, the exhibition had less cohesion than one might have wished. Theme, chronology and genre ceded to the wider focus of looking at Riko's art in general. Friends bought generously from this selection of underpriced art. The show was not reviewed.

I saw Greta enjoy the event. She was grateful for the funds it garnered, able to acknowledge, even if Riko no longer could, that his talent had supported them for another while. Ever the social being, she was glad to be out, look at how people were dressed—a discovery of *disappointing* contemporary fashion—and to observe those coming in off the streets. *Might there be a new buyer for Riko's art?* she asked me.

But after all but their closest friends left, a pall settled on the couple. As agreed upon by the Mikeskas, Mr. Dorsky kept what had not sold. And Riko, who sat through most of the exhibit, became sicker.

One month after the exhibit, Riko was back in Beth Israel. Again there were snows, but none like the previous year's storm. I was able to pick up Greta to bring her to the hospital on most days, but when I couldn't, she and Riko spoke haltingly by phone. It hurt him to speak, but at least she knew he was alive.

The last time I saw them together, Riko had been moved to a private room that somehow had been afforded him. Perhaps the doctors and nurses prevailed to make the hospital itself understand he was too sick to pair with another patient. The floor to the right side of his body was filled with clicking machines checking his vital signs—blood pressure, temperature, rate of respiration, heart rhythms. Since his veins had collapsed on his left side, the intravenous feedings depending from the awkward rolling carrier were dripping into his right arm.

Greta sat in the only chair near his head on his left side. He could see her only if he turned his head uncomfortably. She motioned for me to sit on the bed, also on his left side, so that we looked like three irregularly placed stepping stones, each leading to a different destination. We began a vigil of sorts with stabs at conversation that failed. Because it was easier for him to look at me, Riko wheezed beginnings of sentences, most starting with *I wish*.

He had no need to repeat what he wished had happened, wishes that came hand-in-glove with thwarted ambitions, rage and regrets: he wished the stupidity of the mad-man Hitler had not made them leave Czechoslovakia; he regretted Greta's Jewish roots at the same time he regretted admitting they turned their lives upside down and had destroyed the art of his youth; he wished he had never left England, where he and Greta had witnessed humanity at the pinnacle of honor, and where his self-worth had blossomed. In the United States, Riko regretted he and his art had not been publicly championed; he wished he had made enough money to ensure Greta and he would be safe in their old age. He raged at his old age and helplessness, and often at others who, he felt, had not done enough for him. He was beset by fear for Greta's future, and by his own grief.

In his angriest moments, he railed over his acquiescence to Greta to follow the LowBeers to America so that she might reunite with her sister. He rued her choosing to come to the culturally illiterate United States. Why had he listened to Mimi and Fritz?

Because of their money, contacts and influence, he knew, and because of all the help they had given him and Greta in getting out of Prague, and because America was their only hope, as it had been for so many talented others. He followed because, despite himself, he had fallen for Mimi. All this Greta understood.

At some point during Greta's and my visit with Riko in hospital, his left hand slid off the bed. His wedding band, ignored for so many years, slipped off his finger and clattered dully to the linoleum floor. Greta stared as the ring twirled on its edge then toppled just before disappearing into a heating vent on the floor. Her gaze was uncomprehending, as if she could not absorb what had happened. The removal of that symbolic token of betrothal marked his goodbye to Greta, and both were devastated. I regretted being present for this moment. I had no words of comfort to offer. For however many transgressions had passed between the two of them, their love had endured.

Riko died February 12, 1983. After Greta no longer needed my help getting her to and from the hospital, a curtain fell between us.

21

Sequelae

I was not informed of a service for Riko and did not attend his funeral or burial. I remain ignorant if others went and, if so, who they were.

This is a time for legal matters, Greta said, dismissing me. *I have my baby lawyer*, she said referring to Bill Beecher, the grown son of other loyal friends.

Over the next three years, I became Greta's default button when others couldn't tend. On February 17th 1984, Greta wrote me in a letter I copy here as her writing is unclear in the original.

My dear Denise,

Thank you so much for your assistance. I surely could not have made it without your help. However did you make it possible that I did not see my luggage until I arrived in Palm Beach?? There were my friends (unspecified) and took over.-

They are simply marvelous!-So is the weather. Unbelievable!-I have compatible friends and not a minute of loneliness.-

I think now that I was pretty close to a breakdown.

A good thing you did not come back to Gate 27. We sat there until

3 o'clock. Then we were allowed to board the jet. Small children, and cripples like me, first.-Then we had to sit and wait for 12 planes to go. The captain entertained us by telling us how the computer's malfunction was the cause of our misfortune. Etc. etc.- I sat next to a young woman with 2 children, and beyond the aisle sat 2 young girls who were my nannies.-

Yesterday I accompanied my host to the pool, and, incredibly, I found the young woman who sat next to me on the plane.

This afternoon we went to see a -Woody-Allan-Movie.

So this is my only report. I have to live, to write and to read a lot.-

I hope you remember my arrival on Febraury 29th, at La Guardia, T.W.A., Flight 462 departing at 1:45 from Palm Beach, and arriving at 4:18 p.m. Hope to see your lovely appearance.

Kisses to the whole family

from Greta

Tel. 1-305-967-7679

My assistance was still needed and, clearly, I still was willing to give it. In retrospect, her reminder of when that assistance was required and expected is both sad and risible.

In 1985, she sent me a Christmas card I cherish. Greta pasted on the cover of a two-paged bit of stationery a sketch Riko had made and signed in 1983, the last year of his life. It showed one of his circus acrobats climbing towards a trapeze. On the inside, Greta penned a charitable note.

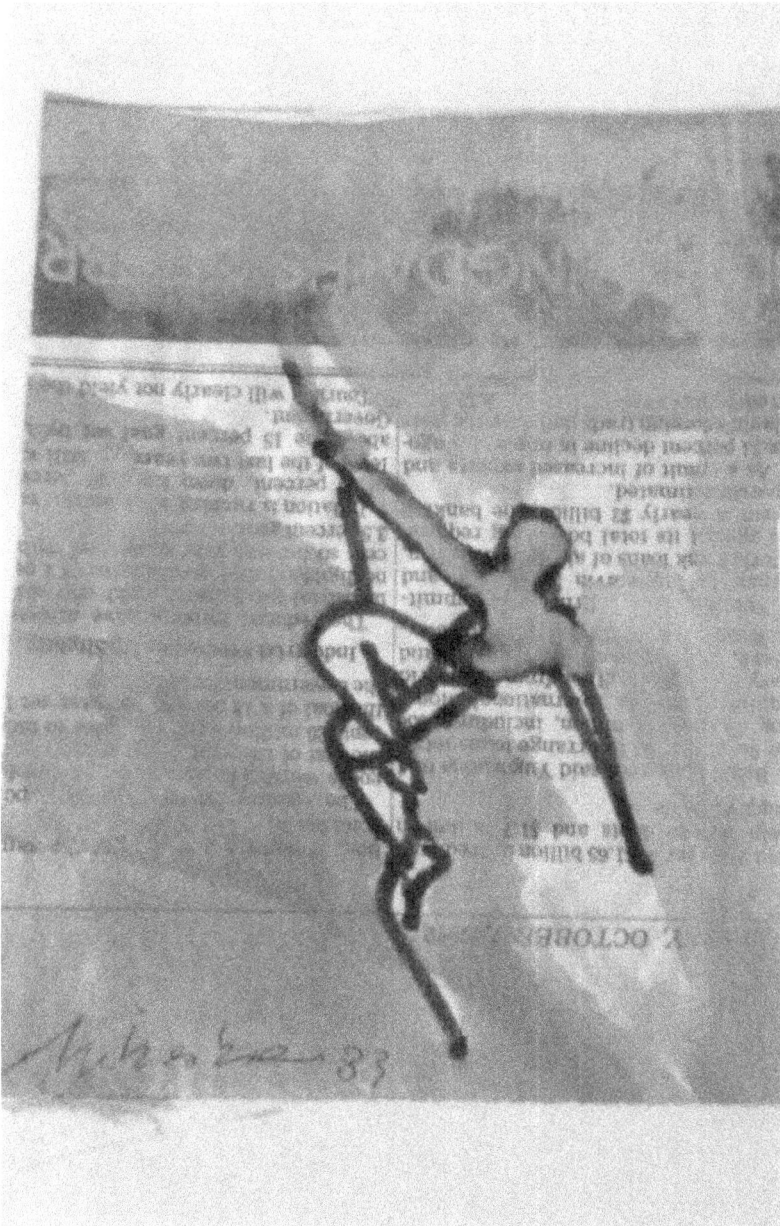

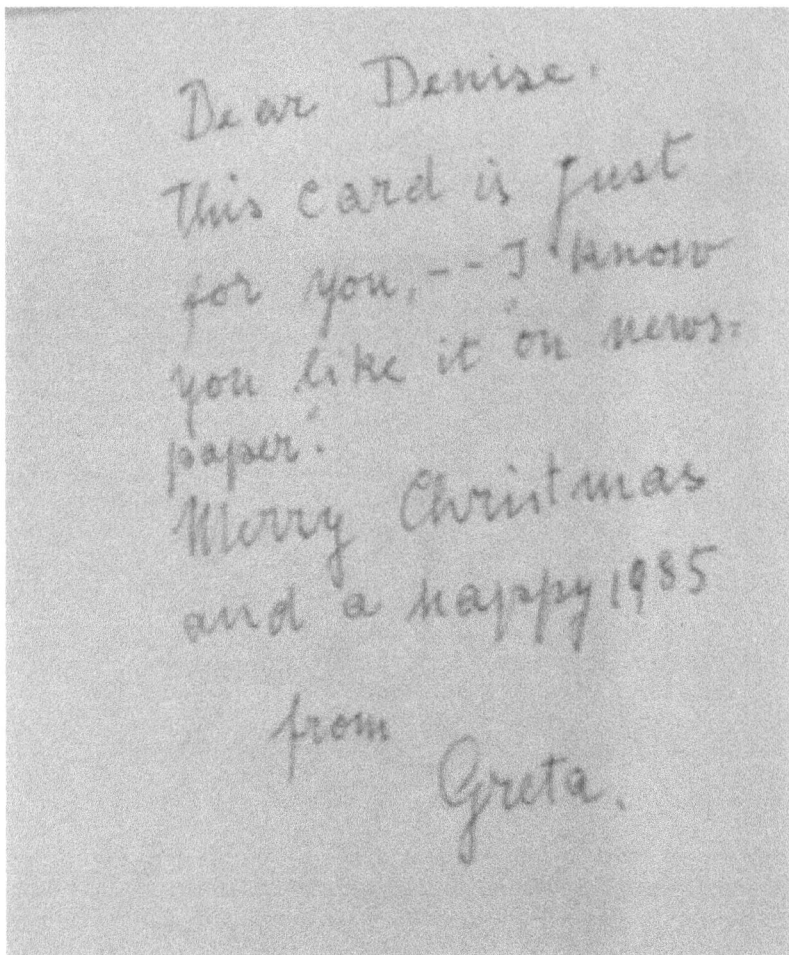

A card from Greta to the author

Sequelae

As early as January, 1986, our relationship had soured. It was prompted by a letter I wrote Greta to let her know that, for professional and personal reasons, I would not be able to give full time to her or to writing about Riko for the next several months. I felt I had done my best to date, and that the manuscript was in solid form to pick up when possible. Greta was furious, and told me my best was not good enough.

In the same letter, almost as an aside, she let me know that Mr. Dorsky, who had hosted Riko's last exhibit in New York, had donated three of Riko's paintings to the Museum in Wichita, Kansas: an abstract of circus performers, a portrait of a young unidentified woman, and a painting called *Gripping Hands*. At the bottom of the letter, Greta added unevenly and almost illegibly, a round stamp claiming 'Estate of Riko Mikeska' with his signature in the center. *This is all we need for an unsigned work*, she wrote. There was no mention of where the actual stamp might be, and as I was not her lawyer, I did not ask her.

Greta (and I) needed a wider-ranging support group. Greta's sister, Anna, her son, Jacques, and his wife, Marilyn, stepped up to attend to Greta, as did the Beechers (including Greta's *baby lawyer*), the LowBeer's daughter, Joan, and Ira (their doctor) and Mary Barash (another love in Riko's life). Friends and students who had stepped back to take a breather returned very occasionally and added what color they could to what had become a very grey life for Greta.

That same spring, Greta fell and broke her arm. She called for my help. I went with her to have it x-rayed, set, re-x-rayed, re-set a few weeks later. Her main question to me was *Have you got the biography published?* My private life and heavy teaching schedule counted not at all for her, but I was able to give her a bit of encouraging news.

Friends, Muriel and Peter Bedrich, encouraged me to submit my manuscript to Peter's firm, Schocken Books, Inc. They looked at the material and expressed interest in the very raw manuscript and in the photographs of Riko's art work. It would be an expensive book to produce, and they wisely wanted to make sure Greta had given me clearance.

Of course she had, I thought. After all, this was her idea and her goal. Everyone I had interviewed had signed off on transcripts I made of our recordings, everyone was keen to have a package published about The Mikeskas. It was a collective effort, every participant as much an artist in creating the canvas on which we had painted this remarkable couple as the depictions Riko and Greta themselves had sketched.

Greta, said I, *the publishers want you to sign a permission slip to make sure we all understand that the material you gave me and told me about Riko's and your lives is accurate and was given freely.*

I will not give it, she answered with no further explanation.

I was stunned into silence and chose to say nothing further, and certainly not to dispute. I knew her well enough by then to know an argument was exactly what charged her. Old she may be, but she still held the murderous verbal sword of the matador.

The reaction of the publishers was sterling. *You were planning on going to Prague, London and Bari to reinforce the material you have, were you not? Go ahead. Sounds as if the rage she has kept in* for so many years is working itself out with her grief. Perhaps she is jealous now that the attention is on him with an actual book in his name. Her reaction may change by the time you return.

And, they added presciently, *you may gain a better perspective of why you undertook this project.*

22

Escaping Vitkovice

IN JULY OF 1986, three years after Riko' death, I found an opportunity to leave my family in safe keeping so that I might research and verify some of the accumulated stories about him and his family in Vitkovice. I flew to Paris, then used a Eurail pass to Prague, where I had booked a room a tram's ride away from the center of town. None of this seemed threatening.

But the staff behind the front desk of the hotel in Prague disagreed. They had read my requisition for permission to travel on to Silesian Ostrava, the city that had swallowed up Vitkovice between the Wars, an integral part of Czechoslovakia over which the Soviet Union still exercised total punitive power. The clerks ran from behind the counter, grabbed me by the shoulders, and pleaded, *Don't go! They still call it 'Black Ostrava,'* as if the color alone might convince me of the town's coal-mining toxicity. *And please don't speak Russian!*

My knowledge of Russian consisted of learning the Cyrillic alphabet to be able to read road signs when we traveled in Russian-speaking countries, but I knew how that beautiful language had become hated under the Communist régime. Ironically for the

Czechs, the preferred language of transaction remained German, the formerly resented language of power. In comparative terms, the Germans had been less destructive than the Russians, so I memorized as much German as I could from the Assimil system of contextual learning and put it into practice. Fortunately, most curators spoke English, as did Soviet-Czech guides attending to the clock tower, the City Hall, the University.

The following days in Prague sent me prowling like a cat. My explorations of the museums and sections of the city both Riko and Greta occupied reinforced what they had told me though, in my estimation, they had not come close to describing the architectural beauties of the city, the bridges crossing the Moldau, the light on the river itself—unusual for two artists. Of greater note in their reporting had been the art of relationships at cafés, the pitting of ideas and attractions that would continue to intrigue.

In the few museums open at limited official hours, I found docents and historians who collaborated to sketch details of art collections, and tell of processes that had saved or destroyed paintings through both Nazi and Soviet régimes. They helped direct me to where Riko's or Greta's work might have hung, but there was nothing on the walls to see. Each official offered a cautious sense of what might remain in hidden collections or storerooms . . . if I had years in which to look for them.

Prague impressed me with its enormous availability of chamber, folk and choral music—in churches, concert halls, and in many smaller venues tucked into buildings along the streets of the Old Town. Young people, steps from one another, handed out fliers for these concerts to which tickets were either cheap or free. I went to as many as I had days for. Not for the first time, I wondered at the absence of music, or even reference to it, in the Mikeskas' home in New York City. Growing up in Prague, Greta practiced the classical repertoire through her piano playing, heard and participated in weekly chamber music concerts in her parent's home. She also attended and liked operas, sang different roles for her co-workers in New York, but for Riko, music seemed to be an art form he had not mined further than tapping out poor rhythms playing his violin either under duress, or to connect to a female; otherwise, Riko never spoke of it. I never heard any playing in their Manhattan home.

I left with potent memories of the synagogues, the crowded cemetery where tombstones leant against each other in seeming sympathy and sorrow, of the ghetto that had survived complete destruction on Hitler's chilling orders to save the area as a place of curiosity to show where once-upon-a-time, a certain people called Jews had lived. The contrasts in the Prague of the Mikeskas' youth and of the contemporary Soviet-ruled city I visited were difficult to encompass, but both were twisted by political pathology.

Armed with the concerns of the hotel staff regarding my going on to Vitkovice, I shouldered a small backpack and clutched onto one of the many slivers of friable paper that made up the tickets to all public transportation. I boarded the afternoon bus that drove me from Prague through the rolling agricultural land of Moravia and through small towns in which each remaining Roman Catholic church's steeple was sacrileged by a hammer and sickle where a cross had been. Three hours later the bus let me off at the station in Ostrava and from there, with another thin round-trip ticket, I took a tram into Vitkovice. I got off at the third stop after the trolley whiplashed round a 90-degree curve, as it must have in Riko's and Doman's time.

Zum Bahnhof, the driver said simply and pointed across the street to the tram stop that would return me to the station. I thanked him.

With the remaining late afternoon light still looking kindly on me, I decided to walk along the clean street that paralleled both the trolley tracks and the river. The river Ostrá (alternately, Ostravice) did, indeed, bisect the town, as I'd been told, but seemed narrower and less deep than the one I credited with powering the coal industry that had made this area the most important iron and steel center of the Austro-Hungarian Empire. An 'empire,' I had to keep on reminding myself, was hardly a negligible political entity, but now it was gone. If the factories were still productive, either the wind was blowing the particulate matter away from me, or there had been control over the carbon emissions; the air looked and smelled fresh. I heard no sounds of industry, as if it might have been a Sunday.

I saw the small houses Riko had described nestle against one another, a few with window boxes, some even with geraniums in them. And, yes, a few windows had the white lace curtains the Mikeska and Rogoisky mothers had labored over to keep clean. I wondered if I rang at the bell of any of these homes, if the inhabitants would let me in; if so, how I would be able to ask all my questions. Would I understand any answers?

As dusk fell, there were no cars on the road, no delivery trucks—not even the small ones I associated with servicing most European towns. The only tram I saw was the one I had taken returning now towards Ostrava. Clearly, it did not have a long run. And where I thought I had been the only pedestrian in town, I became aware of footsteps closing in behind me.

A slight bearded man about fifty years old caught up to me. In Czech-accented English, he rattled off a series of questions.

Who are you? Why are you here? What do you want?

I'm traveling through Europe. A friend of mine who recently died (I hoped for immediate sympathy) *used to live here. I wanted to come see it for myself.*

Who was your friend?

A painter.

Which painter?

Jan Emmerich Mikeska, also known as Riko Mikeska.

Where do his works hang?

The Nazis destroyed most of his work. I'm trying to see if a few canvasses survived.

Did I sense some satisfaction from him in a real smile when I gave him this news? Tiny street lights of meager illumination began to appear. I did not like the man's staccato of questions and excused myself to check into the hotel close to where the tram had let me off.

Had men like this one followed Riko's father? I wondered. If so, how could he not have been discovered in his revolutionary meetings? How deeply rooted was Riko's father's seed of paranoia?

It is the only hotel, my follower scoffed. *If you've come to visit Vitkovice, please accompany me to a cabaret. I was heading there anyway when I saw you.* He failed at a smile. *It isn't far—just an underground cellar. The cabaret is below; we have to hide it from the authorities, but you'll see, it's entertaining; come with me,* he purred into my ear this time, and took firm hold of my arm.

My thoughts of kidnapping, of never being able to let my husband or children know what had happened to their improvident wife and mother began to suffocate me. I fixated on getting to the safety of the hotel. When I wrested my arms from his grip, he took hold again more tightly in a struggle-proof hold and crossed me along a wide diagonal to the other side of the street and the promised underground night spot.

The stench of cigarettes at the entrance of our destination gave me hope; the fug of smoke meant a lot of people. Safety in numbers, safety in numbers I repeated like a mantra as he hobbled me to him down six steep steps. I heard no music, but a traditionally-garbed and kerchiefed woman stood near a coat rack exchanging coats for tickets. Perhaps the band was on a break. Could the man's invitation to witness some nightlife have been legitimate? If so, why force me here, control my every step, deny me my wish to get to the hotel? A dozen surly men paced waiting, it seemed, for permission to go into another room, and when my guide let go of my arm to tell me he needed to speak to another person (to prepare a get-away car? to muzzle me and tie me up? to extort money?), I waited for his back to turn and fled—not before I saw the kerchiefed woman wave me off to get away quickly. I did not stop to thank her for my liberation, and I don't know why the arm-grabbing man did not come after me, but what transpired must have been witnessed by another shadow, because I continued to be followed, this time more discreetly.

I reached the hotel in a lather of terror, tripped through the revolving door that would not move as fast as I wanted it to, and asked the single young clerk at the desk to check me in. *Bitte, ein Zimmer.*

He waved aside my request for a room. He showed me his watch, advanced his finger tip to the next hour, pointed to the dining room, then made the sign of cutting his throat. I took this to mean that dinner service would be over in an hour and that I should hurry.

The hotel dining room walls cracked in all the decrepitude of Soviet architecture. The paint tried a shade between sand and gravel, the lights waned on and off, and in this dimness, a surly young waiter offered me the menu: schnitzel and cabbage. I welcomed not having to discuss options and sank into a small booth where I could watch the door. I was conspicuous enough as a single female in my late forties, and saw the few people in the dining room stop their eating to simply stare at me. I stared back as if I were blind and, as the tables emptied, the initially rude waiter hovered closer.

Lady, I need to escape, he tried first in German, then English. *Take me with you.*

I wondered what my potential kidnapper would do if I had a companion in tow.

Take you with me? Where? I asked.

You go west. I go with you.

I can't help you, I told him, hoping he would not go for a kidnapping routine himself. The fellow looked beaten and unhealthy. Did he not get enough food even working in a kitchen? Surely he might steal a roll or an egg sometimes. I left him a decent tip, then returned to the registry.

The waiter reappeared as if by magic, this time from behind the desk. *Take us both*, he said of himself and the desk clerk.

Let me think how I might help, I said, scanning for time and utterly non-plussed by the scenes that had been playing out since my arrival.

And then the clerk took what I most fear relinquishing in travel: my passport. He promised I might retrieve it on checkout, and climbed with me to my third-floor room. He unlocked the first door that, as in some fine jewelry stores, admitted passage to a small vestibule. This, in turn, faced another locked door. He locked the door behind us before he unlocked the second door, then stopped at the threshold as if to absorb the splendour of the place.

You'll like it here, the clerk said nodding first to the single bed, lamp and cupboard, then to the adjoining bathroom, enormous, but bare of all but a sink and a cheap plastic toilet with a Mickey Mouse cover. He left to the sound of double-locking double doors. I had no key. Never mind imprisonment, what would I do in case of fire?

The outsides of my windows were wrapped in triple curling waves of razor wire to prevent a bone-breaking leap onto the roof of a silent single-storied building whose neon sign blinked

'Casino' across the bleak expanse of concrete below. And if I escaped unbroken, how far might I go without my passport confiscated at the desk?

I revisited stories of Riko arming himself and his family against the perceived enemy. Was I simply imagining mine, or had the warnings of danger by the hotel staff in Prague infected my judgement? I agonized until 4 am when I picked up the room phone by the side of the bed. Miraculously, it connected to the desk, and the same desk clerk was still on duty. (Whatever were his hours?)

I need to leave, I said, figuring that if I could get to the bus station, I might be in safer public view. *I will need you to unlock both doors and to come up with my passport.*

Remarkably, he gave me no quarrel and within fifteen minutes, I was running down the three flights and out the revolving door. Wherever the moon was in its cycle, it hid behind clouds but lent enough light for me to see a greasy-grey sky meld with leadened sidewalks smeared with drizzle, the color and slick I imagined Riko had lived with in the town's polluted air. I reached the near-by trolley stop the driver had shown me the afternoon before, and then I saw another unwelcomed vision: the shadowed shape of a man with a homburg on his head approaching. He came right at me and stood without a word so close to my side, he must have heard the hammering of my heart and the quasi sobs of my breath deafening my own ears. When the trolley came into view, he made sure the two workers at the stop did not get between him and me. He marched me to a back seat, the intimate wall of his body behind me blocking any attempt on my part to turn around, call to the conductor, or try for an escape via more locked doors. To tarry meant to have him touch me from behind, a sensation that brought more threat than continuing ahead. He indicated a seat that faced sideways, and sat close beside me and, as the Ostrava bus station came into view, he said in perfect English:

Get off here and don't look or come back.

Who was he? Had he been there to harm or help me? All that mattered was that I was out and had successfully exchanged my fragile return trip ticket to Prague. The landscape back struck me as mundane. I killed my curiosity to identify indigenous grasses, trees, birds. I had no interest in any of them anymore, but ticked off their repetitions along with the minutes to my arrival at the bus depot in Prague. When I reached the hotel, the desk staff once again ran out from behind the desk, hugged me, and in tears said, *We didn't think you'd return.*

I continued on to Vienna. While en route, but still within the confines of Czechoslovakia, the train stopped in Bratislava. Two male Croatian students boarded the cabin I occupied with two Canadian girls. They entered directly from the platform and sat on one side of the long wicker benches opposite us three women.

We had another 40 miles to go before the border crossing into Austria, so we began a chat that mixed many languages, including Sign. Before long, they offered us some dried apricots and almonds they extracted from a paper bag. We had nothing but water to offer in exchange, and while we accepted their generosity, they withheld taking so much as a sip of our water. I recall we hummed our national anthems, made each other laugh.

The train inevitably reached the border crossing. Two smooth-cheeked Czech border guards with Soviet red stars affixed to their shoulder straps stomped into our cabin, bayonets (!) fixed at the ends of their rifles. We three women opened our backpacks upon rude request and handed over our visas and passports. Done and done. Then they asked the Croatian students to open their single old leather valise (I thought of the wooden one Riko had travelled with, been ashamed of). Systematically, with the ends of their bayonets, the guards proceeded to lift clean modest tee shirts, undershorts, socks from the suitcase. Each article was treated as if it had lain in the sewers for months and dropped on the floor between our feet. When the suitcase was empty, they asked the students for their papers which, thank heavens, were in order. The blackguards left stepping onto the débris they created. None of us women in the cabin knew how to convey our sorrow and misery for the unforgiveable behavior of louts with firepower. We offered, but the students did not allow us to help pick up their now soiled items.

It was from this portion of the journey that I absorbed what Riko, since childhood, understood to his core and suffered through: the devastating power of bullying. Injustice was inherent in that power—and he hated injustice—but it was the administration of that power that galled. How could one effectively fight back without getting maimed or killed? Like a dog, he cowered in fear of making a mistake, of exposing himself to whatever vicissitudes identified him as foreign. The result was Riko's chronic sense of isolation. He fought against it by showing off his languages, erudition and arts of seduction. More pragmatically, I came to see in context how Riko had used his art, his voice and his body for survival.

Was it all their paranoia? Mine? I didn't think so, anymore than it had been for Riko's father, or for Riko himself under the Germans. I was cross at my lost chance to explore the town and area for the three days I had allotted. I wanted to go to the Witkowitzer Bergbau-und-Hüttengewerkschaft Kazimir and Dr. Rogoisky worked for, the newly-named Reichswerke Hermann Göring Conglomerate they continued to serve during the War, the Klement Gottwald Industry it turned into during the Communist years. I wanted to see if the company still existed and, if so, under what guise. Did they still run a school and gymnasium? Would there have been records of those who had worked there seventy years before? Would I recognize the spellings in Czech? Would someone have been kind enough to help me, or would they have been as constrained in action as I? What, exactly, had I hoped to find?

And then I realized I had found what I needed: the little houses; the town bisected by the river; the trolley Riko took to school with his pal, Doman Rogoisky, although the trolley I took lacked the carefree swing of the second car reserved for students. I felt the fear of people in power. For Riko and his family, it had been the Germans—for me, the Communists. Missing were the slag heaps, the stink of burning coal, the line of miners trudging to the maws of the caves. I didn't see them crammed into caged elevators, lunch pails in hand, praying they would survive another day, but it didn't take much to imagine them. We all needed to escape Vitkovice.

23

See the Clearing, not the Dark

MY RETURN TO NEW YORK, with reams of corroborating tales, was met with a steadfast refusal from Greta to publish my material. As with all others whose words about the Mikeskas I recorded and transcribed, I let her read the interviews I made with her, and which she OK'd with pleasure. What I refused was my permission to let her read, edit and control what others had said. She followed up with three unrelated sentences:

You have been tardy with this assignment. True.

It is up to me to filter what you say about Riko. False.

It is of no importance any longer.

OH YES IT IS! I wanted to shout. *There are too many of us who have pledged ourselves to record your histories, and there is more to tell.*

But I didn't have it in me to pursue the project.

When Greta was in her nineties, she entered the Jewish Nursing Home in Riverdale. She was able to do so by taking the practical step of denouncing her conversion to Roman Catholicism when she married Riko and reverting to her Judaic cultural and religious heritage. It happened because she finally accepted the visit from a young rabbi who helped her face her grief over the loss of her family, heritage and country, and to mourn the son she had aborted. Over forty-eight uninterrupted hours, Greta was in such an anguish of tears that the staff wanted to put her in surveiled isolation against possible suicidal depression but, as ever, she rallied.

Years after Greta died, I met an artist who gave art lessons at the Riverdale nursing home. She remembered Greta well for her interest and talent in painting or working with clay. Sounding like the therapists who helped Greta recover her strength after her stroke, the art teacher said *She was the first to show up in class, the last to leave.* If Greta's survival skills were indomitable, her conscience was labile until the day she made the decision that she would die the way the rest of her family had died, as a Jew.

On a dresser close to Greta's bed stood a photo of the Jewish cemetery in Prague. The tombstones rose like so many crooked teeth, chipped, blackened and rotting, veering away from the ghetto that had once existed there. The memorial stones leaned against one another for crumbling support, the support Greta needed and received in her last hours. By that time, I had not seen her in years, but others took over, as they always had in her and Riko's entire lives.

————

What I could not have imagined at that time was the role the Internet would play in resurrecting the Mikeskas.

In March of 2013 in London, I met Ernestine Shargool,

another whom Riko bewitched. She had last seen him in 1974, and although they corresponded for a couple of years thereafter, a complete silence followed. Always in search of re-establishing contact with Riko, she found him when his name popped up on my web page. It said I was writing a biography of Jan Emmerich (Riko) Mikeska, Czech painter.

Ernestine and I started emailing. *Riko changed my life*, she typed, echoing the sentiments of so many others. *Tony, my twin brother, my parents, and I met Riko and Greta on the first day of our first (and last) family holiday at the Casa Antica in Ischia. Tony and I were 23. The date was August 1, 1974.*

It was supper time, our first meal at the pensione. The tables were on the main terrace which overlooked the stepped countryside and the sea below. All the other guests were Italian. Then this fabulous foreign couple came out onto the terrace. I still remember that first time I saw Riko. He had such a presence. His eyes were like blue searchlights that bored straight to my soul.

As with Riko's meeting in the early '70s in Ischia's market place with Veronica Björling, wife of Lars Björling (who originally introduced my family to the Mikeskas), Riko was drawn immediately to Ernestine's distinctive beauty. This time, the blue-eyed blond of fly-away curls he had rescued from the advances of a crudely humorous fennel vendor was replaced by the quiet elegance of a dark-eyed, black-haired patrician grace sitting on the terrace of Casa Antica itself. Riko lost no time in making connections.

A waiter brought a bottle of spumante to our table and explained that it was from Riko, who was celebrating his 70th birthday.

Within a day of their terrace encounter, Greta approached Ernestine with a favor: Riko would like her to sit for him, but he felt too shy to ask directly.

Of course I was surprised, delighted and flattered! And that's how we got to spend so much time together. I would go up to the terrace outside their room in the afternoons and he would paint and talk about everything, and I would listen…I learned SO much from him. For me the time I spent with Riko was the best part of that holiday. Looking back on my life now, it still is one of my most precious memories. I would give anything to hear his voice again.

He never did finish the full length painting he started on (I was wearing an orange shift over my bikini, which he had asked me to wear). Instead he said that he didn't want to pay for my time as a model; he would paint a head portrait of me instead. Sadly, right at the end he did a little more work on it…and rather spoilt it. He asked me if I thought he had spoilt it and I had to admit that I preferred it as it had been before . . . a little more 'airy'.

In the perverse pattern that came to identify Riko, he overworked the painting (a pastel in this case), a habit that stuck implacably and compromised his professional life. It was the craven signature of Riko's seduction, however, that leapt out at me. 'Too shy' to make a proposal, he sent his reliable promoter, Greta, to do so for him. Greta became his procurer.

When Riko married Greta, there is no doubt that apart from his attraction to this remarkably frank, unafraid and daring woman, he viewed her (and she accepted herself) as his Esterhazy, his patron. While she had money, Riko fantasized about being her financial advisor, not provider. When Greta's exile from Prague forced her to leave her money sources behind, I believe she and Riko had a tacit understanding that Greta would continue as the realistic money-maker of the couple; if she couldn't raise the money herself, she would solicit it from others. She accepted the reality that Riko and his works were independently desired objets d'art, so she became the negotiator and offered both. I have no doubt that her financial control of him allowed for a manipulation in their marriage that balanced his philandering.

Ernestine was delighted by Greta's proposition for her to model for Riko. He equally beguiled the Shargool parents with his interest in them while in Ischia, and with letters to them after they left. He flattered Ernestine's equally handsome twin, Tony, asked about his art work.

On February 6th of 1975, back in New York City and six months after their meeting, Riko sent a letter to Ernestine, whom he nicknamed 'Titi.'

My dear Titi, the usual excuses and explanations for my far too long silence, I shall not squeeze into this letter. The Xmas card painted by Tony was nice, he shows that self confidence which one should carry over from the lovely days of Youth into old age. For artists it could be a godsent. Matisse and Monet had it, they did better work while in the seventies than when their beards were just starting to sprout. I wish I had kept some of the carelessness of my Young Years.

When Ernestine and Tony tried setting up a small private English Language School in Naples, Riko offered counsel she needed. Her father was not doing well and her mother did not engage in the manner the twins required. Riko was a parental substitute with incandescent attraction.

Never mind the collapse of (your) School Project. But please finish College and get the degree. It is so important. You will be stronger for it. I have a maître-es-arts-et-sciences from the Sorbonne, just to oblige my father, I never bothered about it later, kept quiet about it even when serving in the Czechoslovakian army and therefore never reached the sublime high of a 'sous (sub) lieutenant' during two years of military service, but when penniless in England and the heads of schools read my transcripts and discovered the degrees I got, the teaching jobs multiplied and kept us alive in dignity on our own . . . One never knows.

The entreaty revealed so much about Riko—his foibles, strengths, empathy, self-irony. He wasn't hectoring, but he was encouraging Ernestine to profit from his own experience—and she did finish college. He knew troubles first-hand, he made clear, but deflected at least the Army experiences with humor. That his teaching jobs had kept them *alive in dignity* stretched truth. Greta, after all, was pulling in as much of a meager salary through her own teaching and fabric designing work as he was, but for the purposes of the letter and of padding his credentials, it did the trick.

He filled the letters with diversions, helter-skelter run-ons, but never strayed far from art or education.

Pleased that you saw some Braques in Rome. I wish I could have shown you an opening for understanding... if there were some good ones. I wish we could one day go to some Museums in Napoli or even better Rome or Florence. During the wintertime when I hardly worked I dug up some of my books on the Prerennaissance and on to Michelangelo and the Borgias. There is a very fine Italian Scholar 'Fusero' who has been shedding some light on the life and doings of Alexander + Cesare + Lucretia and I quite believe what he has found. No whitewash, but he shows great designs they (Borgias) tried to realize by often reproachable means. Let us not forget these means were common in this time. And think of Alfonso and Ferrante of Aragon in Naples!

In August of 1974, he started a letter to 'Titi' in which he complained about the 93 degrees Fahrenheit and high humidity in New York City, about his *asthma attacks caused by golden rod in New York State . . . a disagreeable pollen*, he explained.

He allowed the letter to languish unfinished for six months. Finally on Feb. 6, 1975, he continued:

The Stock (market) debacle of 1969 has dismissed our holdings and we cannot wait anymore for the Upturn the politicians in Washington keep promising. Bad financial worries and the loneliness in this mon-ster of a town makes life bad for old people, rich and poor alike, but for poor it is worse. No pupils, no customers, the $ going up, Studio and Home rent especially. Friends gone to live outside New York or died. A former pupil of mine entered a suicide pact with her husband, so they died. They did not want to end their days in a nursing home. It gives You an idea what even expensive "Nursing Home" are like here.

Enough of that. How is School going? Did Mrs...get in touch with You? I was so pleased that they did not hang my pictures in the lavatory. Such mercies one is grateful.

So it goes. Dear Titi, don't be depressed. Spring is coming do not waste it. We just have to improve our Eyesight and See the Clearing not the Dark.

The vestiges of his German showed up in his occasional capitalizations of nouns and the 'You' to Titi. He closed one of the letters with a special plea that made clear Greta's jealousy of his correspondence with Ernestine:

Please if You answer this letter send it to the Studio address.

Your friend, Riko

Like so many others before her, Ernestine was besotted with Riko, relied on him perhaps more than usual as she was in need of experienced advice at the time. His letters were full of longing, regret, sadness, but also of direction. If Riko recognized the light in his future was extinguishing, he increased the illumination for others. The confidences that won people over to his needs in his earlier years changed into a more selfless interest, ironically compounding his allure. He listened, seemed wise and responsive, and he knew so much—the best of ciceros. When given an opening, his soft voice revealed his erudition, his gentle humor, his gifts for languages, his kindness.

The difference of their ages might have cast Riko exclusively in a parental role, but his personality, looks and vitality, especially in the years she met him in Ischia, opened the possibility for a deeper relationship. How easy it was to fall in love with him! In 1999, still longing for Riko's return but fearing his death, Ernestine wrote *Friend of a Giant*, a poem I have included in full in the notes.

When I met Ernestine nearly forty years after she last had seen Riko, she still missed him acutely. When she heard I had tapes of his recollections, she asked if I might not share them with her. *I want to hear his voice again*. He was a lodestone, his natural magnetism undiminished. She was not the only one continually pulled by his attraction.

He had invited the same reciprocal intimacy with Ed Scheckman when Ed was recovering from the suicide of his first wife. Riko could be a remarkable listener and fine analyst. The con man had the capacity himself to be vulnerable, trustworthy and empathetic. Was there a better seduction?

Now the Internet brought its own kind of compulsive attraction and brought me a recapitulation of Riko's life from other perspectives. Through repeated and persistent searches, artists, art historians and collectors in Czechoslovakia reached out to me first in 2013, and as recently as November, 2015. Might I help with birth and death dates of both Mikeskas? Where might they find Mikeska paintings? In what museums and galleries and private collections did they hang? What had happened to him? To Grete Passer, alternately listed as Grete Schmied Mikeska? The mixing of her names was not surprising, as the paintings Greta finished in the 1920s arced from her maiden name, Schmied, to Passer when she was married to Rolf, to Mikeska, after Riko's public seduction and marriage to her.

As we know, even Mikeska didn't last as her professional name. At Riko's command, she became 'Gill.' The changed spelling of her first name from 'Grete' to 'Greta' was consonant with the Anglicized spelling of LowBeer (from LöwBehr) once they moved to England. Apart from the complexities of spellings, my correspondents asked, did I know of others who were writing about Riko Mikeska in particular? Even after different searches on the Internet, the short answer was 'no.'

Notable among the artists, art historians and collectors was Ivó Habán, Manager of the National Heritage Institute in Liberec who, along with his wife, Anna Habánová, was working on a project dedicated to German-Czech-speaking artists from the interwar period in Czechoslovakia. They had mounted an exhibit, *Junge Löwen im Käfig'—Young Lions in a Cage*, at the Regional Gallery of Liberec, about 145 miles north of Prague, that ran from October 13 to December 31, 2013.

The exhibition included a conference and a catalogue about the Junge Kunst, the art of the young members of the Prague Secession. Mr. Habán had contributed to the exhibition's book with a chapter that included 'biographical medallions' about Riko Mikeska and Grete Passer.

In the pages Mr. Habán sent me about the exhibit, it was one of Greta's paintings that he used as the cover of the book. It showed a young oval-faced girl staring straight at the audience. She is seated on a straight-backed chair over which an écru-colored sheet is draped. The girl sits on this sheet, the better to show off the wild salmon color of her blouse. Her brown hair, cut short and parted like a boy's, has the same brown to gold highlights of the wall that forms the background of the painting, her pointy chin is elongated by the V-neck of the blouse, and her crossed hands sit demurely on her lap. Like Greta, she reveals nothing, but her gaze penetrates. From the accounts she gave me of her engagement at the Reimann School in Berlin, I see the techniques she recalled their teaching her and the academic influences of both Impressionists and Expressionists. I sensed Greta had enjoyed painting the model, an expression of all the specifics she had imbued.

Hanging alongside her painting at the exhibition was a Maxim Kopf of two lovers nude in bed, the male's skin is tan and healthy, the woman's (Marie Duras?) across whose breast he lays his hand, is as pale as a cadaver. Greta's friend, Charlotte Schroetter-Radnitz, who followed her and Rolf to Berlin, also has an entry of sailboats at anchor in Venice's Giudecca. The sudden visibility of artists I had been writing about but seldom, if ever, had seen from this period, reinforced my research. Works by Riko and Greta I missed in 1986 were now in the exhibition's catalogue. On November 27th, 2015, I received an email from Martin Ftacnik, an art collector from Slovakia. Proof of his interest in Riko's art derived from the research he had undertaken of an artist named István Tallós Prohászka. Like Riko, he was born during the Austro-Hungarian Empire and, Mr. Ftachnik wrote, *created the best part of his oeuvre in the '20s and '30s in Czechoslovakia. He had an amazing ability to move on the edge of primitive art and modernity, and at his best, created one of the most original works in the interwar period, influenced by Berlin Expressionism, Symbolism, Secession and local motifs.* He might have been speaking of Riko.

While Mr. Prohaszka stayed put and made his art available, Riko crossed first the Channel, and then the Atlantic. But for a few rare paintings of Riko's from the '20s and '30s his father had saved from the Nazis, or that hung unregarded in odd collections, Riko and his art had disappeared from view. Mr. Ftacnik kept his eyes open for auctions of Czech paintings in general from this era, for Riko's in particular. In 2015, at the New Orleans Auction Gallery in New Orleans, Louisiana, Mr. Ftacnik found one.

He continued his letter: *I was in touch with Ivó Habán (I admire his work) over the past three months regarding this painting… and he also believes that this should be from around 1930–'32. Perhaps it was even exhibited at one of the Prager Secession exhibitions (more probably the second one). The motif comes from the southern France, where he used to go. The dimensions are 78x95, I will leave the metric conversion up to you.* (My math measured 30x37 inches. I saw no title.)

It was an immense ordeal to get it to Europe, not least because they managed to send me a completely different painting at first attempt, so it took me about 4 months to get it right.

My own guess is that the photo dated from 1929 or '30, the time Riko and Greta were in Juan-les-Pins, before Riko came down with typhoid fever.

Mr. Habán, Mr. Ftacnik and I were encouraged by our mutual chase of other Czech painters from the interwar period, and we tried to help one another. Immensely gratifying to me, after the multiple forays into the complexities of Riko's and Greta's lives, was that the discipline and passion by which they chose to live had been rediscovered and validated. The Second World War, which had uprooted and destroyed most of their art and families and sent them into double exiles, did not leave them with enough elasticity to return home, but through the Internet, their art had done it for them.

Riko and Greta demanded high recognition as the formidable teachers and artists they were, as exemplars of an artistic, intellectual and cultural time, as true believers in art as a path to immortality. Ultimately, time worked in their favor and in mine. The Internet (as unimagined in their lives as the role of the CIA as a patron of the arts had been) connected me with the world of artists, historians, students, and archivists in a communal dig to find traces of a once-celebrated artist, the people, wars and artifacts that surrounded him.

As to resolving society's debt to an artist in exchange for the artist's fulfillment of a cultural expectation, it strikes me the equation is imprecise. There are more intimate ways to measure the reciprocity of artistic bonds.

When Riko was teaching in West Runton, one of his young pupils had been collecting her drawings and paintings as a gift for her father when he returned from the War. One day, the Headmistress drew Riko aside to let him know the little girl's father had been blinded in an explosion. Without divulging he knew about the father's accident, but understanding the father would be furloughed as soon as the hospital discharged him, Riko suggested his pupil start sculpting in readily accessible clay.

First in coarse lumps, then in increasingly refined shapes, the young girl fashioned a progression of horses. She responded to Riko's concentration on her and proved inspired under his guidance. She found fun in the urgency she sensed in him for her to arouse her own curiosity, to elicit it in others, and to fashion something memorable.

When her father came home, the little girl offered her creation of three-dimensional figures that her father could hold, trace with his fingers, and comment on. Like the artist 70,000 years ago who cross-hatched an ochre stone, her art arrested attention, satisfied and expanded curiosity. It all mattered.

Notes

Notes

Introduction

p. 1

Red ochre cross-hatched stone found in western South Africa, 70,000-100,000BCE

Franco-Cantabrian lions, 30,000BCE

Venus of Willindorf, 25,000BCE

Chapter One—A Proposal

pp. 6, 114, 131, 154, 158—<u>Fritz LowBeer</u> (alternative spellings: Loef-Behr, Löw-Behr, LöwBeer; I have chosen the one he used in the United States), 1906-1976. Of a prominent Jewish family in Czechoslovakia, Fritz inherited a great fortune through textiles and the manufacture of dress shirts. He became a collector of fine East Asian art. The Löw-Beer East Asian collection is now housed in the Linden Museum in Stuttgart. (<u>http://www.tugendhat.eu/en/fritz-low-beer-as-a-collector-of-asian-art</u>). In honor of his 100th birthday, the Museum organized an exhibit, *In the Sign of the Dragon*, on the Beauty of Chinese Varnishes, and augmented it by producing a fine catalogue.

He and his wife, Mimi, were generous and effective friends to both Riko and Greta in managing their escape from the Nazis in Czechoslovakia, and in arranging their immigration to the United States in 1948. Both intellectuals, he and Riko thrived on a battle of wits.

pp. 6, 38, 178, 194—<u>Marcel Marceau</u>, French actor and mime, 1923-2007. For all Riko's attraction to Marceau's depiction of the mute clown, 'Bip', as part of the universality of the extreme emotions and myths circus personalities exhibit, Marceau carried greater weight for Riko in his wide range of human expression (YouTube: *The Waiter*, for example) and the entanglement of good and evil (YouTube: *The Hands*). There is little doubt that Marceau's mime acted out for Riko his perceived mute state in America.

Chapter Two—Meeting Riko

pp. 13, 158, 190—<u>Dorothy Dehner</u>, 1901-1994, American. Known for her sculpture, which ranged from Giacometti-like fineness of lines to the sturdy forms of Henry Moore. Her painting styles showed clear influence of Cézanne and Van Gogh, a quality Riko would have recognized, admired and envied.

Notes

Chapter Three—Meeting Greta

p. 16—<u>Spanish Flu</u>—In 1918, towards the end of the First World War, it became evident a serious outbreak of viral infection was affecting soldiers and civilians alike. The vectors were identified as birds and, through later mutation, pigs. Though the origin was thought to be from a French farm in Etaples near the Pas de Calais in Normandy, later research suggested the virus may have been carried to pig farms by Chinese laborers working behind British and French lines. In 1917, a virus that had caused a serious upper respiratory influenza in China was identified as identical to the one that caused the Spanish Flu. The reason for the name is that during the War, with its monstrous casualties, the Allies did not want to admit they were fighting a disease as a second enemy. Spain, which was neutral during the War, felt free to report on the deadliness of the disease, especially as their King Alfonso XIII was sick with it; hence, the influenza became known as the Spanish Flu.

The result of sending the more seriously affected soldiers home spread the disease to places as far flung as Kansas, Samoa, New Zealand, the Arctic, India. The pandemic killed 20% of those affected. Worldwide, the numbers of deaths have been estimated between 50-100 million. With the already compromised immune systems of soldiers under the stresses of chemical and combat attacks, the flu killed otherwise healthy young men at a rate higher than usual. The Spanish Flu killed more soldiers than military combat did, and may have tipped the balance in favor of the Allies in winning the War, as they contracted the disease later than the enemy.

It was the first of two pandemics involving the H1N1 influenza virus, the second wave occurring in the 1990s and 2000s. In 1919, cholera, diphtheria, typhoid and yellow fever were still killing large numbers of people, so the significance of the Spanish Flu was tempered.

See: John M. Barry, *The Great Influenza*, Viking, 2004.

Chapter Four—Putting Pieces Together

p. 25—<u>Battle of Hastings</u>, October 14, 1066, otherwise known as the Norman Conquest, when Duke William II of Normandy (William the Conqueror) defeated King Harold II, the last Anglo-Saxon King at Hastings in England. William the Conqueror was crowned the first Norman King of England at Westminster Abbey on Christmas Day, 1066. French became the language of the court, but melded with Anglo-Saxon to ultimately create the English language we speak today. Riko studied the depictions of these battle scenes from the Bayeux tapestries shown yearly at the Bayeux Cathedral while he was in Brittany.

p. 25—<u>Magna Carta</u>—issued by "Bad" King John in 1215 to cope with the crisis brought on by his abuse of his barons and 'free men'. It guaranteed to them the right to justice and a fair trial through the judgment of their peers. Everybody, including the King, was to be subject to the same laws. It took the better part of the 13th century, overcoming Pope Innocent III's and the barons' wish to exclude serfs and non-free labor, to amend the charter to include all men. The Magna Carta became the basis for the British and American Constitutions, as well as for the UN Charter on Human Rights.

When Riko encountered a situation he found unjust anywhere, he would mutter: *No Magna Carta here.*

pp. 26, 28, 41-2, 47, 50-1, 53, 98—<u>Crankshaw, Edward</u>. *The Fall of the House of Habsburg* (New York City: The Viking Press, 1963), p. 33, 58-59 on language and views of Karl Marx; pp. 76-77 on the financial ruin of the Monarchy; p. 92, role of the Rothschilds as financiers; p. 120, excerpt from the Austrian dramatist (1791-1872) Franz Grillparzer's satirical verse concerning the Emperor Franz Josef; p. 121, historian, Josef Redlich's, interpretation of Emperor Franz Josef's governing philosophy; p. 254, first mention of Czech autonomy and wish to have racial equality and universal suffrage written into the Constitution; p. 300, language ordinance putting Czechs on an equal footing with Germans, giving them a greater advantage over Germans in Bohemia, since every Czech civil servant had to know German, but few Germans knew Czech.

pp. 26, 68, 73—Pablo Picasso, Spanish. Born in Málaga in 1881, died in France in 1973. Riko considered him to be the all-around artist whose draughtsmanship, invention, playfulness, excellence were without peer. Riko's only painting in homage to this painter was his own version of Picasso's *Guernica*.

Picasso's *Absinthe Drinker*, 1901. Now hangs in The Hermitage Museum in St. Petersburg, Russia.

Chapter Five—Entrapment or Negotiation?

pp. 36, 67, 70, 169, 171—Rembrandt Harmenszoon van Rijn, Dutch, born in Leiden, 1606, died and buried in a numbered, but otherwise unmarked grave, as a poor man, a debasement Riko felt keenly about. Probably more than any other painter, Riko admired Rembrandt, appreciated his skills in etchings, and honored his deep knowledge of the Classics and of Bible stories. Riko's tours of museums always included stops before Rembrandt paintings and etchings.

p. 41—<u>West, Rebecca</u> (Dame Cicely Isabel Fairfield DBE). *Black Lamb and Grey Falcon* (New York: The Viking Press, 1941)

Chapter Six—Compilations

p. 49—<u>Jan Matejko</u>, 1838-1893, Krakow, Poland. Best known for his depictions of historical events, Riko's fascination with him was in Matejko's depiction of hands. His self-portrait shows Matejko sitting in an arm chair, both hands resting visibly in different positions on the arms of the chair. Matejko had made many sketches for the self portrait, and it is these sketches of hands to which Halina refers in her observations of Riko studying when he came for dinner at the Rogoisky household.

Matejko held importance to the Czechs, since his father was a Czech who tutored and performed music in Prague. Matejko was offered a post at the Prague Academy of Art, but chose to remain in Krakow at their own academy. His best known work was of the court jester to King Sigismund I (1500s), Stanczyk. Questions exist as to whether or not Stanczyk was a true historical figure; nevertheless, he persists as representing the conscience of the nation. Riko would have been educated to this bit of Polish history through his mother. In ethics and art, Matejko captured Riko's imagination and respect.

pp. 49, 82, 98—*Personal correspondences* with <u>F. James Rybka, MD</u>, Musician, biographer of *Bohuslav Martinů: The Compulsion to Compose*. Scarecrow Press, Inc., 2011. Dr. Rybka suggests that Riko's consistent lifelong difficulties with music, whether playing or listening to it, may have been a congenital kind of deafness, a form of *amusia*.

p. 50—<u>Cervantes, Miguel de Saavedra</u>, 1547-1663. Spain. Author of the first Spanish novel with the eponymous hero, Don Quixote, who fights for the underdog in a series of fantasies, that allowed for political commentary under the guise of comedy.

$$\mathcal{N}otes$$

Chapter Seven—World War One, Art to the Rescue

pp. 53-55—<u>Austro-Hungarian</u>s consisted of a group that considered itself Austro-Hungarians per se, along with a federation of Bohemians, Moravians, Silesians, Slovakians, Ruthenians (see map, p. vi and all references to Edward Crankshaw and F. James Rybka in notes)

pp. 54, 124, 131—<u>Sudetenland</u>, that part of Czechoslovakia comprising the northwestern portions of Bohemia and north Moravia in the Sudeten Mountain range sitting like a jaunty cap on the region defined as Czechoslovakia at the end of the First World War. The population was predominantly German, and when the economic depression of the late thirties affected the region, the Sudeten Germans opted to ally themselves with the rising economy of Nazi Germany rather than the falling one of Czechoslovakia.

p. 54—<u>Karl Marx</u>, 1818-1883. German philosopher, economist, social thinker and co-author with Friedrich Engles of *The Communist Manifesto*.

p. 56—<u>Karl Harrer</u>, not to be confused with the journalist of same name who wrote for the Nazi party. There is an Austrian painter, born 1881, by the same name, who did achieve some renown with his painting, but whether or not he is the Karl Harrer who taught Riko is impossible to say.

p. 56—<u>Anton Klinger</u>, undisclosed origins, possibly Austrian or German, as he taught at Riko's German High School in Ostrava.

p. 56—<u>Salo Salomonovič</u>, only testimonials extant are from the files of Yad Vashem in Jerusalem. The files deal mainly with the suffering of Czechs at the hands of the Germans. Riko's art school friend from Vitkovice and Paris was caught and exterminated during the Second World War.

pp. 57, 63—<u>Hanns Heinz Ewers</u>, 1871, Düsseldorf-1943, Berlin. Although Riko dismissed the short stories of Hanns Heinz Ewers as merely 'sexy', they were in fact known to dwell on pornography, blood sport, torture and execution. He wrote a trilogy of three novels in which his protagonist, Frank Braun, is his alter-ego. In one novel, *Alraune*, Frank Braun helps in the impregnation of a prostitute with the semen of an executed murderer to create a female homunculus very like the Frankenstein monster.

Ewers wrote a critical essay on Edgar Allen Poe, another master of the literary horror genre. That Riko reacted to Ewers's ability to elicit powerful erotic emotions is clear.

p. 57—<u>Edgar Allan Poe</u>, 1809, Boston-1849, Baltimore. Credited with being part of the American Romantic movement, this poet, editor, literary critic wrote mystery stories of macabre elements including the emerging field of Science Fiction. He was proficient in cosmology and cryptography, a favorite of both Riko's and Greta's.

p. 57—<u>Heinrich Cristoph Kolbe</u>, 1771-1836, Düsseldorf, Germany. Predominently a portraitist of the Rhineland.

p. 57—<u>Feodor Dietz</u>, 1813-1870, German painter of historical battles and deaths of royalty. Riko would have absorbed Dietz's forms, colors, moods and lighting in his paintings of the First Schleswig War of 1848, then of his pictorial and word accounts of his fighting in the Franco-Prussian War.

p. 57—<u>Alfred Kubin</u>, 1877, Bohemia, Czech Republic-1959, Austria. Another one of the depressive painters Riko empathized with. Kubin was part of the Blaue Reiter Group. He illustrated in spidery lines the stories of Edgar Allen Poe, Oscar Wilde and Fyodor Dostoyevsky. He tried copying with his own ink and wash technique, the velvet textures of Odilon Redon's and Max Klinger's works. Riko especially admired the latter.

pp. 57, 95—Jugenstil, so named in Munich, but of German origin, became an international philosophy and style incorporated in art, architecture, jewelry, furniture, textiles, interior decorating, utensils and lighting. It embraced the organic forms and structures in Nature, enhanced curved lines that came to be known as *violent curves or whiplash*. In Vienna, Riko and Greta would have seen Otto Wagner's Karlsplatz Stadtbahn Station; in Paris, Hector Guimard's Metro entrances readied for the Paris Expo of 1900. They would see the Liberty style of Jugendstil in the architecture of the Liberty's of London store during the War, Charles Rennie MacIntosh's versions in Scotland, and Lewis Comfort Tiffany's Art Nouveau glass creations in New York City. It was an all-encompassing style that thrived between 1890-1910 and included Vienna's Gustav Klimt, Jan Toorop, whom Riko met in Holland, and their own Czech illustrator/painter, Alphonse Mucha. The Catalan architect, Antonio Gaudí, most spectacularly gave us representations of Art Nouveau in Barcelona with his splendidly curved Casa Batlló, the Cathedral Familia de la Santa Sagrada, and his Parque Guell. Jugendstil was very much the style in which Riko and Greta perceived the world in their growing years.

p. 59—Peter Behrens, 1868, Hamburg-1940, Berlin. Painter and architect who moved away from the curves of the Jugendstil to an austere, industrial-like paring down of function vs. form. Le Corbusier and Ludwig Mies van der Rohe would embrace this Modernism.

One of Riko's main teachers in Vienna's Akademie der bildenden Kuntz, the one who introduced him to Ludwig Otto Haas Heye; in short, two professionals who turned Riko's career to fine arts.

p. 59—Alfred Roller, Austrian painter, graphic and set designer, Born in Brno, Moravia, 1864-died 1935 in Vienna. One of the founders of the Vienna Secession, along with Josef Hoffmann and Gustav Klimt. A fine draughtsman and illustrator, famed for his posters concerning Jugendstil exhibits. Designed sets for Richard Wagner's *Tristan and Isolde*, Richard Strauss's *Der Rosenkavalier* and *Die Frau Ohne Schatten*. Became head designer for the Vienna State Opera House. One of Riko's teachers in Vienna.

pp. 60-63, 66, 134—Ludwig Otto Haas-Heye, 1879-1959, German born fashion designer and professor of art at the Berlin Academy of Art. The first professional who helped Riko come into contact with the academic world of art in Berlin and who later reconnected with him in Paris and London.

Chapter Eight—Peripatetic Education

p. 61—Richard Strauss, German composer, born in Munich in 1864, died in Garmisch, 1949. Like Gustav Mahler, one of the late German Romanticists to follow Richard Wagner. Riko's main brush with him seems to be when Riko met Professor Haas Heye in Vienna, and was shown the estate in which Strauss lived. There was never indication of much interest in music in Riko's life (more so in Greta's), but what might have resonated for both the Mikeskas is that during WWII, Strauss's Jewish daughter-in-law, Alice, was interned in Theresienstadt along with Greta's niece Charlotte. Only the latter survived (see Chapter Twelve). Strauss tried distancing himself from the Nazis, never fully succeeded, and was merely tolerated by Goebbels until they could find someone more completely aligned with the Nazi Party. Strauss wrote the Olympic Hymn for the summer games in 1936.

p. 61—Pauline von Metternich, Vienna, 1836-1921. Born into Imperial Hungarian and Austrian families, she became a prominent socialite in the courts of Dresden, Paris and Vienna, promoting the music of Richard Wagner and Bedřich Smetana, and influencing the mores of imperial courts. Riko's main attraction to her was as a model for the most distinguished painters of the day.

p. 61—<u>Bedřich Smetana</u>, Czech composer, born in Bohemia in 1824, died in 1884. Considered the father of Czech music with his operas and, most famously, *Ma Vlast (My Homeland)*. His struggles to learn from the music of Franz Liszt and Richard Wagner were stymied by the Czech State's political insistence that he remain free of German influence. This is a topic that ran like a live wire through Riko's life. Whether or not Smetana's music moved Riko, his political and emotional life did, especially knowing that Smetana had suffered deafness and a mental breakdown, the latter a result of the trials between following his musical education and his patriotism.

p. 61—<u>Richard Wagner</u>, 1813-1883, German composer, conductor, polemicist, theatrical director, known for his idea that music was subsidiary to the drama of opera. He wrote both libretti and music for his operas, from *Rienzi* through the Ring Cycle. He was twice exiled to run away from debts, in and out of love many times, and disliked by Riko for his anti-Semitic views. That Wagner would have figured prominently in the lives of artists and intellectuals from the 19th century on is indisputable, and that he had his own opera house in Bayreuth riled both Riko and Greta.

p. 61—<u>Edgar Degas</u>, French painter and sculptor, born and died in Paris, 1834-1917. Though mostly known for his horses, female dancers and nudes, he painted historical tableaux that added to his allure for Riko. Ingres' famous and oft-quoted advice to Degas also rang true for Riko: *Draw lines, young man, and still more lines from life and from memory, and you will become a good artist.* Though recognized as an Impressionist, Degas denigrated the Impressionists' passion for painting "en plein air," often preferring the intimacies of indoor spaces, like Mary Cassatt's. His virulent anti-Semitism (most politically evident in his anti-Dreyfus sentiments), like Wagner's, would have had little practical effect on Riko's and Greta's appreciation of his artistic genius and range.

p. 61—<u>Eugène Boudin</u>, 1824-1898, French painter Riko studied for his depictions of skies and seascapes, elements that came to be crucial to Riko when he was in Brittany. Boudin's *Sailboats at Trouville*, like Riko and Greta, crossed the ocean to reside in the USA (Mellon collection in Yale University).

p. 62—<u>Wolfgang Amadeus Mozart</u>, 1756-1791, Austrian musical genius.

p. 62—<u>Franz Léhar</u>, 1870, born in Slovakia, Austro-Hungary, died near Salzburg, 1948. Composer, best known for his operettas, pleasing to Hitler and Goebbels, but modified by their wish to get rid of his Jewish wife. They finally declared him an honorary Aryan. His operettas interested Riko to the extent that Max Reinhardt (to whom Professor Heye introduced Riko) was producing them. It is far more likely that Greta went around humming his melodies than that Riko invested himself in them.

p. 62—<u>Max Reinhardt</u> (nee Goldmann), 1873, Austro-Hungary, died in NYC, 1943. Famed for establishing the most important German language acting school in Vienna, as well as the Salzburg Festival with Richard Strauss and Hugo von Hofmannsthal. His escape to America resonated with the Mikeskas and their interest in film. Riko, remembered meeting him in Vienna with Professor Heye, and followed his career with the singular interest of another émigré.

p. 62—<u>Rudolph K. Kommer</u>, 1885-1943, a shadowy German figure wrapped in mystery regarding his possible role as a double agent during WWII. Inevitably associated with Max Reinhardt. Evidently, he was present when Riko met Max Reinhardt with Professor Heye in Vienna.

p. 64—<u>Wilhelminian Society</u>—Riko alludes to a period in Germany from 1890-1918 of social conservatism, great strides in industrialization, development, grandiosity of a military force, and a special romance in promotion of a naval force, costumes and all, including the spiked helmet. It coincided with Victorian attitudes in England as well as the Belle Epoque in France. In terms of art, it is the first time we encounter the term "degenerate art," coined by the Germans.

p. 67—E.A. Barber, British. 20th century Hellenic authority, editor and author who exposed moral arguments relating to justice. He used the Scriptures and the dualism of Platonic philosophy to bolster his arguments. He collaborated with J.B. Bury on several historical treatises from the conquests of Alexander the Great to those of the Romans and their annexation of Egypt. His particular contribution dealt with Alexandrian literature and poetry; in other words, subjects that illuminated and enlivened Riko's artistic and intellectual curiosity.

pp. 67, 68—Emil Orlik, Born in Prague (Austro-Hungary) in 1870, died, 1932. Among his students were Paul Klee and George Grosz, after Orlik returned from Japan, where he had travelled to learn the art of woodcutting. Riko found his work a font of inspiration and admired his draftsmanship.

p. 67—Michelangelo di Ludovico Buonarroti Simoni, 1475-1564. Florentine sculptor, painter, poet and architect considered to be one of the greatest artists of all times. He was a contemporary of the equally gifted Leonardo de Vinci, hence considered him a rival. Notably, the Medicis supported him, and it was this kind of patronage Greta tried to guarantee for Riko in the United States.

p. 67—Johan Sebastian Bach, 1685-1750, German musician and prolific composer noted for his weekly cantatas at church and for the St. Matthew and St. John Passions. He fathered over twenty children and promoted the work of his wife, Anna Magdalena Bach, for whom he composed a book of evolved piano exercises. With Riko's 'amusia' (see

F. James Rybka entries in notes), it is unlikely he could have appreciated Bach's phenomenally clever inventions, but Greta, as a pianist, did.

p. 68—<u>Ludwig von Beethoven</u>, 1770-1827, German composer of orchestral, choral, operatic, instrumental, solo and mass music. Deaf mid-life, he nevertheless composed prolifically and for varied voices and timbres, notably for string quartets, which may define his highest art.

pp. 68, 95—<u>Gustav Mahler</u>, 1860-1911, Bohemian "German-speaking Jew"—the definition that seemed de rigueur in the transitions in the first half of the 20th Century. Being a German speaker (Jewish or not) underscored what Riko's father, Kazimir, insisted on for the promotion of his son. Mahler was a composer and conductor who brought the Austro-German idiom in music into the modern era.

pp. 68, 80—<u>Paul Cézanne</u>, artist, born and died in Aix-en-Provence, France. 1839-1906. Hailed by Picasso as *the father of us all*, Cézanne is credited with bridging the art gap between the Impressionists and the Cubists and Expressionists. His work was placed in the Salon des Refusés, created by Napoleon, for artists not painting traditionally. Riko felt Cézanne was the most influential painter in his academic career as he guided the eyes of painters and viewers alike to understand the geometric shape hidden in organic subjects. Riko used Cézanne's palette as the basis for many of his paintings. He also honored Cézanne's death of pneumonia caused by remaining in a field to paint it during a fierce rain storm. Riko deemed those two ultimately murderous hours of discipline and curiosity appropriate for an artist who needed to *get it right*.

p. 68—<u>Paul Seurat</u>, 1859-1891, Paris. Father of Pointillism, where the brush strokes are so short, they appear as dots. He studied the physics of color, melded the art of painting to a scientific base. Although Riko never copied his style, he appreciated yet another impressionistic interpretation and technique.

p. 68—<u>Otto Dix</u>, 1891-1969, German. Both Riko and Greta were drawn philosophically to the realistically grotesque renderings of war as seen through the eyes of an experienced soldier who fought on the Western Front during World War I. His depictions of the decadence of the Weimar Republic, when defeated post-War Germany was suffering financial catastrophe, was a period both Mikeskas experienced first-hand in Berlin in the '20s. As a painter, Riko appreciated Dix's going back to the Old Masters' technique of thinly glazing over tempera. Dix was a founder of the Dresden Secession, but later joined the Berlin Secession, an indication of the foment of the movements surrounding the Prague Secession, of which Riko was a co-founder.

p. 68—<u>Ernst Ludwig Kirchner</u>, 1880-1938, German Expressionist, one of the founders of *Die Brücke, The Bridge.* Expelled from the Berlin Academy for *degenerate* art. Found sympathy with Riko and Greta for his outcry in 1933: *Here (Germany) we have been hearing terrible rumours about torture of the Jews, but it's all surely untrue.* He committed suicide by shooting himself in Switzerland.

p. 68—<u>Paul Klee</u>, Swiss, 1879-1940, well known to Riko for his involvement with the evolution of Cubism, and for his long attempt at figuring out colors, helped by his and Riko's mentors in Fauvism, Robert Delaunay and Maurice de Vlaminck. Known for his fey watercolors and collages on textiles as well as paper.

pp. 68, 77—<u>Fernand Léger</u>, French painter, sculptor and film maker, proponent of Cubism reduced to elemental vs. ornamental forms, exemplified in the human figure which, for him, had plastic vs. sentimental value. Another World War I veteran, he pared his ideas into abstractions. He taught at Yale during the Second World War, but returned to France thereafter. Like other contemporaries, Riko followed his influences in France and in the US.

p. 69—<u>Princess (later Queen) Juliana</u>, (Juliana Louise Emma Marie Wihelmina) born in Noordeinde Palace, The Hague, 1909-died in Soestdijk Palace, Baarn, The Netherlands, 2004. Hugely popular Regent who ruled for 32 years.

p. 70—<u>Meindert Hobbema</u>, born and died in Amsterdam, 1638-1709. Like Rembrandt, part of the Golden Age of Dutch painting. Student of both Salomon and Jacob van Ruisdael, his hallmarks are landscapes which often include roads going through forests, water mills, dark foregrounds balanced by light skies. Riko sought to capture the particular northern light in the Netherlands, such as he had seen in the paintings of Rembrandt and Hobbema (who almost exclusively used only his last name).

p. 70—<u>Franz Hals</u>, born in Antwerp in 1582, he became a lifetime resident of Haarlem. He made his living principally from painting portraits and insisting his subjects come to him. With good tutorial credentials, he nevertheless advanced an auto-didacticism in painting layers with brushstrokes that veered from supremely careful to seemingly slapdash. Viewers respond to the immediate liveliness of his canvasses. Also part of the Dutch Golden Age.

p. 70—<u>François Rabelais</u>, 1483-1494. French Renaissance writer and physician, whose lusty writings about a father, Gargantua, and his son, Pantagruel, became icons of exaggerated appetites. Once the academics learned not to shun him, he has been appreciated through the ages. Riko read him in German translation.

pp. 70, 71—<u>Vincent Van Gogh</u>, 1853-1890, Dutch artist whose works largely reflect his life in France, where he died with some form of mental illness. Throughout his life, he had been visited by hallucinations, which influenced his colors, textures and compositions more than his subjects. In his studio, Riko had a well-thumbed copy in English of Vincent's letters to his brother, Theo.

p. 71—<u>Jan Toorop</u>, 1858, Indonesia-1928, The Hague. An artist whose curiosity and talent led him to many styles and countries. Brought *Japonisme* to Europe. He was the one who met Riko in the Netherlands, gave him the few lessons time would permit, and insisted Riko go to Paris to firmly lay his foundation as a painter.

p. 72—<u>Pierro della Francesca</u>, born 1415 and died in 1492 in the Republic of Florence. One of the great Renaissance masters, who studied the portrayal of perspectives aided, no doubt, by his interest in mathematics. He was one among many (see below) Italian Renaissance masters Riko studied on his own and in classes from high school on.

p. 72—<u>Andrea Mantegna</u>, 1431-1506, present day Italy. Credited with a sculptural approach to painting, influenced perhaps by his interest in archeology, he became Venice's most notable painter. He was the son-in-law of Jacopo Bellini (1400-1470, Venice), himself the inheritor of an art education from the Gothic masters: Brunelleschi, Donatelo and Masaccio. All of these formed the agar in which Riko's germinating interests in art, architecture and fresco painting grew.

p. 72—<u>Tommaso do Ser Giovanni di Simone *Masaccio* (Maso, meaning short or clumsy, and short for Tommaso)</u>, born 1401, died in Rome in 1428. Praised by Vasari for recreating life-like figures and establishing the vanishing point to give perspective. Early death of unknown causes.

p. 72—<u>Giotto di Bondone</u>, Italian painter and architect of Gothic period. 1267-1337. Designed the Arena Chapel in Padua and the Campanile for the Cathedral in Florence. Much more work is attributed to him, although art historians cannot vouch for their accuracy. He and Cimabue were bridges from Byzantine to Gothic Italian styles. The colors used in the Italian Gothic and Renaissance and Medieval periods live on undiminished in museums all over the world, including New York City's Metropolitan Museum, where Riko used to refresh his own thoughts and instruct those of others.

p. 72—<u>Leonardo di ser Pierro da Vinci</u>, 1452-1519, Italian polymath (painter, inventor, scientist, music devoté, architect), was Riko's favorite alongside the above four Italian Renaissance artists, all recorded meticulously by Giorgio Vasari (1511-1571) in his *Lives of the Most Excellent Painters, Sculptors and Architects*. Riko studied their paintings obsessively as a student, and felt they were his greatest teachers in perspective, naturalism, expression of three dimensions, and architectural strength. Riko constantly referred to Vasari's book.

pp. 72—<u>Jan Van Eyck</u>, 1390, Belgium, died 1441. The Ghent Alterpiece, and the Arnolfini portrait at the Metropolitan Museum of Art in New York City, are two celebrated masterpieces, lauding Van Eyck's attention to detail, use of glazes over paints, and attention to the Virgin Mary in all her historical states. All aspects of Van Eyck's work instructed Riko, whose sense of humor appreciated Van Eyck's play of words on his own name. Van Eyck signed with variations of his motto *ALS IK KAN* (*AS I CAN*, the *IK* and *EYCK* phonetically interchangeable). To gild the lily, Van Eyck wrote in Greek characters. His portraits, often in three quarter view, would influence Hans Memling and Petrus Christus, whose variation on a wedding scene also hangs in the Metropolitan Museum, and which Riko would stand in front of, wondering at the iconographic details for hours.

pp. 72, 94—<u>Alfons (Alphonse) Maria Mucha</u>, born in Brno, Moravia, in 1860. Recognized today for his "Art Noveau" illustrations (he distanced himself from that term, preferring his work be termed simply Czech). A chance to enter a poster for a performance of a Sarah Bernhardt play with only two weeks' notice put his name on the map. Celebrated by his contemporaries and fellow Czechs, including Riko and Greta (see her years in Berlin, Prague and Paris). Died in 1939.

pp. 72, 95—<u>Gustav Klimt</u>, 1862-1918, Austrian painter associated with Symbolism, but popularized by erotic portrayals of females, often garbed with plentiful gold leaf.

p. 72—<u>François Auguste Rodin</u>, French sculptor, born 1840, died 1918. Despite traditional academic training and no will to establish a new genre of sculpture, Rodin eschewed classical smoothly surfaced traditions to embody down-to-earth characters (*The Burghers of Calais* at the Metropolitan Museum being one of the prime examples), molding the clay in folds, as if with angry hands. Those same folded faces will find expression in the busts of Matisse and Picasso.

p. 73—<u>Emil Filla</u>, 1882-1953, Moravian. Artist, whose trajectory followed that of Riko's in the sense that both belonged to popular art groups of the period (Filla to Manes, Riko to the Prague Secession, both in Prague), admired the same artists in the Fauves and German Expressionist Movements, joined the Cubists in experimentation. Filla was interned at Dachau and Buchenwald during World War II.

p. 73—<u>Otto Guttfreund</u>, Czech artist, born in 1889 in Bohemia, died in Prague's Vlatava (Moldau) River in 1917 at the height of his career. Like many of his generation, he wound up fighting in the First World War with the French Foreign Legion, ending up imprisoned for almost four years. He studied in Paris under Rodin. Guttfreund's roughly surfaced sculptures show that influence. Even if he did not coin the term for his style, he accepted it as Cubo-Expressionistic.

p. 73—<u>Georges Braque,</u> 1882-1963. French painter influenced by Picasso, Matisse, Cézanne, Gauguin, and proponent of both Cubism and the Fauves with their brash bright colors. He is quoted as saying he believed that volume, line, mass and weight defined a beauty the artist then interpreted with his impression. Although Picasso took the limelight, Braque is recognized for his equal artistic excellence. Riko and Greta thought highly of both.

pp. 73, 77—<u>Albert Gleizes</u>, 1881-1952, French painter, mostly in individual cubist style. Along with Jean Metzinger, he wrote the first treatise on Cubism, entitled *De 'Cubisme'*, in 1912. He lived in Pelham, NY for four years during which he promoted modern art. His group, consisting of André Lhote, Marie Laurencin, François Léger and Robert Delaunay, formed the nexus and precursors of artists both Riko and Greta encountered at the Café du Dome, Les Cloiserie des Lilas, La Rotonde, La Coupole in Montparnasse. They were all pieces in the stew of art bubbling in Paris at the time, the ones with whom Riko enjoyed his discussions on art, his *badinage* and with whom he felt he *belonged*. Greta's involvement may have been as much social as artistic, but that was before she and Riko had met.

pp. 73, 78—<u>Jean Metzinger</u>, born in Nantes, France, 1883, died in Paris, 1956. One of the originators of Cubism, especially involved with the mathematics of it. Close friends with fellow Cubists, Fauves, and post-Cubists: Fernand Léger, Juan Gris, Albert Gleizes, André Lhote, one of Greta's teachers while she was in Paris.

p. 75—<u>Jean Poleront</u>, no history beyond his teaching at the École des Beaux-Arts. Riko despised him for his cruelty and lack of talent.

p. 76—<u>George Keller</u>, known only through Riko's account, and that third-hand from Ilse Gruenfeld's brother to her, and then to Riko as a possible help in connecting to other artists in Paris. As it happened, he and Riko did not meet.

p. 76—<u>Gustav Eiffel</u>, 1832-1923. Noted French meteorologist and student of aerodynamics, Eiffel is best known for his eponymous tower in Paris readied for the Universal Exposition of 1898, and for his contributions to the construction of the Statue of Liberty. His work on bridges (spanning the River Douro in Portugal, for one), aqueducts, canals (Panama, for which he designed a lock), construction of the

Nyugati Railroad Station in Budapest (on the Vienna-Budapest line) revealed his will to show the metal construction of each of his engineering accomplishments. He paved the way for le Centre Pompidou in Paris, among other showplaces, where the importance of exposing the inside engineering became the outer shell. Riko and Greta roamed the Paris of his design, came to applaud the Smithsonian Institution's granting Eiffel the Samuel P. Langley Medal for aerodynamics, an expertise that played towards the USA's man-on-the-moon initiative. Greta and Riko had watched the landing in July of 1969 with the same awe the world felt.

p. 76—Augustus Saint-Gaudens, American, 1873-1943, *the red-bearded giant* Riko referred to was a graduate, though not a contemporary at the Ecole des Beaux-Arts in Paris. They never met, but Riko and Greta came to know well Saint-Gaudens's statues of Admiral Ferragut and General Sherman, both in New York City. Saint Gaudens could not have accomplished his work without the expertise of Parisian metal workers, nor without the pedestals the American architectural firm McKim, Mead and White designed. He was a contemporary of John Singer Sergeant's and of Marie Cassatt's when both these artists were working in Paris.

p. 76—Admiral David Glasgow Ferragut, American, 1801-1870. Played an important role in the American Civil War, ultimately named first Admiral of the US Navy. Famous for defeat in one battle on the Mississippi, but ultimate glory to control the river in the Battle of Mobile. When warned against the tethered mines ("torpedoes") in the bay, he ordered the captain of the ship to proceed. Remembered for the slight misquote: *Damn the torpedoes, full speed ahead.*

p. 76—General William Tecumseh Sherman, 1820-1891, American, Head of the Union Army during the Civil War. His capture of Atlanta secured President Lincoln his second term. Sherman was derided for his *scorched earth* methods, which enabled him to march across the South to the Atlantic. He accepted the surrender of the Confederate states of Georgia, Florida and Carolina and left behind a cogent account of the Civil War.

p. 76—<u>Marie Cassatt</u>, 1844-1926. She was one of many Americans who settled in Paris in the 19th century to study painting and create her work. Instead of being drawn to the outside light that her fellow Impressionists preferred, she chose to paint intimate interior scenes devolving around familiar occupations she saw her sister and children involved with: reading, writing letters, giving baths. Friend of John Singer Sergeant, who also painted indoor scenes, though with a great deal more drama in theme, light and color.

p. 77—<u>John Singer Sargeant</u>, 1852-1925. Became a famous American portraitist, but painted in other genres as well. Spent most of his life in Paris, but travelled widely to London, Italy, the Middle East, and from Montana to Maine in the United States. Hugely influential and closely studied by Riko.

pp. 77, 115, 202—<u>Andre Dérain</u>, 1852-1925. Riko revered Dérain as a teacher in Paris, and as a colorist who, along with Henri Matisse, founded the Fauves, a collection of painters who chose to portray scenes in wildly accentuated color, hence being dubbed the *wild beasts*. Riko studied with him in Paris, was witness to Dérain's friendships with Guillaume Apollinaire, the writer, as well as with Picasso and Matisse.

p. 77—<u>Amédée Ozenfant</u>, 1886-1966, French, Cubist who became a great proponent initially on the use of color as a subservient element to form, but revised his thoughts over the years to suggest such things as color charts for architects to use.

pp. 77, 94—<u>Alexander Archipenko</u>, born in the Ukraine in 1887, died in 1964. Studied in Kiev as an artist, sculptor and graphic artist. Plastic possibilities in sculpture appealed to him said to *portray Cubism in three dimensions.* Continued on to Paris where he stayed until 1923, and where his works were exhibited in the Salon des Indépendents as well as the Salon d'Automne. Also found favor and exhibited his works in the biennales in Italy. His figures are limned to an almost stylized form (DBD), as if he is foretelling the ultimate simplicity that will come with Brancusi. Came to the United States after 1923 and became a US citizen in 1929. Another of the greats who added to Riko's education.

p. 77—<u>Alberto Giacometti</u>, 1901-1966. Italian-Swiss sculptor, painter, draughtsman, print-maker, known primarily for his attenuated figures, an irony considering one of his mentors was Rodin of famously bulky human forms. He was one of the ones Riko saw frequently in the café's in Paris and liked him enormously for his self reflections and honesty on why he ended up painting and sculpting the way he did. When Riko said *he was always looking for his brother, Diego,* it was because Alberto liked to use Diego as a model. Riko and Alberto were part of that mass of students who would go repeatedly to the Louvre to study and copy everything in sight but, as Alberto said, he still was *trying to understand.* Late in life in the United States, when still attempting to explain to people why he sculpted his figures as such thin rails, he suggested he was sculpting not the model, but the shadow. For all their friendship in Paris, there is no indication that there was any attempt on either man's part to reunite in New York.

pp. 78, 80—<u>André Lhote</u>, born in Bordeaux 1885, died in Paris, 1962. Along with the aforementioned painters, he was a student at the Ecole des Beaux Arts in Paris, and influential in the Cubist movement. Travelled extensively through Europe, Egypt and Brazil.

Appointed by UNESCO as President of the International Association of Painters, Engravers and Sculptors. Taught Greta alternately with Metzinger in Paris.

p. 78—<u>Henri-Emile-Benoît Matisse</u>, 1869-1954. French artist whose colors and abstract forms influenced Riko and all Impressionists.

p. 78—<u>Nils von Dardel</u>, 1888-1943, Swedish artist, post-Impressionist. Café cohort of Riko's and Greta's. Moved to the United States and died there before the Mikeskas arrived.

p. 78—<u>Man Ray (Emmanuel Radnitsky)</u>, 1890-1976, American artist who divided his years between New York, Paris, and Los Angeles. Best known as a Surrealist for his contributions in photography, the Dada movement, film, and experimental works in collaboration with, among others, Francisco Picabia and Salvador Dali.

p. 78—<u>Kiki (Kiki de Montparnasse/Alice Prin)</u>, 1901-1953, French lover of eight years and model for Man Ray's photographs while in Paris. Bawdy, entertaining, famous and funny, a subject of Hemingway's writing.

p. 78—<u>Willy Guggenheim (Varlin, name adopted in honor of a union syndicalist)</u>—1900-1977. Swiss lithographer and drawer of humorous cartoons. Shared lodgings with Riko in Paris. Part of the café groups.

p. 80—<u>Georges Feydeau</u>, 1862-1921, French playwright thought to anticipate the theatre of the absurd with his zany comedies of sexual mores and manners during the Belle Epoque.

Notes

Chapter Nine—Greta

p. 83—<u>Schmied children</u>: one stillborn, Gertrude, Carla, Erich (died of scarlet fever at age 5), Margareta (Greta), Hedwich, Max Egon, Anna. Only Greta and Anna survived the Holocaust. In the picture, Greta is third from the left.

p. 87—<u>Richard Klenka</u>, one of the few 20th century Czechoslovakian architects to have studied in Paris, greatly influenced by both Jugenstil coming from Vienna and Art Nouveau from Paris, best known here for architecting the house in which Greta grew up on Maiselova Street. https://www.google.com/maps/@50.090393,14.418287,3a,75y,2 42.9h,90t/data=!3m6!1e1!3m4!1seauS55u5n6yFazhNDoGWm-w!2e0!7i13312!8i6656in

p. 87—<u>Biedermeier</u>, a curious title born of conflating the names of two writers but characterized by several components: a defined period of time from 1815 to 1848, affecting a style in music, literature, the visual arts, interior design and architecture that fell away from the Romantic flourishes to adopt the clean lines introduced by Napoleon Bonaparte's preference for the Roman Empire style. The period of reordering European boundaries and alliances after the French Revolutionary War and the Napoleonic Wars came about through the Congress of Vienna, and was characterized by civility and a prop-agation of the arts that travelled into the newly reordered countries, mainly into the Baltic states. In architecture and interior design, the artists concentrated on using local woods such as cherry, oak and ash to avoid the heavy taxes and transportation costs involved with the preferred (by the social classes) use of mahogany. Biedermeier exerted an enormous influence on the future of Bauhaus and Art Deco, the decorative milieu of the young Mikeskas.

p. 87—Mordecai Maisel, 1528-1601. Jewish sage and philanthropist who was, along with his family, thrown out of Prague in the pogroms of 1542 and 1561. He accumulated enough wealth to return to Prague to underwrite the building of four of its synagogues, two ultimately destroyed by fire in the 1700s. Revered for his promotion of Jewish religion and culture and noted in this account for having a street named after him just outside the present Jewish ghetto in Prague. Greta Schmied grew up in a house on Mordecai Meisel Street.

pp. 87, 88—Franz Kafka, 1882-1924. Bohemian Czech Jew whose strife with his over-bearing father and understanding of the quarrels between the use of German, as opposed to the demeaned Czech, resounded with Greta. Kafka was good-looking, involved with the political topics of the day, a depressive (*I have the true feeling of myself only when I am unbearably unhappy*). He is considered one of the best European writers of the 20th Century. Greta's managing to have him become her tutor was critical in her development. Kafka and Max Brod used to encourage one another to read Greek classics in the original language, and it is thus that they started tutoring Greta and her female siblings in Plato's *Protagoras*. They also managed to speak in French, the language Greta wished to learn so she could make out what her parents were saying when their children were not supposed to understand. He, Max Brod, and Felix Weltsch were an inseparable trio until the two latter left for Israel on the last train out of Prague in 1939.

Kafka, Franz. *Diaries* (New York: Schocken Book, Inc. 1948, 1949) pp. 300, 301.

p. 88—<u>Max Brod</u>, 1884-1968. Bohemian author, composer and journalist, perhaps best known for his friendship with, and biography of Franz Kafka, for encouraging and promoting the writer Jaroslav Hašek to publish *The Good Soldier Schwjk* and, likewise, for helping promote composers like Franz Werfel and Leos Janácek. A fervent pro-Zionist Jew, Brod escaped Czechoslovakia in 1939 to immigrate to Israel. As Kafka's executor, he took with him letters and manuscripts Kafka had asked him to burn, saw to it, instead, that Kafka's works were published.

p. 88—<u>Felix Weltsch</u>, 1884-1964, the first, including Franz Kafka and Max Brod, in the triumvirate of tutors Greta arranged. Like Kafka and Brod, he was a German-speaking Czech Jew, a philosopher, an active polemicist. He escaped Czechoslovakia in 1939 leaving with Brod on the last train out of Prague.

p. 89—<u>Dora Diamant</u>, born in Poland, 1898 and died in Berlin in 1924. Best known as Franz Kafka's lover (he died in her arms in 1924 at a sanatorium where he was being treated for tuberculosis), and for her work in theatre. She married and moved with her husband to Russia, but escaped the Soviet Union to find her way to England in 1939. She was interned in a camp on the Isle of Man for a year, then released to work in London theatre, where she promoted the Yiddish language theatre.

p. 89—<u>Sigismund Schlomo Freud</u>, Pribor, Czechoslovakia (at that time part of German section) 1856-1939, London. Founded with Alfred Adler the Vienna Psychoanalytic Society as father of psychiatry. Renown for his theories of the *ego*, *super-ego* and the *id*. As far as Greta's story goes, he is of minimal importance as by the time she was growing up, it was Alfred Adler whose explanations of the *inferiority complex* suited Greta. *He helped me get my divorce. 'You are not always in love with only one person,' he told me.*

p. 89—<u>Alfred W. Adler</u>, Austrian medical doctor and psychologist, 1870-1937. Great favorite among Greta's circle of friends, particularly with her cousin, Charlotte, daughter of Greta's oldest sister, 'Lotte.' Charlotte introduced Greta to Adler and to the LowBeers, who were so multiply helpful to Riko and Greta. Charlotte survived Theresienstadt (*Thanks to you and Riko, who taught me to paint*), and was the one who informed Greta of the loss of their whole family except for Greta's sister, Anna. Certainly, the introduction to Adler was critical when he encouraged her to divorce Rolf Passer, hence the beginning of the Riko and Greta history.

p. 92—<u>Tomáš Masaryk</u>, Moravian, born 1850-died 1937. First president of the Czechoslovakian Republic, who remains the symbol of democracy for his country. He was a politician, sociologist and philosopher, whose motto was *Do not fear, do not steal.*

p. 93—<u>Rolf Passer</u>, 1893, Czech physicist, Greta's first husband. Last census 1940 had him in Beverly Hills, California Possible death in 1972.

pp. 94, 98—<u>Charlotte (Lotte) Schrötter-Radnitz</u>, 1899-1986, Prague. Friend of Greta's from Prague who married Richard Schrötter (see below). All three were students of Professor Thiele's at the Prague Academy of Art where they mixed with Utrillo and Soutine. Charlotte and Richard again followed Greta and her first husband, Rolf Passer, to Berlin to continue their art education. When Greta left Berlin for Paris, Charlotte and Richard moved to Venice where both exhibited at the 1926 Venice Biennale as representatives of the Czech government. Like Greta, they were Jews who had to flee the Nazis. Charlotte was able to stay in Venice, during the War thanks to Bernard Berensen, noted art critic. She and Richard divorced before the War. It is probable he left for Australia, perhaps the un-named contact in Riko's father's letter alluding to having Riko and Greta escape to Australia themselves.

pp. 94, 98—Richard Schrötter, Czech artist, 1893-? Possibly died in Australia. See above for his painting career. Where Charlotte chose landscapes predominantly, Richard painted interiors and some portraits. In Prague and Berlin, he and Charlotte were friends with Oskar Kokoschka and Egon Schiele.

p. 94—Moritz Melzer—German painter, born in German-ruled Bohemia in 1877, died in Berlin, 1966. One of Greta's principal teachers at the Reimann School in Berlin in 1921-'22. He was another proponent of expressionism whose work was deemed *degenerate* during the Second World War.

p. 95—*sound-mosaics* (Mahler), *'cadences and colors* (Klimt) are phrases Joseph Horowitz used in a magnificently detailed review he wrote in 1986 in New York's *Keynote* magazine devoted to the arts in the City. Mr. Horowitz's article was entitled *Mahler, Klimt and find-de-Siècle Vienna.* From September through October of 1986, there was an exhibit at the Museum of Modern Art called *Vienna 1900: Art, Architecture, & Design.* Correlating with these paintings culled from 1898 to 1918, and represented by Egon Schiele, Oskar Kokoschka and Gustav Klimt, the 92nd Street Y in New York City organized a series of concerts by composers from this same time span to show the syncretism in art and music.

On July 4, 1986, the art critic John Russell wrote a review for *The New York Times* specifically on the Vienna 1900 curated at the Museum of Modern Art by Kirk Varnedoe, and on July 14, 1986, Kay Larson, art critic of *New York* magazine followed it up with a much more detailed sense of what turn-of-the-century Vienna itself was like: *beautiful and doomed, like any proper Germanic heroine of the period. Its gilded elegance still haunts us...*

p. 95—Marton, Kati. *The Great Escape: Nine Jews Who Fled Hitler and Changed the World.* New York, Simon and Schuster, 2006

p. 96—<u>Prague Secession</u>, Czechoslovakian anti-Germanic and an-ti-academic art movement begun in 1887, named by Josef Mànes, who objected specifically to the old and rigid system of exhibiting art, and to the over-powering pan-Germanic influence that had ruled over Czechoslovakia during the Austro-Hungarian Empire. The Secession helped usher in Art Nouveau, also known as Jugendstil, characterized in Vienna, Paris, Berlin, Glasgow, Helsinki (among other capitals) by organic swirling lines and detailed decorations in architecture, de-sign, jewelry, clothing, furniture. Riko, Oskar Kokoschka, Emil Filla were among those who helped carry the Secession during the 1920s. The Prague Secession took off after 1929.

p. 96—<u>Maxim Kopf</u>, born in Prague in 1892, died in Vermont, USA in 1958. Friend, celebrated painter and sculptor in the Prague Secession, and admirer of Riko's work. Kopf travelled widely around Europe and to the Pacific Islands—the Marquesas, Tahiti. He mar-ried the writer and political scientist, Mary Duras, who was jealous of Max's friendship with Riko, and of Kopf's granting Riko his students when Kopf left for Tahiti. His marriage to Duras ended in 1933.

p. 96—<u>Mary Duras (Marguerite Donnadieu)</u>, born in Saigon, French Indochina, 1914, died in 1996 in France. She adopted the name Duras after her father's village in Lot-et-Garonne in France in the '20s. From 1942-44, she worked for the Vichy Government at the same time that she worked as a French Communist in the Resistance. Best known for her book *Hiroshima mon Amour*. Beaten by her family as a child in Indochina, she grew up feisty. Riko and Greta saw her as obdurate, jealous, bright, focused on herself and her writing.

p. 96—<u>Willy Novak</u> (unclear timeline). Apart from being an artist in Riko's circles, Novak's caché may be in his enrollment in Professor Franz Peter Kien's art classes at the Academy of Fine Arts in Prague before the War, but his life stays hidden compared to Kien's, a Jew who was sent to Terezin, made secret depictions of the camp that showed it was not the show-case camp the Nazis portrayed.

pp. 96, 103, 134—Oskar Kokoschka, 1886-1980, Austrian Expressionist artist, poet and playwright whose academic training in Vienna, Berlin and Prague preceded Riko's. He, too, rebelled against the decorative art of the day to support the Prague Secession. Both suffered under Nazi rule, and both escaped to England during the War, where his and the Mikeskas' paths crossed many times.

pp. 97, 116-117—Jan Löwenbach, 1880-1972, Czech attorney, writer, and music critic who, from 1941 until his death lived with his wife, Vilma, in the United States. Through his writing and personality, he promoted the works of Czech artists in general, but of composers specifically, such as Bedřich Smetana, Antonín Dvořák, Leos Janáček, Max Brod and Bohuslav Martinů. Although the Mikeskas chose to live apart from the Czech community in the United States, they certainly had to be aware of the Lowenbach's influence in promoting artists in general.

p. 97—Bohuslav Martinů, 1890-1959, Czech composer. See biography F. James Rybka. *Bohuslav Martinů: The Compulsion to Compose.* Lanham, Maryland: The Scarecrow Press, Inc., 2011.

p. 97—Sidonie-Gabrielle Colette, 1873-1954, French writer of renown, whose sexually and maritally complicated personal life led her to write about feminist liberation. She survived the Second World War in Paris, but feared for the arrest of her third husband, a Jew. Her literary output, from the *Claudine* novels initially usurped under the name "Willy" by her first husband, to *Gigi*, was huge. She was nominated for the Nobel Prize for Literature in 1948.

p. 98—<u>Max Jacob</u>, 1876-1944. French poet, painter, writer and critic, close in friendship to Pablo Picasso whom he introduced the Georges Braque. He was felt to be a link between the Symbolists and Surrealists. He died in Drancy before being shipped off to Auschwitz.

p. 98—<u>Guillaume Apollinaire</u>, 1880-1918. Polish-French poet, playwright and defender of Cubism and Surrealism. He was a popular figure in the cafés in Montparnasse and Montmartre. He died of the Spanish Influenza.

p. 98—<u>Bram (Abraham Girardus) van Velde</u>, born in 1895, The Netherlands, died 1981 near Arles, France. From impoverished beginnings, he achieved significant fame as an intense colorist and abstract expressionist. Heavily influenced by Matisse, then Picasso. He exhibited at the Salon des Indépendents in Paris four times, 1928, '32, '40, '41. The last two times were jarring in that the Nazis were on the look-out for 'degenerate' expressionist art, but somehow, van Velde's passed. In the 1960s, at the time that Riko was also exhibiting at some of the better New York City galleries, van Velde had three exhibits at the Knoedler Gallery—1962, '64, '68. Although Greta and Riko did not mention him apart from this entry, it is highly likely that they would have visited all three exhibits numerous times. Bram's brother, Geer, with whom Bram was close, was also an accomplished painter.

p. 98—<u>Albert Schweitzer</u>, 1875-1965, born in Alsace-Lorraine when it was under German rule, and died in Labaréné, Gabon (formerly Equatorial French Africa), site of the hospital he established with his anesthesiologist wife, Hélène Bresslau. Perhaps the most luminary person Greta met in a life full of people of extraordinary historical, cultural, political, artistic and musical significance. Known primarily for his theological studies on his quest for the life of Jesus, his study and playing of J.S. Bach's music—principally the chorals—his receiving the Nobel Peace Prize in 1952, and the delivery of his speech,

"The Problem of Peace", his work to counter the brutality of 'civilized' societies (so-called by themselves) against the colonized, resulted in founding and maintaining the hospital in Gabon which Greta wanted to visit. Certainly Greta and Riko admired his attempts, along with those of Albert Einstein's, to work against the use of nuclear tests and weapons after the atomic and hydrogen bombs in the 1940s and '50s.

Chapter Ten- Friends and Flight

p. 103—<u>Mae West, Clara Bow, Charlie Chaplain</u>—Popular Hollywood actors spanning the eras of silent to talkies in the movies.

p. 104—<u>Paul Joseph Goebbel</u>, in office as a member of the Nazi party from March 13, 1933 to April 30, 1945, capping his last official day as a less than 24 hour Chancellor of Germany. His most enduring legacy was as Hitler's Minister of Public Enlightenment and Propaganda.

p. 107—<u>General Friedrich August Hayek</u>, Viennese, 1899-1992. Austro-Hungarian-born philosopher associated with the economics of conservatism. Highly regarded and decorated in Great Britain and the United States. Awarded the Nobel Prize for Economics along with Gunnar Myrdal. Riko was keen to imbibe all the knowledge of economics possible from him during their short encounters on the Croatian island of Hvar as Riko fancied himself a financier and wanted to control Greta's inheritance.

p. 107—<u>Duke of Windsor</u>, Edward VIII—1894-1972. Riko and Greta met him through F.A. Hayek on the Croatian island of Hvar during one of their last summers there. Certainly, Greta and Riko were titillated by his notoriety in his abdication of the British throne to marry the twice-divorced American, Wallis Simpson. They looked askance at his seeming sympathy with the Nazis in France at the beginning of the war, and saw this verified when the British government sent him and Wallis to spend the war years in the Bahamas. After the war, they returned to France, where he lived out his days.

p. 108—<u>Karl Gunnar Myrdal</u>, Swedish economist, sociologist and politician, born 1898, died 1937. Nobel Laureate with Friedrich Hayek (whom Riko met in Hvar) for their pioneering work in the theory of money and its fluctuations, and analysis of the interdependence of economic, social and institutional phenomena in the study of race relations. Myrdal wrote a book, *An American Dilemma: The Negro Problem in Modern Democracy* which influenced the 1954 U.S. Supreme Court decision *Brown v. Board of Education of Topeka.*

Chapter Eleven–First Exile

p. 113—<u>Edvard Beneš</u>, 1884-1948. Second President of the Czechoslovakian Republic, after Tomáš Masaryk, between 1935-'38, then again between 1940-'48. Fierce patriot, he led the Czech movement abroad during the First World War, and in 1940, organized the Czech government in exile by moving to Putney in England. It is here that Riko and Greta, along with their Czech friends, Eve Korner, Erika Kalmer and others, formed the nexus of Czech transactions, spying and news publications. He was succeeded by Emil Hacha as president of the Czech Republic in 1938. After Hacha's death, Beneš returned to the presidency and in 1943 chose to sign an entente with the Soviet Union rather than with Poland. He formed a coalition government with Klement Gottwald, who ultimately undermined him. Under Gottwald's Soviet fist, Beneš lived to see the demise of the Czech independence he had fostered.

p. 113—<u>Emil Hacha</u>, 1872-1945. Famous Czech lawyer, specialist in English Common Law and in International Law, appointed by Tomáš Masaryk as president of the Supreme Administrative Court, translator of Jerome K. Jerome's *Three Men in a Boat* and short-term third president of the Czech Republic between 1938-1939, when Beneš resigned to form a government in exile in London. It was Hacha who faced Hitler's Hobson's choice to cede the Sudetenland to Germany without force, or cede it under force. France and the United

Kingdom further pressured him to allow for immediate annexation of the Sudetenland to Germany; if not, *they would become uninterested in the fate of Czechoslovakia*. He fainted in front of Hitler when made to wait for hours to decide the fate of his nation, suffered successive heart attacks, and died in jail under suspicious circumstances in 1945.

p. 115—<u>Blaue Reiter, the Blue Rider</u>, 1911-1914. An art movement founded by Russian and German artists rebelling against the strictures (as they saw them) of the Munich academic community. Along with the also short-lived art movement Die Brücke, The Bridge, the artists of the Blaue Reiter comprised the fundamentals of Expressionism. Among them were Wassily Kandinsky, Franz Marc, August Macke. The beginning of the First World War signaled the end of their movement, but not before they left a huge imprint in their syncretism of colors, music and art. They, along with the Fauves and the art of André Derain, in particular, influenced Riko.

p. 115—<u>Fauves</u>, a school of painters using broad brushstrokes (though not exclusively) in bold colors that thrived from around 1900-1910. Henri Matisse and André Derain were the main proponents. Derain's intense colors had a huge influence on Riko. Derain became his friend.

p. 115—<u>Maurice de Vlaminck</u>, French, 1876-1958. Along with Matisse and Derain, one of the proponents of Fauvism. He blamed Picasso for its downfall in favor of Cubism.

Chapter Twelve—Keeping Contact

p. 121—<u>Tobruk</u>, Famous desert battle at the Libyan-Egyptian border fought during the Second World War in 1941 between Axis and Allied forces. The battle lasted 241 days, commanded on the German side by *The Desert Fox*, Field Marshall Rommel, and by Field Marshall 'Monty' Montgomery on the British side. The American allies under General George S. Patton's 2nd Armored Division helped in the victory, but his style was badly received. The details of Greta's first husband, Rolf Passer's role in the battle remain undetailed, but it is clear he was injured and evacuated to England where he contacted Greta and Riko, and where Riko collaborated with his illustrations and paintings on a book about the battle.

p. 122—*The Good Soldier Schweik* (Svejk and Schwejk are variants), by Jaroslav Hašek, is a dark satire on the absurdity of war and obedience to military discipline. Wittingly or not, Riko displayed the same sort of passive aggression the hero of the novel, Josef Svejk, shows while in the Army. The novel reflects the conflict Riko, among many Czechs, had with the ruling Germanic Empire. In the book, Svejk does not understand fighting for an Empire for which he feels no loyalty. Riko and Greta had a much-read copy of this book written in Czech in their apartment in New York. It was Max Brod, Greta's tutor as a child, and Franz Kafka's executor, who also promoted the publication of *The Good Soldier Schweik*.

p. 124—Kristallnacht, November 9-10, 1938. Precursor of the Final Solution practiced over two days throughout Austria (Vienna its epicenter) and Germany when a paramilitary force, the 'SA' and non-Jewish civilians joined forces to smash carefully pre-marked Jewish homes, businesses, hospitals, schools, synagogues, and follow this up by incarcerating 30,000 Jews in concentration camps where atrocities were committed against the inmates.

Chapter Thirteen-England During the War

p. 131—Bohuš Beneš, nephew of Eduard Beneš, who along with Tomáš Masaryk, forged the independence of the Czechoslovakian Republic after the First World War. He was a great proponent of Czechs in exile in England during the Second World War and did his utmost in keeping contact with those left in their homeland. He became a fierce opponent of the Communist regime after the War.

Notes

Bohuš came to the United States, where he lectured frequently about both Tomáš Masaryk and his son, Jan. Riko and Greta came to know him in London through Eve Korner and Erika Kalmer.

p. 131—In a letter to me dated October 29, 1984, after a visit I had in London with both Eve Korner and Erika Kalmer, the latter wrote me in answer to my queries about their contemporary cultural lives between the Wars in Czechoslovakia:

I cannot say there was anything special influencing our lives in the period between the wars but for the then current world affairs and events. Otherwise, life in the Democratic Republic was quite normal and pleasant and our generation did not necessarily have the feeling that it was a newly formed independent state. In spite of the Czech and Slovac lands having belonged to the Austrian-Hungarian monarchy, the Czech language had been kept alive, so there was quite a lively cultural life in every aspect. Here are a few names:

WRITERS AND POETS: *Karel Čapek*
Vítěslav Nezval
František Langer
Jaroslav Seifert (Nobel Prize 1984)
Jiri Wolker
Franz Kafka
ARTISTS: *Švabinsky*
Vicenc Mucha
Karel (?) Feigl
P. Kremlička
Oskar Kokoschka
COMPOSERS: *Karel Janáček*
Martinů
Weinberger

p. 131—<u>Dr. Cisaz</u>, no references found

pp. 132, 141—<u>Jan Masaryk</u>, son of Tomáš Masaryk, Czechoslovakia's founder and first president of the Czech Republic. Like his father and the Beneš father and son duo, he fought against the repressive Communist regime that followed the Nazis in Czechoslovakia after the War. The manner of his death remains in dispute. The Communist party declared he committed suicide, but others believed he was pushed through a window to land in a courtyard to his death.

p. 139—<u>Johann Christoph Friedrich von Schiller</u>, 1759-1805. German philosopher, poet, historian, playwright and physician who, among other accomplishments, encouraged Goethe to finish his poems. Riko loved Schiller's language, and taught his poetry whenever he could.

p. 139—<u>Christian Johann Heinrich Heine</u>, 1797-1856, German poet, essayist and literary critic, chiefly known for his *Book of Songs*.

p. 139—<u>Johann Wolfgang von Goethe</u>, 1749-1832, German author of lyric and epic poetry, diplomat and civil servant. Along with Schiller, whose plays he premiered, Goethe was an early participant of the *Sturm and Drang* literary movement. Riko recited the works of these poets from memory and taught them to his English pupils during the War.

p. 144—<u>Terezin (Czech name)/ Theresienstadt (German name)</u>, fortress that took ten years to construct starting in 1780 under Joseph II, Habsburg Emperor, against Prussian invasions. He named it after his mother, Maria Theresa. It was strategically placed between two rivers, the Elbe and the Ohre, in the Sudetenland portion of Czechoslovakia and through most of its existence was used as a political prisoner's camp, first against the Prussians, then against prisoners of war in World War I, and ultimately, against the Jews in World War II. Hitler's and Goebbel's propaganda program required them to come up with a so-called model internment camp to dispel horror stories travelling west of appalling conditions in other detention centers the world knew about. By the 14th of June, 1940, this Jewish ghetto within the prison fortress was created. Musicians were ordered to band together to play for the Führer and visiting dignitaries, though the Führer never came. Many drawings children made while in Terezin have been preserved. Some play up to show the good times required of them, others portray the sickness, starvation, filth and misery of the conditions. It was while in Terezin that Messiaen wrote his *Quartet for the End of Time*.

Chapter Fourteen—Second Exile, Welcome to America

p. 157—F. James Rybka, MD, *Personal correspondence*. Like Greta and Riko later on, the Löwenbachs ended up in London during the War. Rolf would have had the opportunity to meet him there again and to reconnect to the Czech artistic community that Eve Korner and Erika Kalmer opened up for Greta and Riko. However, the Löwenbachs' time in London was brief. By the time Martinů arrived in New York in 1941, and the Mikeskas in 1948, Jan Löwenbach was already active as a copyright lawyer and co-publisher of the *Newyorkske Listy*. There is no indication that the Mikeskas ever tried to connect to the Czech community in New York City. I never heard Riko describe himself as a Czech artist, but simply an artist.

p. 157—George Winthrop Sands, 1908, Poissy, France, died in the United States in 1986. Orphaned by age 6, his guardians alternated between his father's mother, Anne Harriman Vanderbilt, who lived in France, and his uncle through marriage, Ogden Mills who lived in Westbury, Long Island. His adult experiences were congruent with those of Riko's in terms of being in Europe during the War, losing an infant son, and experiencing many failures in his professional life. He was friends with Ed Scheckman who introduced him to Riko and, along with Fritz LowBeer, the three became the Three Musketeers with Riko as their d'Artagnan. He went from wine importer to M.D.

p. 157—<u>Anne Harriman Sands Rutherford Vanderbilt</u>, grandmother to George Winthrop Sands (above). She was the heiress of the Vanderbilt railroad fortune. She lived in France during WWI, hosted parties there and in New York at her mansion 660 Fifth Avenue (corner of 35th Street) to help the War cause. Riko was overwhelmed by her wealth and position in Society at the same time he felt sadness for his friend, Win, for his isolation as an orphaned child.

p. 157—<u>Ogden Livingston Mills</u>, 1856-1972. American business man, philanthropist, race horse owner and breeder who acted as guardian to 'Win' Sands, Riko's friend. Riko found the legacy of wealth attendant on Win almost incomprehensible. Ogden's father left Ogden and his sister an estate valued at over $36 million in 1910. The sadnesses in Win's life made Riko think of him as *a poor little rich boy.*

p. 160—<u>Albert Einstein</u>, born in Ulm, Germany, 1879, died in Princeton, New Jersey, in 1955. Renown for the four theories he proposed in 1905 that changed the world of physics, nuclear physics and astrophysics. His General Theory of Relativity called forth such attention, that to evade people stopping him on the street to ask for an explanation of *that theory*, he apologized saying he was sorry but that people often confused him with *that Professor Einstein*. Riko identified with him as a co-refugee, a new American citizen, and for his support of causes such as Civil Rights, Zionism, and for his opposition to the military use of the atomic power he helped harness.

p. 160—<u>Edward Teller</u>, Hungarian physicist, 1908-2003. Popularly known as 'the father of the hydrogen bomb,' Teller disliked the title. He is best known for his work on the Manhattan Project along with Robert Oppenheimer, its director, whose clearance he came to question when interviewed by the Atomic Energy Commission. Teller was brilliant, complicated (as was Oppenheimer), very difficult to get along with and volatile in character. He remained an expert advisor through the Reagan years in military matters, but personally was unpopular.

p. 160—<u>Arnold Schönberg (Schoenberg)</u>, Vienna, 1874-Los Angeles, 1951. Austrian composer and painter associated with the Expressionist Movement. For his paintings such as 'the Red Gaze', showing a simian with red rimmed eyes, and his string quartet, *Verklärte Nacht* (published in 1899), he earned Hitler's designation of a Jewish artist producing *degenerate* art and music. He immigrated to the United States in 1934, settling in Los Angeles after a short period in Boston. He was immensely influencial for the articulation of his twelve tone scale, but also for the depth and breadth of his musical education, learned and practiced in Vienna and Berlin at the Prussian Academy. He was the subject of a portrait of Egon Schiele in 1917 and of a painter-like black and white photograph by Man Ray in 1927, years that coincided with Riko's life in Prague, Vienna, Berlin and Paris. His music was of no interest to Riko but, as an immigrant who made it in the United States, Schönberg threatened Riko.

p. 160—<u>Bertolt Brecht</u>, born in Augsberg, Germany in 1898, died in East Berlin, 1956. Playwright, poet and theatre director, Brecht made his name in portraying man in society. Constantly recognized and praised for his language, the Berlin critic, Herbert Ihering, wrote in 1922: *It is a language you can feel on your tongue, in your gums, your ear, your spinal column.* Brecht collaborated with many great names in theatre in the era Riko and Greta were also in Berlin. Horrified by the carnage of WWI, and encouraged by his father, Brecht enrolled in the University of Munich to take medical courses as a way of staying out of the conflict, although war would be a major theme in his works. A staunch Marxist, he skirted around the Baltic countries, staying mostly in Finland, during WWII. He came to the United States, but after being called to testify before the House Un-American Activities Committee (HUAC), he delivered gibberish through his translators and left for Germany shortly thereafter. His musicals, often in concert with the composer Kurt Weill, became hugely popular in the United States and elsewhere. His contributions added to the agar in which Riko and Greta grew their inspiration.

p. 160—Otto Ludwig Preminger, born in Austro-Hungary in 1905, died in New York City in 1986. He was offered work in Hollywood before the outbreak of WWII, so suffered none of the indignities most of the émigrés from Europe experienced. Actor, film director and producer on Broadway and in Hollywood, he was responsible for a long-list of hits and was nominated for two Academy Awards as Best Director (*Laura*, being his breakthrough film). His career was stormy, if successful.

p. 160—Friedrich Christian Anton 'Fritz' Lang, born in Vienna of Czech parentage in 1890-died in Los Angeles, 1976. Renown for his film-making during the Weimar years and his association with German Expressionists, he created a silent film, *Metropolis*, which dealt with the inequities between the workers and ruling classes of a factory, and the capture and remaking into a robot of a beautiful woman sympathetic to the workers. Its plot is dark as is his film *M*, the first talkie made in Europe. He escaped the Nazi putsch to go to Hollywood, where he established the genre of the film noir. He joined the list of extraordinary Jewish talent that fled Europe because of the Nazis, and gained popularity and respect on this side of the Atlantic. He was nearly blind when he died in Los Angeles, and much revered by fellow directors. Riko and Greta were, of course, conversant about him and other émigrés who won fame, whether in science, maths, physics or art, in the United States.

p. 160—Mies van der Rohe, 1886-1969, self-described as a German-American architect who helped move architecture through classical and gothic style into modernism, a 'skin and bones' use of industrial steel and plate glass that can be seen in most prominent American cities. The Seagram's Building on 53rd Street and Park is a fine example.

p. 160—<u>Walter Adolph George Gropius</u>, born in Berlin, 1883, died in Cambridge, Massachusetts in 1969. A protégé of Mies van der Rohe (above), he, too was influenced by the roots of Cubism and Expressionism, but created an art form, Bauhaus, that encompassed sculpture, architecture, furniture, decoration, and handicrafts just as the Jugenstil had done fifty years before in Vienna. Although Riko felt as a young student that perhaps architecture would have offered him a discipline by which to work, he seldom spoke of architects or architectural styles except for likening the towers in San Gimignano to those in Manhattan when he first arrived in New York.

p. 162—<u>Bedřich Smetana</u>, 1824-1884, Bohemian composer who came to be known as the "father of Czech music" for his promotion of the Czech aspirations towards independence, finally achieved after World War I. He composed operas, but may be best known abroad for his *Má Vlast* (My Homeland). He became deaf ten years before his death in a mental asylum.

p. 162—<u>Gioacchino Rossini</u>, born in Pesaro, Papal States in 1792, died in Passy in France in 1868. His immensely popular operas *L'Italiana in Algeri, Le Comte Ory, La Cenerentola* gave Greta musical fodder to sing and act out at her job in New York City.

p. 162—<u>Charles-François Gounod</u>, French composer, 1818-1893. Like Rossini, Gounod's contribution to Greta's life was through giving her arias from *Faust* and the *Ave Maria* to sing aloud and in jest at work. Greta's grounding in piano was serious and gave her a cultural edge Riko never acquired. (See F. James Rybka on amusia in his biography of *Bohuslav Martinů*.)

p. 162—<u>Pyotr Ilyich Tschaikovsky</u>, born and died in Russia, 1840-1893. This Romantic composer, like Rossini and Gounod, furnished songs for Greta to sing—all in German, as she noted. Both Riko and Greta found sympathy with Tschaikovsky for his depressive disorders and for his experiences with cholera. That he was part of the *mighty handful* of five composers in St. Petersburg, or that his range of education allowed him to be a fine critic did not interest the Mikeskas, whose musical needs were narrow.

Chapter Fifteen—Perilous Steps

p. 169—<u>Sir Cecil, Maurice Bowra</u>, 1898-1971, British classical scholar and literary critic.

Chapter Sixteen—The Caprices of War

p. 171—<u>Frances Stonor Saunders</u>, born, 1966. British journalist and historian. *Who Paid the Piper? The CIA and the Cultural Cold War. Granta, 1999*. (In the United States) *The Cultural Cold War: The CIA and the World of Arts and Letters, 1999*. ISBN 0 56584 596 X
The Independent: Modern Art with CIA Weapon. Saturday, October 21, 1995.

p. 172—<u>Truman Garcia Capote</u>, 1924-1984. American novelist, playwright, actor and screenwriter. Charismatic personality helped by his avowed homosexuality and involvement with the artistic community in NYC in the 1960s. Made famous by his novella *Breakfast at Tiffany's* and his crime novel *In Cold Blood*.

p. 172—<u>Paul Jackson Pollock</u>, 1912-1956. American painter of the abstract expressionist movement Riko stepped into when the Mikeskas arrived in New York. Pollock is known for his style of "drip painting."

p. 172—<u>Mark Rothko</u>, 1903-1970. Russian-American painter who eschewed but was associated with abstract expressionism. During his studies at the Parsons School of Design, he met Arshile Gorky, who introduced him to the American Avant-garde. He believed in art as being "a toll of emotional and religious expression." Many believe this culminated in his Rothko Chapel, now in Houston, Texas. Like Riko, he was profoundly influenced by Greek mythology and came to be known as the artistic "mythmaker." Also like Riko, he believed in a sexual/seductive ingredient to art. *It is a lustful relationship to things that exist.*

p. 172—<u>Willem de Kooning</u>, 1904-1997. Dutch-American Abtract Expressionist forming part of the New York School. He numbered among the few 'chosen' by the OSI/CIA in their promotion of American artists who exhibited artistic freedom as opposed to the art emerging from the repressive Soviet régime during the Cold War.

p. 172—<u>Robert Motherwell</u>, 1915-1991. American painter, print and collage maker, editor who coined the phrase *New York School* to describe his works along with those of Willem de Kooning, Mark Rothko and Jackson Pollock. He was influenced by the Surrealists in France.

Chapter Seventeen—Adaptations

p. 175—<u>Georg Ehrenfried Grosz</u>, born and died in Berlin, 1893-1959. His caricature-like drawings and paintings of people and life in Berlin in the 1920s excoriated the city's depravity which advertised everything for sale. Grosz spared no feelings in showing viewers the horrors of war, prostitution, corruption. He moved to the United States with his family in 1934, taught for many years at the Art Student's League in New York, and softened his painting themes and styles while in America; however, he returned to Berlin in 1959 and died after falling down stairs. There is no evidence Riko sought him out or that their lives crossed in any way other than in Riko's admiration for this artist, Communistic in belief and Expressionistic at base. He was associated with the Dada movement, of which Man Ray was an exponent in photography.

p. 175—<u>Wassily Wassilyevich Kandinsky</u>, born in Moscow in 1866, died in Neuilly-sur-Seine, France in 1944. From studies in law and economics, Kandinsky tried his hand at art aged thirty and found ease and success in his new medium. He is known for his Fauves-like colors and for the painting *The Blaue Reiter*, painted in 1903 to express the movement of the same name. Philosophically complex, under the often discredited Mme. Blavatsky, he became a theosophist. In art, he came to postulate the point and the line as the two sole components out of which all art emerged. Riko's appreciation of him would be through his association with the Fauves before he came to America.

p. 175—<u>Cornelis Theodoris Maria Kees Van Dongen</u>, born in Rotterdam in 1877, died in Monaco in 1968. Another proponent of Fauvism and, therefore, a painter Riko paid attention to after his student days with Derain. Van Dongen was known for his 'Bohemian eroticism' and for his portraits that used a great deal of green in the way Alice Neel and Lucien Freud would come to use it during Riko's time.

p. 175—<u>Egon Schiele</u>, 1890-1918. Austrian protégé of Gustav Klimt, and part of the eclectic group including Vincent van Gogh, Jan Toorop (whom Riko met and had lessons with in the Netherlands), and the Norwegian painter who painted the essential, Edvard Munch. He died, along with his six-month pregnant wife, of the Spanish flu, but in his short life created many spidery, angular, graphic-if not pornographic- drawings and paintings, including self-portraits sometimes in the nude. His colors were sparse and lush.

His work, along with Edvard Munch's, Pablo Picasso's, Paul Klee's, and those of almost the entire panoply of Expressionist painters between 1920s and 1930s earned the title of *degenerate art*. In 1937, Adolph Hitler said: *For all I care, those prehistoric Stone Age culture barbarians and art-stutterers can return to the caves of their ancestors and there can apply their primitive international scratchings.* [p. 313 of

Sue Prideaux's book, *Behind the Scream on Edvard Munch's life*; Yale University Press, 2005]. Riko and Greta bathed in their art, debated it at their cafés, and honored the artists.

p. 175—<u>André Breton</u>, 1896-1966. French poet and writer of anarchistic sentiments. Considered to be the founder of Surrealism stemming from the Dada art forms he associated with in Paris. He escaped to the United States in 1941 thanks to the efforts of Valerian Fry and Harry Bingham. He was a great collector of ethnographic artifacts.

p. 175—<u>René Magritte</u>, Belgian artist, 1898-1967. He turned perceptions upside down by inviting viewers to truly define what they were looking at in a witty way, *Ceci n'est pas une pipe* being the foremost example of the difference between reality and the depiction of it. His observations about light (the sky remains light long after the shaded houses and streets have put their lights on), about the viewers' ability to fill in what is missing (the 'fill-in-the-head'—author's definition—painting of a suited torso with a bowler hat above a space) bridged the gap from Impressionistic influences to pop art.

He produced fake paintings of Picasso's, Braque's and de Chirico's during the first World War, an exercise to forge bank notes he collaborated on with his brother in the needy post-war period. He joined the ranks of all the artists Greta and Riko grew up with, even if not known on a personal basis.

p. 175—<u>Roy Fox Lichtenstein</u>, 1923-1997. American pop artist whose use of Ben-Day dots became his signature style in portraying comic book characters.

p. 176—<u>Andy Warhol</u>, 1928-1987. Charismatic American artistic icon of Pop culture that exhibited what he made fun of. Noted as an illustrator, artist, silk-screen maker of political figures (Mao) and movie stars (Marilyn Monroe, Elizabeth Taylor), film-maker of movies of unusual length but little action, host of parties at his famour Factory populated by other icons of the '60s, for example, the model Twiggy and the musician Lou Reed.

p. 176—<u>Larry Rivers</u>, Bronx born Yitroch Loiza Grossbergh, who changed his name when playing sax with a Greenwich Village band which included the name *Larry Rivers*. Musician, film-maker, and artist, his brand of non-narrative Pop art riled Riko. He saw it as soulless and vapid.

p. 176—<u>Lascaux</u>, series of caves of pre-historic art over 17,000 years old discovered in 1940 by an eighteen year-old near the village of Montignac in the Department of the Dordogne in France. They display painted drawings of animals, and stand as the ultimate proof of the human need to create art.

p. 177—<u>Ieoh Ming (I.M.) Pei</u>, Chinese American architect, born 1917, and famous for the glass Pyramid in the courtyard of the Louvre in Paris, the J.F.K. Library and the East Wing of the National Gallery in Washington, D.C., and for the Museum of Islamic Art in Doha, Qatar. Known for elegant simplicity of line, use of stone and water in his sculptures.

p. 177—<u>Barnett Newman</u>, American artist, 1905-1970 whose interest in myths and the primitive unconscious found expression in multiple paintings of rectilinear lines and colors that evaded Riko's engagement. Riko found Newman's sculpture, Broken Obelisk, at the Museum of Modern Art worthy of admiration for its risk and design.

p. 177—<u>Thomas Kennerly 'Tom' Wolfe, Jr.</u>, American author and journalist born in Richmond, Virginia in 1931. He found favor with Riko with his non-fiction book called *The Painted Word* which, if short of mockery, pointed out the dependence on fads and written explanations to sell contemporary art which, otherwise, he felt had questionable inherent meaning.

Chapter Eighteen—Riko as a Teacher and Painter

p. 184— June C. Singer, Abbreviation from *The New York Times* obituary: *Singer, June C., painter and interior designer, died February 16, in Springfield MA, at 91. Born June 21, 1920 in Manhattan, Mrs. Singer spent most of her life there. She was proud to be a native New Yorker and deeply loved the city's spellbinding mixture of creativity, culture and history. She married noted New York pediatrician Dr. Milton Singer in 1941. Dr. Singer had a practice in Manhattan, was on the staff at Babies Hospital, and was Director of the Pediatric Cerebral Palsy Clinic. Mrs. Singer studied painting under Czechoslovakian artist Riko Mikeska and maintained a studio on 17th Street. She traveled and painted extensively in Europe in the 1970's and 1980's. After Dr. Singer died in 1972, Mrs. Singer started an interior design company, June C. Singer Interiors. She pursued that career intensely and successfully, attracting such well known clients as Vincent Sardi and Audrey Hepburn. She continued working well into her eighties.*

p. 185—Hans Holbein the Younger, 1497-1543, Swiss German artist who was encouraged by the philosopher and humanist, Desiderius Erasmus, to move from Basel to England, where he became Henry the VIII's appointed court portraitist. Unique in his abilities to capture character in paint—on canvas and in enamel miniatures— he recorded the history of a turbulent age. It is Hans Holbein the Younger portraits of Thomas Cromwell, Thomas More, Henry the Eighth, his six wives, and Desiderius Erasmus (see below) that captivated Riko's unbridled admiration.

p. 185—Thomas Cromwell, Earl of Essex, KG, 1485-1540. Of humble origins, he became a lawyer and statesman and rose to spend the last eight years of his life as the Chief Minister to Henry VIII. He helped Henry VIII unite his government by defining laws and administrative procedures, breaking with Rome's Papacy, and increasing his land holdings. Cromwell's helping move from Royal Supremacy to Parliamentary terms signaled the importance of the English Reformation. It also threatened the King, who had him beheaded for his troubles.

p. 186—Thomas More, 1478-1535, contemporary of his countryman, Thomas Cromwell. Also a lawyer, More served Henry VIII as secretary and personal advisor. As a philosopher and humanist, in 1516 he wrote a book called *Utopia* about an ideal island nation in which the workers were valued. This aspect of his writing later drew praise from the communists in the USSR, where several cities commissioned a statue in his honor. He was violently anti-Reformation, anti-Martin Luther's proclamations in particular. He refused to acknowledge Henry the VIII's annulment of his marriage to Catherine of Aragon, and equally refused to admit the King as Supreme Head of the Church of England. For his refusal to take the Oath of Supremacy, he was convicted of treason and beheaded. In 1935, he was canonized.

p. 186—Desiderius Erasmus Roterodamus, born in 1466 in Rotterdam, died in Basel, 1536. Recognized as a Dutch Renaissance humanist, his philosophy embodied his disciplines as theologian, social critic and classical scholar. He maintained his belief in Roman Catholicism, eschewing the reforms of Martin Luther.

p. 186—Henry VIII, born in 1491, Henry ascended the throne as the second Tudor King, following his father, and reigned the rest of his life to 1547. Remembered, among many things, for his break with the Roman Catholic Church to establish the Church of England, and giving himself the Divine Right of Kings. Those in his court who did not bow to this decree were beheaded (see Cromwell and More above). He is also remembered for his six wives and for his daughter, Elizabeth, who became the first Queen of England. For Riko, he exemplified generous patronage.

p. 186—<u>Anne Boleyn</u>, 1501-1536, second queen of Henry the VIII, not properly considered his wife as there was no annulment of his marriage to his first wife, Catherine of Aragon. In an effort to marry Jane Seymour, Henry accused Anne of being unfaithful, a crime punishable by death. Despite Anne's profession of innocence of the King's charge, Henry had Anne beheaded in the Tower of London.

p. 186—<u>Jane Seymour</u>, 1508-1537, third Queen (properly second wife) of English King Henry VIII. His favorite. He mourned for three years after her death of puerpural fever after giving birth to Henry's only son, Edward VI.

p. 186—<u>Agnolo Bronzino</u>, 1503-1572, Italian Painter, described by Giorgio Vasari in his *Lives of the Painters* as a Mannerist who rendered naturalistic representations more complex. Widely admired by Riko.

p. 186—<u>Diego Velázquez</u>, Spanish, 1599-1660. Velazquez was portraitist to King Philip V of Spain's royal court as Hans Holbein the Younger was to Henry VIII's. Widely admired by the Impressionists and Symbolists and even Dada painters, Edouard Manet, Pablo Picasso, Salvador Dali, and Francis Bacon painted tributes to him. Riko's admiration of him was more tempered in comparison to Hans Holbein the Younger.

p. 187—<u>Lerida</u>, city in western Catalonia, Spain.

p. 187—<u>Fraga</u>, town in Catalonia conquered by Moors by Count Ramon Berenguer IV of Barcelona in 1149. King Alfonso I died in 1134 trying to keep the walls of the town secure against the Moors.

Unusually, Riko seemed confused in giving this history while taking a tour of viewers around the Frick (see King Ferrante of Aragon in Naples below).

p. 190—<u>Marcel Duchamp,</u> 1887-1968, born and died in France after having lived in the United States long enough to become an American citizen. Protean in his interests and talents, from painting, sculpture, chess-playing, music and collaborating with writers and librettists, he decried the *retinal* art of Matisse, for example, to depict a more rigorous intellectual form best shown in his painting of *Nude Young Man on a Train*, and *Woman Descending a Staircase*. He enjoyed explorations into Dada, an outer fountain shaped like a urinal gaining notoriety. Riko did not like him.

p. 191—<u>Roland David Smith,</u> American sculptor and painter, 1906-1965. Part of the abstract Expressionist movement in the United States, he worked sculptures, frequently in series, in burnished steel. He and his wife, Dorothy Dehner (Riko's studio neighbor), chose to live away from the maelstrom of artists in New York by settling up the Hudson in Bolton Landing, New York.

Chapter Nineteen—The Dream Birds Take a Long Time Before they Reach the Blue Yonder

p. 200—Author's note: I did reach Bari and Ulriche Bozzi, widow of Aldo Bozzi, who treated me to the splendours of the Italian table and her stories about both Greta and Riko. She admired Greta for her steadiness, Riko for his erudition and ability to sketch portraits.

He told me not to spoil our daughter, to read the classics to her, to take her to museums. And, yes, he did change my way of looking at art forever. He made me grow up. I should say that Riko changed my way of seeing and my mentality. He left me more open, receptive, and sensitive about the future. And then, he made me love painting that at first I did not understand. After I had known Riko, I put more weight on substance than on form.

She and Aldo built a house in Lake Garda in the hopes they might treat Riko and Greta to vacations there.

Riko wrote me how miserable he and Greta were, how poor, how difficult life was in America. He never asked for favors, but we wanted to give him one. It was too late. By the time we had our house built, Riko was deathly ill.

In London, I met Eve Korner and Erika Kalmer, a duo that had seemed interchangeable so close were their names and resemblance in intelligence, charm, generosity and fun. I was impressed by the quality of Riko's and Greta's friends. The people who had been so good to them during the War continued to be good to them through me. They hosted me at their respective flats for teas, and the stories I collected are ones the readers already know. As I scrutinized the small Mikeska paintings that hung on the walls of each home, I was aware of the paucity of paints and materials Riko had at his disposal during the War. The canvasses were small, pigments limited, but each landscape or still life told a story the artist and recipient shared intimately. The women treasured the experiences of his paintings as much as the art itself. The only new angle on Riko was that he liked to cook, had pretenses of being a great chef (his tea shop during the war harkened to those fantasies), but failed unless he was preparing the Christmas carp dinner he recalled with undying nostalgia and hunger. To these remarkable people, I remain especially grateful.

p. 206—Ringelnatz's poem, translated by Catherine A. Lillie

An M.

Der du meine Wege mit mir gehst,
Jede Laune meiner Wimper spürst,
Meine Schlechtigkeiten duldest und verstehst –
Weißt du wohl, wie heiß du oft mich rührst?

Wenn ich tot bin darfst du gar nicht trauern.
Meine Liebe wird mich überdauern
Und in fremden Kleidern dir begegnen
Und dich segnen.

Lebe, lache gut!
Mache deine Sache gut!

To M.

Companion constant at my side,
Who sensed my very eyelash quiver,
Endured my malice more than any should abide –
Do you know how passionately you make me shiver?

Once I'm dead and gone, don't dare to mourn
My love's sojourn
Will extend across time and, robed in unfamiliar dress,
Find you and bless

Live well, laugh loud!
Do yourself proud!

Notes

Chapter Twenty—Discoveries and Farewells

p. 209—Artists whose works were similarly on exhibit with Riko's at the Burgos Gallery, for example, were de Chirico, Fernand Léger, Rice Pereira, among others.

Chapter Twenty-three—See the Clearing, not the Dark

p. 245—<u>Lucrezia Borgia</u>, daughter of Pope Alexander VI and sister of Cesare, reputedly murderous and scandalous. Patrons of great artists of the Renaissance, including Michelangelo, Leonardo da Vinci, and poet Ludovico Ariosto, known most famously for his *Orlando Furioso*.

p. 245—Ferrante (Ferdinand) of Aragon in Naples, 1104-1134, died in the Battle of Fraga in an unsuccessful attempt to keep out the Moors. Riko made reference to this history when lecturing during his informal tour at the Frick Museum in NYC. In his letter to Titi he nudges her to look up the event Ferrante organized when he invited his enemies to a peace-making banquet at his castle, then murdered them in gruesome ways, fed some of the bodies to the crocodiles living in the moat surrounding the castle, and mummified others to be left in the dungeon dressed in their original costumes.

p. 247—In churches, synagogues, museums and galleries, I searched for and found, but could not photograph, only three Mikeska paintings, one thought to be by Greta, but left unsigned. The Director, Markéta Theinhardt of the National Gallery (known as the Modern Gallery before the War) kindly guided my search, limited as much by the politics of the day as by the rarity of finds.

p. 249—personal correspondence.
   "I (Martin Ftacnik) purchased the painting this year here:
   New Orleans Auction Galleries
   333 St. Joseph Street"

Friend of a Giant

You were a Giant and snow was your hair,
Your eyes were blue searchlights that stripped my soul bare.

Your voice was the whisper of wind in the trees,
Your words were the birds, your tears the salt seas.

The little men shouted and shrieked all day long,
But all I could hear were the words of your song.

You were my Gulliver, wise BFG,
You called me your Child, you taught me to see.

The little men scampered and scurried around,
From your shoulders I laughed at those mice on the ground!

You were Chagall, I played Mona Lisa,
Sat looking all skwonk, like that old Tower of Pisa.

You gave me your hat when the time came to part,
I made it my ship to sail close to your heart.

Our letters flocked home like migrating swallows,
You wrote of yesterdays, I of tomorrows.

Now I don't even know where your skeleton lies,
But I know that I still see the world through your eyes,

Those eyes that saw angels, dragons and clowns
In New York and Paris and war-rubbled towns.

That portrait you painted will be till my end
My proudest possession: it's signed 'To my friend'.

© Ernestine Shargool
In loving memory of Painter and Philosopher Riko Mikeska
'skwonk' is a Zimbabwean word for 'wonky'.

Acknowledgements

My THANKS GO TO ALL who contributed to the creation of this profile of two remarkable artists, Riko and Greta Mikeska. Their family members, friends, students and colleagues gave me permission to use transcripts of our talks and correspondences and these, in turn, allowed me to flesh out the lives of two people I met only in their advanced years. I encountered great generosity, honesty and care to ensure the Mikeskas' lives and art endured. Verbally, by letter, via phone calls and, ultimately, by email, I collected facts and sentiments from Prague, London, Bari and New York City. I trust I have included the salient recollections expressed by the following people. In alphabetical order, they are: Nava Atlas, Ira Barash, Mary Barash, Arthur Beecher, Lenore Beecher, Patricia Beecher, William Beecher, Joan Berkovitz, Lars Björling, Veronica Björling, Aldo Bozzi, Rudolfine Bozzi, Ulriche Bozzi, Martin Ftacnik, Denis Gouey, Bernard Gurevitz, Anna Habánová, Ivó Habán, Judith Hines, Nicola Incisetto, Hala Janizewski, Erica Kalmer, Ernst LowBeer, Mary Marquardt, Gene Poll, Doman Rogoisky, Celia Rozen, Ann Sabo, Arthur Sachs, Edward Scheckman, Jacques

Schmied, Marilyn Schmied, Ernestine Shargool, June Singer, Chaim Tabak, Teena Vallerine, Eve Whyte, Horst Winkelman, Susan Witter, Michael Zwerdling.

Special thanks go to Jacques Schmied, Greta's nephew, and to Chaim Tabak for providing me with photographs of most of the paintings extant from Riko's collection, and the few artifacts that remain from Greta's.

For translations from Czech, Italian, and German, special thanks go respectively to Hala Janizewski, to Adelaide Goitein, and to Catherine A. Lillie.

Interest in my subject gained me many readers who encouraged me to go on. Pedal points in this respect have been Ann Darby and Augusta Gross. In groups of three, Barbara Salvatore, Virginia F. Schwartz, and Leslie T. Sharpe, poets of the English language, were there early and consistently for me among the Walton Writers' Group, and gave me guidance angels wish for. Later, and up to publication, another three stand out for their persistent editorial expertise, humor, wisdom, magnificent writing, and educated sense of history: Catherine A. Lillie, Paul Pitkof, and Sidney S. Stark. They helped sort the complexity of two personalities of multi-faceted backgrounds who lived through the most turbulent times in the 20th Century. I could not have done without them. What faults remain are mine alone.

My thanks go, as ever, to the splendid librarians at the New York Public Library and at the New York Society Library, havens of enlightenment. The librarians guided me through microfiche files, map collections, newspapers, historical documents

Acknowledgements

and books, then gently reminded me where I might find the most silent corners to read in on any one day.

Profound thanks to Katie Holeman, artistic designer of the book and ultimate friend, whose humor and positive spirits led me to believe this book really would appear to a larger public.

I thank Jimmy Rybka, friend, educated reader and mentor on Czech history and the world of music and writing during the period Riko and Greta were concentrating more exclusively on art. I strongly recommend his book on Bohuslav Martinů, a personal as well as professional biography of this magnificent Czech composer whose life had its own demons and benefits.

And then, there is my family to thank. I had no idea that my promise to Greta in 1982 would sling-shot me into the age of the internet over thirty years later to find those who had known the Mikeskas in Prague, England, Scotland, Italy, New York. Through all these years, my family gave me patience, financial support, kindness, editorial skills, humor, their own considerations of this challenging couple, and always tolerated the enforced separations. All these add up to a lot of love. I cannot sufficiently praise and thank my husband, Tom, our children, Andrea, Erika and Seth, who lived through these tales from their perilous inception. You are my bread, salt and water.

About the Author

Of Brazilian-Chilean-French origins, fluent in four languages, and a traveler to the seven continents with her husband and children, Denise B. Dailey adapts easily to international subjects. Her ability to listen to people in multiple languages, and her passion to share their stories, inform and propel most of her writing, from short stories to travel journals, the most recent being _Listening to Pakistan_. Denise has a B.Sc. from McGill and an MFA from Columbia Universities. She has taught English as a Second Language at UN schools and in the School of General Studies at Columbia University.

www.ingramcontent.com/pod-product-compliance
Lightning Source LLC
Chambersburg PA
CBHW060228050426
42448CB00009B/1344